CURRENT RESEARCH
IN EGYPTOLOGY 2005

CURRENT RESEARCH IN EGYPTOLOGY 2005

Proceedings of the Sixth Annual Symposium

which took place at the

University of Cambridge, 6–8 January 2005

edited by

Rachel Mairs and Alice Stevenson

Oxbow Books

Published by
Oxbow Books, Oxford

ISBN 978 1 84217 229 2

This book is available direct from
Oxbow Books, Oxford

www.oxbowbooks.com

and

The David Brown Book Company
PO Box 511, Oakville, CT 06779, USA
(Phone: 860-945-9329; Fax: 860-945-9468)

Cover: Nefertari and Anubis from the sarcophagus chamber of Nefertari's tomb (QV 66)
Courtesy of the Getty Conservation Institute. © The J. Paul Getty Trust 1992.
All rights reserved.

Printed in Great Britain by
Short Run Press, Exeter

Contents

Preface..vii

Symposium Papers Not Included in This Volume..ix

Bringing Egypt Out Of Academia: Outreach and Inclusion in the Petrie Museum
   (*Yvette E. Balbaligo*) 1

Pepi I and the Temple of Satet at Elephantine (*Richard Bussmann*) 16

The Unique Amun-Re at Luxor Temple (*András Gulyás*) 22

Ostraca, Literature and Teaching at Deir el-Medina (*Fredrik Hagen*).....................38

Children and the Dead in New Kingdom Egypt (*Nicola Harrington*)......................52

'It is better to be silent than speak in vain': The Challenge of Producing Proverbs
   in Demotic and Greek (*Nikolaos Lazaridis*)...66

Egyptian Artefacts from Central and South Asia (*Rachel R. Mairs*) 74

Investigating Ancient Egyptian Towns: A Case Study of Itj-tawy (*Claire Malleson*).............90

A Study of Ramesside Royal Women's Tombs in the Valley of the Queens
   (*Heather Lee McCarthy*)...105

Designing Materials for Language Self-Instruction: A Case Study
   of Middle Egyptian (*Anne Morrison*) 123

New Considerations on Campbell's Tomb (*Mike Stammers*)................................138

The Material Significance of Predynastic and Early Dynastic Palettes
   (*Alice Stevenson*)..148

Egyptian Royal Women and Diplomatic Activity during the New Kingdom
   (*Georgia Xekalaki*)...163

Preface

The sixth annual Current Research in Egyptology symposium took place from Thursday 6th – Friday 8th January 2005 at the University of Cambridge and was attended by over 100 delegates. CRE was founded with the purpose of providing a forum for Egyptology graduate students, who had yet to find a permanent academic post, to exchange and generate ideas. Originally, it was envisaged that this would involve the graduate community of the British Isles but over the years the conference has attracted increasing international participation. This was notable at the 2005 conference, with delegates from across the United Kingdom and Western Europe, as well as North America and Australia, and we hope that this trend will continue in the future.

A total of 33 papers were presented, with further participation in the form of poster sessions. Thirteen of these papers are published in this volume. The range of topics covered was truly representative of the diversity of research currently being conducted by graduate students in Egyptology, ranging from the Predynastic to the Roman periods, and from reports on archaeological fieldwork to linguistic analysis.

In introducing the papers contained in the present volume, we cannot hope to do justice to the full scope of the material covered and issues raised by them. If we were to suggest a general theme, however, it might be that of exploring the borders and parameters of the discipline of Egyptology. The public face of Egyptology, and the way in which it responds to the needs and concerns of its wider constituencies beyond academia, is the major subject of two of the papers presented here, but is an issue which prompted much wider debate at the symposium. Another key concern was Ancient Egypt's relationship with the world beyond its borders and, alongside this, the interaction of Egyptology with the study of other areas of the ancient world. In a wider interdisciplinary sense, we may note among many of the papers published here, and presented at the conference itself, an increasing engagement with the theory and methodology of archaeology and the social sciences. This is of particular value in developing critical and reflexive approaches to the primary data at our disposal. These concerns – on framing questions, constructing avenues of approach, and situating Ancient Egypt within its wider disciplinary and cultural contexts – are important if we are to promote and sustain a constructive dialogue. We hope that CRE VI provided a useful forum for voicing and exploring them.

In the course of organising the conference and preparing this publication we have inevitably incurred many debts of gratitude, which we are pleased to have the opportunity to acknowledge here. Thanks are due to Kathryn Piquette, Yvette Balbaligo, Peter Robinson (for his work on the CRE website) and Henriette Koefoed. Generous grants from the Thomas Mulvey Fund (University of Cambridge) and the Royal Historical Society enabled us to cover various logistical expenses, and the Thomas Mulvey Fund also provided a subvention towards publication costs. The Centre for Research in the Arts, Social Sciences and Humanities (CRASSH) at the University of Cambridge kindly hosted the conference reception, and the staff of Queens' College provided assistance in arranging accommodation and the conference dinner. The main conference sessions were held at the Faculty of Law and thanks here are also due to the Faculty's receptionist Norma Weir.

In response to previous concerns (Piquette and Love 2005, viii) that any dialogue concerning the role of graduate students in shaping the future of the discipline must also include Egyptians themselves, a CRE bursary for Egyptian students has been established. It is hoped that this will fund, or at least subsidise, the cost of participation for one or more Egyptian graduate students. A number of donors very generously contributed towards the establishment of this bursary and we hope to see this project continue and expand in the future.

Finally, our sincere thanks to all the anonymous senior academic referees who gave freely of their time and expertise to review the articles submitted for the present volume.

Further details may be found on the CRE website (www.currentresearchegypt.fsworld.co.uk), which also contains details of past conference and publications.

Rachel Mairs and Alice Stevenson
October 2005

References

Piquette, K. and Love, S. 2005, Preface, in K. Piquette and S. Love (eds.), Current Research in Egyptology 2003: Proceedings of the Fourth Annual Symposium University College London 2003. Oxbow, Oxford.

Symposium Papers Not Included in This Volume

Charlotte Booth (Birkbeck College): *Nubians in Egyptian Art.*
Published in expanded form in Booth, C. 2005, *The Role of Foreigners in Ancient Egypt: A Study of Non-Stereotypical Artistic Representations.* BAR International Series 1426. Archaeopress, Oxford.

Mike Brass: *Investigating the Origins of Social Complexity in Early Saharan Pastoralists.*

Paulo Carreira (Classical University of Lisbon): *Akhenaten's Offering Scenes and Hymns to the Aten.*

Benoit Claus (Université Libre de Bruxelles / Universität Basel): *Realms of Memory in Ancient Egypt: Museon and Library in Egyptian Temples.*

Paul James Cowie (Macquarie University, Sydney): *Reassessing the New Kingdom Egyptian Empire in the Levant.*

Karen Exell (University of Durham): *Why did the Egyptians Make Monuments?*

Steven Gregory (University of Exeter): *The King in Time and Space: The Expression of Spatial and Temporal Aspects of Ancient Egyptian Kingship.*

Tom Hardwick (Worcester College, Oxford): *Fragments from Sinai: Discoveries in the Ashmolean Museum, Oxford.*

Marwa Helmy (Katholieke Universiteit Leuven): *Socio-Economic Aspects of Mortuary Remains in Predynastic and Early Dynastic Egypt – Energy Expenditure Analysis Revised.*

Ole Herslund (Carsten Niebuhr Institute, Copenhagen University): *'God is Up': The Ritual of Amenhotep I, Embodied Structures and Ritualized Agents in Ramesside Deir el Medina.*

Amandine Marshall (University of Lille): *The Fly and the Lion as Examples of Royal Rewards.*

Sally McAleely (Institute of Archaeology, University College London): *More about Flower Arranging in Ancient Egypt: Some New Kingdom and Graeco-Roman Period Archaebotanical Remains Examined from a Material Culture Perspective.*

Jan Moje (Institut für Ägyptologie, Münster): *Research in the Hieroglyphic Palaeography of Some 19th Dynasty Private Stelae.*

Rune Nyord (Carsten Niebuhr Institute, University of Copenhagen): *The Body in the Hymns to the Coffin Sides.*
Published as Nyord, R. 2006, The Body in the Hymn to the Coffin Sides, *Chronique d'Égypte* No. 161, Vol. 81.

Pippa Payne (University of Cambridge): *In Excess of Fifty Dogs.*

Vanda Raimundo (Oriental Institute, Lisbon University): *Cosmetics: Beauty and Seduction in Ancient Egypt.*

Jenna Spellane (Trinity College, University of Cambridge): *The So-Called 'Daily-Life' Mummy Boards from the Tomb of Sennedjem at Deir El-Medina.*

Geoffrey Tassie (Institute of Archaeology, University College London): *Single Mother Goddesses and Divine Kingship: The Sidelock of Youth and the Maternal Bond – Revisited.*

Barbara Tratsaert (Ghent University): *Wadi Bakariya, A Roman Gold Mine Settlement in the Eastern Desert of Egypt.*

Paula Veiga (Lisbon University): *Health in Ancient Egypt.*

Bringing Egypt out of Academia: Outreach and Inclusion in the Petrie Museum

Y. E. Balbaligo

Introduction

The Petrie Museum of Egyptian Archaeology at University College London (UCL) is a distinguished collection of Egyptian artefacts created through the bequest of the writer Amelia Edwards and named after W. M. F. Petrie, the prolific archaeologist and first professor of Egyptology in England. Since the museum was established in 1892, the role of the museum, and of museums in general, has changed. Museums are no longer seen as solely guardians or keepers of collections. Museums now make artefacts accessible to people and enable them to explore collections for inspiration, learning and enjoyment (definition from the Museums Association 1998). Museums are also tied to the cultural and social values of their times and there is now an emphasis on making museums inclusive institutions that are accessible to a diverse body of people. This paper will focus on the Petrie Museum and discuss the current initiatives to target diverse audiences beyond the students the collection was originally intended for, and how they are making the past accessible to new audiences and why. By discussing the current outreach initiatives, it is hoped that they will illuminate the relationship between how contemporary social agendas affect museums and how this can potentially have an impact on the development of Egyptology. These issues will be framed within debates in museology and public archaeology, in order to bring these two complementary disciplines to Egyptological audiences and show how this existing body of literature can contribute to the debates within Egyptology about who the past is for and how we, as a discipline, interpret and present the past. The ultimate aim of this paper is to share good practice and highlight the strengths of the Petrie Museum.

The Petrie Museum and its social context

It is acknowledged that museums are a significant and powerful vehicle for the public construction of the past and for public involvement in archaeology (Merriman 2004b, 85). Archaeology, however, is inescapably highly politicised. It is embroiled in social and cultural debates about the past and its meaning for the present, and has significance beyond the accumulation of abstract knowledge about the past (Smith 2004, 1). As cultural houses for archaeological objects, museums are ultimately about the development of cultural identities as well as notions of citizenship, and these are all inextricably bound with politics. In 1997, the new Labour government saw a shared culture as a vehicle for increasing social cohesion through individual self-fulfilment, awareness of citizenship and communal participation. Thus, ideas of social inclusion are enshrined in governmental policy by the Department for Culture Media and Sport (DCMS) and the Social Exclusion Unit (formerly in the Cabinet Office and now in the Office of the Deputy Prime Minister), in an attempt to enhance the cultural life of Britain and to make British society inclusive to all people. Museums therefore have the potential to be "agents of social change" where museums are "often the focal point for cultural activity in the community, interpreting its history and heritage. This gives people a sense of their own identity, and that of their community" (DCMS 2000, 3; see also 1999; 2001; Dodd and Sandell 2001). The emphasis on dismantling barriers to accessing museums and on providing services for a much broader range of people has the potential to contribute to greater social equality. While the concept of social inclusion has become embedded throughout central government policy, critics have argued that the assignment of social goals to cultural organisations is tying them too closely to the state and eroding their autonomy and reducing the arts to a tool for governmental control (Sandell 2002, 18). However, museums and galleries have the potential to contribute towards the combating of inequality and they do have a responsibility to do so. This requires museums to become responsive, not to short-term, party political objectives but rather to longer-term paradigmatic shifts in thinking, whilst being contemporary and also understanding their position in their own social structure. The Petrie Museum is a Designated museum with an outstanding collection and receives significant funding from DCMS. As well as serving its primary users – the staff and students at UCL – it must also demonstrate its worth to a wider audience who will benefit from the collection. While it is accountable to external funding bodies, the Petrie is also bound to its parent institution, UCL.

The university context of the Petrie Museum

As a university museum, the Petrie receives most of its funding from UCL and was founded with the same libertarian ethos. The university is also home to four publicly accessible museums, of which the Petrie is one, and twelve departmental collections, unified under the name 'UCL Museums and Collections'. These museums and collections cover a diverse array of subjects from science and archaeology, to geology, natural history and art, and were gathered and developed from the 1820s to assist UCL's academic staff in their teaching and research. Previously all collections existed separately, however in 1998 UCL invested further resources into the care and management of the collections and for the first time centralised its management systems. All of the museums and collections work towards collective goals and this can be seen in the UCL Museums and Collections mission statement of the *5 Year Strategic Plan 2004–2009*, a document which provides a focus for shared common objectives and to give the museums a framework within which to work and measure success (see Ambrose and Runyard 1991; Davis 1996). The mission statement is to "inspire learning, support research and stimulate enjoyment for the benefit of UCL and the wider community, based on the sustainable use of the collections" (UCL Museums and Collections 2004, 1; *cf.* previous mission statement in MacDonald 2000, 68). This statement mirrors the current definition of what a museum is and it defines who its users are. One of the ways in which to ensure sustainable use of the collections is in the audience it attracts. Although the priority audience is UCL's staff and students, all the museums are expanding to serve the wider community and to be more accessible and inclusive. While all the museums target the same audiences, the Petrie's audience base is more diverse. It is taking advantage of its special appeal to certain interest groups, as well as actively creating new audiences and targeting new communities so that the collections can continue to be appreciated and used.

A significant problem shared by all the museums is the low usage of the collections. Outside of the Egyptological community, too few people are aware of the Petrie's collection. Even within UCL, many students are surprised to learn that UCL has four museums and even more collections. Thus, they are under-utilised and under-appreciated. The total direct users (as opposed to virtual users) is estimated at 17,000 per year (UCL Museums and Collections 2004, 1). This is a common problem faced by university museums and a problem also faced by the Oriental Museum at the University of Durham, which houses an Egyptian collection (Karen Exell, personal communication). Low usage of the collections is also closely connected to physical access and the visibility of the museums. All of the UCL museums are located within the main UCL campus and its opening hours are constrained by staffing levels. Access to the Petrie is further restricted as it does not have an easily accessible public entrance (see MacDonald 2000, 67). Other problems faced by the Petrie include insufficient funding – a perennial issue for all museums, especially university museums (MacDonald 2000, 68) – as well as limited accommodation and space for the collection. Accommodation has long been an issue, as its present location was supposed to be temporary. Of the 80,000 objects in the collection, 6% are on display, and the Petrie is currently housed above UCL's main boiler where building work is frequently carried out. In the past, air conditioning and the roof and drainage system have caused irreversible damage to part of the collection. Low lighting and the labelling of the objects have also been areas of dissatisfaction for visitors, as a degree of specialist knowledge is required to understand the context of the objects. These are problems with its present location, however the relocation of the Petrie to a purpose-built museum would eradicate these problems and this is discussed below.

The Petrie Museum is attached to the Institute of Archaeology at UCL, where undergraduate and postgraduate students use the collection for courses in the archaeology of Egypt and Sudan, museum and artefact studies and conservation. Furthermore, the Petrie is closely linked to the postgraduate courses the Institute offers in Museum Studies, Public Archaeology and Cultural Heritage Studies, and is thus uniquely placed to benefit from research conducted in these areas. Although the Petrie is primarily a teaching collection, it nevertheless "remains little known and almost underused by Institute of Archaeology staff teaching courses" (MacDonald and Shaw 2004, 112); there is, however, potential for cross-disciplinary usage. As well as being linked through teaching, many of the initiatives at the Institute tie in with initiatives at the Petrie. One of the current activities is the attempt to diversify archaeology. The driver for this initiative is the Race Relations Amendment Act (2000), where it is the duty of universities to make race equality central to the way public authorities work. In 2001, UCL agreed to Corporate Equality Objectives which apply cultural diversity, and UCL has produced a Race Equality Action Plan for 2002–2006, which covers equality issues in the management of college. The Institute has agreed a Strategic Plan (2004–2006) which acknowledges some of the difficulties involved in recruiting a diverse staff and student body. At the time of writing, the Institute of Archaeology is in the process of establishing a Diversity Working Group which will report directly to the Institute's Policy Group to evaluate the way it recruits staff and students and structures courses. Archaeology as a subject does not have a strong record of ethnic minority staff recruitment and this goes back to very low levels of ethnic minority student recruitment. Furthermore, the curriculum at the Institute has been viewed as rather traditional and Eurocentric, reflecting archaeology's long preoccupation with area studies and great civilisations, rather than, for example, themes of potential topical interest (MacDonald 2004). This focus on diversity is also reflected in wider archaeological thought as seen in the strategic aims of DCMS (outlined above), the Council for British Archaeology and English Heritage, amongst others. In the long term, the outcomes of the diversity initiative at the Institute have the potential to impact upon visitor numbers and further use of the Petrie.

The role of outreach

The two main priorities for the UCL Museums and Collections are to increase the use of the collections for teaching, learning and research, and to increase the access and use of the collections for widening participation and wider public audiences (UCL Museums and Collections 2004, 2–8). UCL's Widening Participation Unit plays a similar role where the aims are to "raise awareness of higher education among under-represented groups, to increase the number of students from under-represented groups attending programmes at UCL and to maintain and increase the progression and retention rates of under-represented groups at UCL" (Widening Participation website). For the Petrie Museum, the UCL community who usually use the collections consists of undergraduate and postgraduate students of the Institute of Archaeology, as well as Continuing Education colleges and other lifelong learners. Increasing the numbers of users can be achieved by diversifying who the users are, and this is currently done with an Education and Access Officer through educational channels; two outreach workers who work with Egyptian and Sudanese communities and African and African Caribbean communities and supplementary schools; and a virtual outreach curator.

Outreach has become fundamental to the process of changing the role of museums within their communities and establishing relationships with new audiences. It has become a means of introducing museum subjects and collections to audiences that have tended to be excluded from museums and galleries by a variety of barriers (Martin 1996, 38). Museums now no longer need to be conceived of as a building to which visitors are enticed, but as a service which tailors its work to different target audiences. As a result, outreach work has become an important means of service delivery – both as an end in itself and as a way in which the museum can publicise itself (Merriman 2004b, 95). By using outreach workers, the Petrie makes its collection accessible to communities outside of the confines of the university and traditional Egyptology audiences, by taking knowledge and objects *out* of the museum to other communities. Here, museum objects, through loan boxes and portable exhibitions, are a starting point for activities and workshops. Outreach workers also bring groups *in* to the museum to contextualise what has been learnt, introduce them to the displays and the university environment, and utilise the Petrie as meeting place for further discussions. This has strengthened the connections between the museum collection and local communities and has extended the educational role of the museum, as well as increasing the numbers of visitors.

At present it is difficult to measure the impact of outreach work and its social value (for example see Scott 2002), as its effects are not immediately evident. It has the potential, however, to have long-term benefits for individuals and the museum itself. It provides a service to people who do not usually go to museums and it has increased the local and cultural relevance of museums to the communities they are serving. Outreach work is raising the profile of the Petrie and demonstrating the value of the museum and its services to the university and other funding bodies. For individuals, it is acknowledged that museums can have an impact with wide-ranging outcomes: from the personal and psychological, such as self-esteem or sense of place, to the pragmatic, such as the acquisition of skills to enhance employment opportunities (Sandell 2002, 5). Outreach at the Petrie can further personal development by introducing people to the culture of ancient Egypt and Sudan, and tied in with UCL Widening Participation initiatives, introduce young people to a university environment.

Although there is no guarantee that new audiences, particularly the 'socially excluded' who would not normally consider visiting museums, are reached (Merriman 2004b, 96), the Petrie are targeting specific groups to ensure that outreach workers are made the most of. In 2000, the Petrie commissioned research into understanding attitudes of existing users such as academics and amateur enthusiasts, and non-users, from modern black and Egyptian communities in London as well as children (MacDonald 2000; MacDonald 2003; MacDonald and Shaw 2004). It is the first time that the Petrie has asked these communities for their opinions and the findings of this study are a basis for audience development and communication, as well as the current initiatives that are in place.

Museums visits have always had a place in mainstream education. However, outreach with schools expands the educational role of the museum through better interaction with objects to understand the past (see Stone and Molyneaux 1994; Stone and MacKenzie 1994; Hooper-Greenhill 1999). The Education and Access Officer is responsible for promoting UCL Museums and Collections to schools, families and life-long learners. This role has involved developing partnerships with primary and secondary schools in London boroughs. The services and programs offered vary from museum visits, to handling sessions with objects in classrooms, an after schools group and enrichment clubs, as well as teachers' packs and digital resources. Outreach work in schools is largely responsive, where primary and secondary schools call the Petrie and request talks, outreach sessions or visits. The activities are tied in with certain Key Stages in the English National Curriculum. At Key Stage 2 (for 7 to 11 year olds), there is an option in History to focus on ancient Egypt, which encourages the study of aspects of everyday life through archaeological evidence (MacDonald 2000, 79; MacDonald and Shaw 2004, 114). The Education and Access Officer also recruits student volunteers at UCL and gives training to enable them to take loan boxes out to schools to run outreach sessions.

Archaeology summer schools are also organised, where Camden Council have targeted hard-to-reach groups. Past successful summer schools include: *A Slice of Camden,* which introduces primary school children from Camden in London to local history, heritage and archaeology through handling sessions and mock excavations; *Mummified,* which involved handling objects from the Petrie collection and visits to the Egyptian galleries in collaboration with the British Museum; and *Splash,* a summer school for teenagers on Marine archaeology, held at a diving school and the Institute of Archaeology. Pupils were given introductions to handling objects, principles of archaeology and wreck-diving, and a practical element of underwater archaeology in a swimming pool with mock-salvage exercises. Using the collections supports and enhances what pupils learn at school and introduces subjects they may not know about. It also introduces the concept of university in a very low-key way, to hopefully raise aspirations (Celine West, personal communication).

A loan box is another way that museums have attempted to widen hands-on access to objects, as well as breaking long-held taboos about being allowed to touch and handle objects (Merriman 2004b, 93). This method is also one of the oldest forms of museum outreach and a vital component of educational outreach (Merriman 2004b, 95; see also Hall and Swain 2000; Paris 2002). The Petrie loan box is used by outreach workers and there is also one available for teachers to borrow. The box has been adapted for Key Stage 2 and for themes in Islamic Civilisations for Key Stage 3 (for 11–14 year olds), to take Islamic and modern Egyptian perspectives into account. The box currently contains real Egyptian objects from the pharaonic, Coptic, Medieval and modern periods, as well as resource packs with activities suggestions. Objects in the box include a bronze figure of the goddess Bastet (*c.*525 B.C., unprovenanced – see Figure 1), a black steatite Coptic cross from Koptos, and modern rosary and prayer beads. With these particular objects, questions about different religions and beliefs, aspects of daily life and

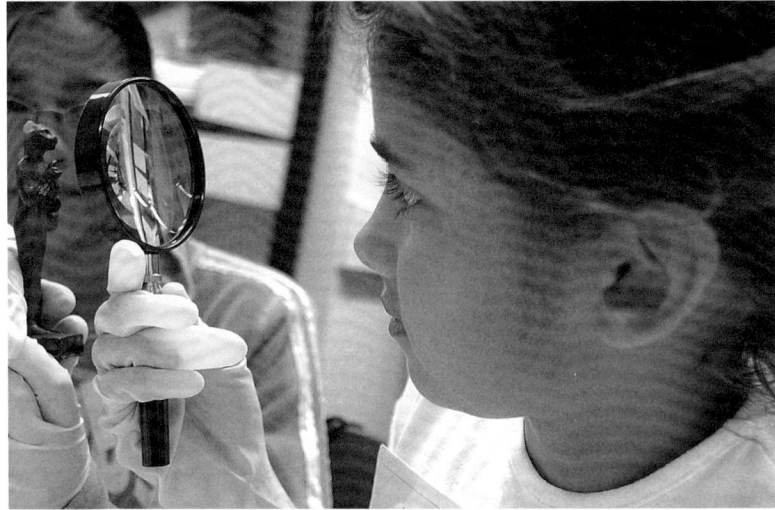

Figure 1. *Outreach session with primary schools; learner looking at a statue of Bastet from the Petrie loan box, 2004 (photo: Petrie Museum of Egyptian Archaeology, University College London).*

chronology can be explored, as well as identifying materials, manufacture, function and usage. This range of objects demonstrates evidence for the relationship between ancient and modern Egyptians, and the culture's continuation and relevance. There are many benefits of using real objects in learning and working with audiences, especially the young. They provide a direct link with a topic or the past and can enhance young people's interest in and understanding of a subject, while encouraging them to use all their senses – especially touch, sight and smell. They help to develop the important skill of drawing conclusions based on an examination of evidence, together with an understanding of the limitations and reliability of evidence. In schools, they are ideal for generating group and class discussion, all while promoting the value of museums and encouraging young people to visit museums with their families to further their learning, as well as for fun (from UCL Museums and Collections website). As the loan box is portable, object-centred learning is also used at public events which generally coincide with national events such as Black History Month, Family Learning Week, the Big Draw and National Archaeology Week. Furthermore, in presenting images of the objects, there is a movement to showing them being actively used and this can be seen in the Petrie's updated information leaflet which also has a section in Arabic and shows the diversity of the Petrie's users.

Reaching new communities

In 2002, two additional outreach workers were employed to work with Egyptian and Sudanese, and African and African Caribbean communities and supplementary schools. MacDonald (2000, 79) states that "the decision to target people of Egyptian and African descent was made in recognition of the fact that the [Petrie] collection may have a special significance for people who see their roots in Egypt specifically or Africa generally. Many black people regard ancient Egypt as a culture that has been appropriated by Eurocentric archaeologists and historians. Some would say that an Egyptian museum such as the Petrie, with its roots in Western archaeological practice, has a duty to explore alternative views of its subject matter". These two outreach posts have been hugely successful and have transformed the services offered by the Petrie. The success in reaching communities is also due to the Petrie's location and the ethnic diversity of London.

The Egyptian and Sudanese outreach worker Okasha El Daly has been establishing contact with a range of Egyptian and Sudanese communities in London, also in conjunction with the Egyptian Cultural Bureau in London. Historically, it is perceived that modern Egyptians have not been as engaged in the study of ancient Egypt as Western scholars, and that Medieval Arabs had no interest in ancient Egypt. Reid (1984, 233; see also Reid 2002) has stated that "Islamic identity has tended to crowd out feelings of kinship or curiosity about ancient Egyptians and Western imperial domination set back the growth of indigenous Egyptology, which might otherwise have taken root fifty years before it did". However, El Daly (2005) has demonstrated that Medieval Arabs had a great appetite for historical research, where they learnt about the ancient culture through direct contact with Copts, and observed monuments and artefacts. Furthermore, some Arab scholars had access to ancient scripts and correctly deciphered aspects of demotic, hieratic and hieroglyphs. El Daly's research is the bridge between Medieval Arabs and modern Arabs, showing them that their ancestors were interested in their past. It is also an invitation to modern Arabs to re-examine their relationship with their past, as presently, for Egyptians, it has been noted that there is a gap between modern Egypt and the past as it is seen as being for tourists (Hassan 1998; 2003; El Daly 2003). Before the research undertaken by the Petrie, El Daly states that "no one had ever asked Arabs for their opinion" (Okasha El Daly, personal communication).

Outreach activities have included setting up discussion groups and exhibitions, and giving lectures in Arabic to adult Arabic audiences including Iraqis, Syrians and Palestinians on aspects of these cultures, as well as lectures on ancient and Medieval Egypt. Furthermore, there is an emphasis on working with Arabic women, as women are not traditionally seen as being interested in archaeology. The same expertise in the Petrie has been used by the British Museum. Okasha El Daly was a consultant for the *Sudan: Ancient Treasures* exhibition (September 2004 – January 2005) where he translated the catalogue into Arabic. This was an important step in showing Sudanese people that an authoritative institution such as the British Museum was taking an interest in their culture. This will become more important as the exhibition is to go on tour, with the hope of attracting more Sudanese visitors.

As well as working with adults in the UK, Okasha El Daly has given lectures in Arabic and English in Egypt and he has worked with children from preparatory schools, using the outreach in the Petrie as a model. However, an infrastructure for outreach work does not exist in Egypt and they do not have the same access to loan boxes or teaching resources as exists in the UK. Outreach in Egyptian schools has been done with slides and replicas of objects, as it is prohibited to use authentic ancient Egyptian artefacts. The aims are to make modern young Egyptians identify with ancient Egyptians and show how they can be relevant to their lives, through themes such as tolerance with foreigners and migration, religious worship, and skills such as organisation and timekeeping. Conducting outreach with young Egyptians is a way of introducing sound knowledge from reliable sources, with the potential to train and recruit the future generation of Egyptian archaeologists. These types of activities need to be made sustainable in Egypt, but more pressingly, they need to be driven by the Egyptian government, education ministers and the media as a form of mass communication. This can only be done successfully if there is dialogue and cooperation between these institutions. While much more needs to be done, the work done so far has raised the profile of the Petrie Museum with the Egyptian and Sudanese communities in the UK and in Egypt.

The outreach work with African and African Caribbean communities and supplementary schools in London, carried out by Kenneth John, has focused on the Africanisation of Egyptology. The rationale for an African-centred Egyptology is that "many people in the past were taught that Egypt was the only country in Africa that produced anything worthy of praise or emulation by the rest of the world. This resulted in a long-standing agreement between scholars, historians and politicians, to relocate Egypt, the agreed location being the Middle East. This sustained the belief that Egypt is not an African country and that its greatest achievements had very little to do with black Africans" (Kenneth John, personal communication). While there is a long history of black scholarship on ancient Egypt and its relationship to the rest of Africa (for example Asante 1992; 1995; 2000; Celenko 1996; Mudimbe 1988), there is evidently a great and powerfully-felt need among African and African Caribbean people to reposition ancient Egypt within Africa. Furthermore, within Egyptology, there has been work towards relocating Egypt back into Africa (for example see O'Connor and Reid 2003). The work done by Kenneth John is rooted in communities, with people who do not normally engage with institutions, bringing the Petrie Museum to communities to encourage, inspire, educate and enlighten, thereby showing that museums are a viable prospect for young people. Community resources that are ideal for partnering and promoting what the Petrie has to offer, have been established because some organisations did not want to get too involved with the existing mainstream outlets. While mainstream education is more focused on achieving academic results based on the national curriculum targets, these do not require a specifically African or Caribbean point of view. Here there is scope in the long term for museums and collections to be used to tackle underachievement within certain communities and ethnicities.

Kenneth John has been building links with education departments in London boroughs such as Ealing, where progress has been made to introduce black history into mainstream teaching as well as black history after school clubs. One of the main undertakings has been forming the *Splendour of Egypt* Project with other heritage organisations including the National Archives, the British Museum and the British Library. The project uses a variety of methods from workshops, staging dance performances and the African martial art Kazimba, to engage with local African and African Caribbean communities in London and the project has provided many opportunities for young people to develop skills through new experiences. The project, however, is not only about research and visits to museums, as learning, community development and social cohesion come out of fun recreational activities. Kenneth John has also set up and contributed to many discussion groups including the 'Nubian and All African People Study Group' who meet in the Petrie on Friday evenings for discussions and object handling, and the 'Nubian Women's Development Initiative' based in Luton, Bedfordshire, who frequently visit the Petrie. In these discussion groups, many subjects relevant to Africa and African people are explored, including the tenets of an African-centred Egyptology (see Figure 2). Kenneth John says that "in the past, African peoples have not had a space to discuss these issues, but using the Petrie Museum as a meeting place engages people who would not usually access museums or educational establishments" (Kenneth John, personal communication). It is hoped that people will use the museum and resources of the university at other times and that they will become more confident about using these services in the future.

Tenets of African Centred Egyptology
- The ancient Egyptians were black skinned people.
- Ancient Egypt was more advanced than other cultures or societies of that time.
- Egyptian culture had (and still has) a tremendous influence on European cultures.
- The religious and cultural beliefs of East, Central and West Africa had more influence on the development of ancient Egyptian culture than did the Greeks, Romans or Asiatic civilisations.
- There has been a vast racist conspiracy to prevent dissemination of evidence for the above assertions.
- Black History Month activities and events are only social and political tools used to develop the self-esteem of African, Caribbean and many other people of 'colour'. These events have no real credibility in academic fields and so need not be taught or promoted in mainstream education from primary right up to university level.
- What is taught at home, in supplementary schools and community settings is often inaccurate and grossly exaggerated.
- By concentrating only on past achievements of African people there may be a danger of limiting potential for future ambition and aspirations.

**Do you agree or disagree with any of the above statements?
Has this been your experience?**

Figure 2. Tenets of African Centred Egyptology; thought provoking and challenging statements explored in groups.

Moving beyond outreach

There can be no doubt about the value of outreach work for the Petrie and the schools and communities they have impacted upon. However, there is a need to embed the education and access role in the long term, to continue the work with primary and secondary schools in London boroughs and build long-term relationships. It is hoped that the education and access service will become more strategic and better used, with regular outreach across many schools. Within schools, it is hoped that pupils will learn about different ways to see objects, that the loan box will be used in a multidisciplinary way with more teachers borrowing the loan box and not lack the confidence to use it (Celine West, personal communication). Furthermore, raising awareness of the museum in schools will hopefully attract more visitors into the museum. The two outreach posts have grown considerably and more emphasis has been placed on re-shaping mainstream resources than on producing specific resources for target groups. It is clear that the groups worked with so far regard it as most important that the museum focuses on broadening and improving its mainstream provision as this will be more lasting and sustainable. In organising workshops Kenneth says "people have wanted me to come into schools, to entertain and keep children occupied. Though that has a potential to change individual lives it doesn't lead anywhere. Keeping children entertained is counter-effective as they don't see the academic value of what I'm doing. The way forward is to work more with schools and other authorities, for outreach to be mainstreamed and for communities to take more ownership" (Kenneth John, personal communication). As well as doing outreach, Kenneth does *inreach*, organising consultation sessions and raising significant issues with staff and museum professionals. He also represents the Petrie and the communities he works with on many committees and advisory boards. Through these initiatives, he is involved in shaping the future heritage provision in London, and by becoming part of the decision-making process, this has the potential to influence policy-makers' agendas.

Although the outreach initiatives have been successful and popular, there are big resource issues as the posts are not full-time and work is dependent on staff with short-term contracts. As most outreach work involves building relationships with new audiences, the work is staff-intensive and working with communities has meant developing the need to respond rapidly to opportunities such as putting an exhibition together or attending conferences and lectures at the last minute. Sadly, at the time of writing, funding for the outreach posts came to an end in July 2005 as they are not a core-funded activity. The posts and services are currently being evaluated and bids have been submitted to the Heritage Lottery Fund and other funding bodies. Museums frequently operate in a project-funded culture which is largely wasteful because of the time and resources needed to get people into place. In the case of the Petrie, outreach is a long-term need and not a project, but unfortunately ambition exceeds resources (Sally MacDonald, personal communication). However, the Petrie outreach workers have been role models to the people they have worked with and ambassadors for the museum. Successful outreach depends on the people who do the outreach and how they engage with the public and this work requires a certain type of person (Kenneth John, personal comunication). The work done by the present outreach workers have set wheels in motion and it is hoped that one day, these initiatives will lead to work that really is sustainable and posts that will be permanent.

Digitising Egypt

A museum website is fundamental for audiences who cannot access the museum, for further information about the collections, the museum's history and practical matters such as opening times. The Internet is one of the principal ways in which access to archaeological collections is being promoted and it is growing, allowing them to be accessed in ways that ways that extend far beyond the capacity of the physical museum space (*e.g.* Merriman 2004b, 90). While digital media clearly provides a new dimension to the accessibility of museum archaeological resources, such as through online object databases, the web is also generally limited to those with the resources who can afford it. Furthermore, Merriman (2004b, 91) states that non-visitors tend also to be non-users of the Internet, except perhaps in the case of young people, who are more likely to be Internet users but less likely to visit museums. Nevertheless, the Petrie website is an essential tool for information dissemination and for marketing, and it has been translated into Arabic. For schools, there is a range of online educational resources for different ages and abilities, such as *Textiles in the Petrie Museum*, aimed at 14–16 year old students studying Textiles, and information for teachers to help plan a meaningful visit with the *Egypt in Africa Pack for School Visits*, for teachers of 7–11 year olds. For academics and researchers, the Petrie has developed a full online illustrated catalogue of its 80,000 objects that is continually edited and updated. Further learning resources include *Digital Egypt for Universities*, a rich source of information on ancient Egypt, illustrated by objects from the Petrie collection and 2D and 3D reconstructions. This site also aims to support learning across many disciplines including architecture, art, medicine, science, religion, literature, gender studies, cultural studies, museum studies (Digital Egypt for Universities website). The material is presented by theme, place and time, rather than as structured learning courses, thus learning is shaped by the experience of the user.

The world of the virtual museum is expanding and allows geographically-dispersed institutions and collections to be united. The Petrie's outreach curator has documented and photographed Egyptian collections in museums to create a shared online resource, reuniting dispersed material from excavated sites. The Accessing Virtual Egypt website enables virtual access to the collections of ancient Egyptian and Sudanese objects in five museums, of material known to have been excavated by Petrie or by the organisation he initiated, the British School of Archaeology in Egypt. As well as the Petrie Museum, some of the objects excavated by Petrie can also be found in the Bexhill Museum, Brighton Museum and Art Gallery, Buckinghamshire County Museum and Ipswich Museums Service. The aim is to virtually bring together these collections and make them available to the public for the first time. Though it is not intended as a comprehensive and definitive catalogue of these artefacts, it is a way to improve access to the objects and encourage further research. A further website that brings together objects excavated by Petrie is the Virtual Kahun website, a joint project between the Manchester Museum and the Petrie Museum. This website gives users the chance to explore Kahun in virtual reality, where every excavated building can be visited, many of the artefacts excavated can be virtually 'handled' and the collections can be searched. The site aims to increase children's knowledge and awareness of ancient Egyptian material culture through online, database-related educational resources. Many of these resources can be used in the classroom or in conjunction with museum visits.

The Petrie's digital initiatives are one of the activities to benefit from 'Renaissance in the Regions' funding – an investment from central government to enable regional museums to raise their standards and deliver real results in support of education, learning, community development and economic regeneration. The Petrie has successfully bid for funding to establish the Egypt Subject Specialist Network (ESSN), a digital project which aims to collect information from every collection in the British Isles with Egyptian objects. These records will be accessible on Cornucopia – a fully searchable online database of collections held by cultural heritage institutions throughout the UK, which has been developed and managed by the Museums, Libraries and Archives Council (MLA). This database allows those institutions to record and maintain collections descriptions and details in a unique shared national resource. The Cornucopia database will provide a collections level description and will start collecting information on the state of conservation and archives to be able to get more funding for a dedicated curator, as there are few specialist curators. Once objects are in a better condition, they can be made more accessible. Current partner museums for this project include the British Museum, Ashmolean Museum, Fitzwilliam Museum, Bolton Museum and Manchester Museum. This project is due for completion by the end of March 2006. These new digital initiatives are not only a tool for academics, researchers and students of all ages, but the disparate museum objects and site inventories from the same archaeological excavations by Petrie can be 'virtually' reunited once again.

Other notable initiatives in the Petrie include the introduction of an MLA funded 'positive action' traineeship which provides training for person of an ethnic origin to work in a museum and undertake a postgraduate qualification; visiting scholars to look at specific objects, such as Islamic objects in the collection; new approaches to visible storage to increase access to the collection; an experimental project to barcode objects so they may be more easily located; experimenting with new ways of labelling dense displays; foreign loans; and the development of Petrie travelling exhibitions. Day to day activities include ongoing cataloguing of objects for the database, conservation and, of course, an active *Friends of the Petrie* programme.

The future of the Petrie Museum

The dream of a new building for the Petrie Museum has been in the making for many years and this dream is being planned with a purpose built space called the Panopticon. In December 2004, the Panopticon received planning permission from the London Borough of Camden and has received strong endorsement, including a commitment from the Heritage Lottery Fund. For the first time, the entire collection will be displayed and stored appropriately. It will contain on-site conservation facilities and a climate-controlled environment to ensure that the collection can be conserved in an environment that is both protective and accessible, where visitors will be able to see how objects are conserved. The Panopticon will have a significant impact on the interpretation and teaching of Egyptology, as the displays and access to the collection will enable new and interdisciplinary ways of working. It will open up new ways of access for communities and local groups to continue the work that has been started with the outreach programmes. The Panopticon will also house the Library Special Collections, a collection of books and manuscripts covering a wide range of subjects, dating from the medieval period to the present day; the UCL Art Collection which comprises more than 10,000 paintings, drawings, prints and sculptures that date from 1490 to the present day, including prints by Dürer and Rembrandt, works by 18th and 19th century British artists such as Turner and Constable; and temporary exhibition spaces to present a rolling series of exhibitions and associated activities, based both on the other UCL collections, as well as Community Partnership Exhibition, with exhibitions of interest to local Camden residents. The building will provide a new public entrance to the university's central campus and will contain two lecture theatres, study space for students and researchers, an activities room for schools, community groups, local societies and other visitors to London and a café. Initial plans for the design of the Petrie Museum and other aspects of the building have been completed (see Figure 3), and extensive consultation with community and special interest groups, as well as non-users, has taken place to help plan how the new museum might look and operate. This type of consultation will be ongoing and services continually evaluated.

Figure 3. Visualisation of how the exterior of the Panopticon housing the Petrie Museum might look, designed by Opera, 2004 (photo: Petrie Museum of Egyptian Archaeology, University College London).

At the time of writing, the Panopticon has the full backing of UCL and the Heritage Lottery Fund, and the Petrie has extended their fundraising period and expect to submit the Stage 2 bid to the Heritage Lottery Fund in December 2005. For this vision to be fully realised, significant funding is required, however, with its own building, it is hoped that the Petrie will be seen as more fundable as it will have direct public benefit and the public outside of the university will be able to access it more easily. The opening of the Panopticon is now scheduled for 2009.

Concluding remarks

Some of the issues discussed here are also problems for other university museums as well as national museums. The initiatives set out in this paper specifically show how the Petrie Museum is responding to external factors, like governmental and university targets, and also how it is managing its social responsibility as an Egyptian museum to audiences who may have been excluded in the past. By diversifying its users through outreach work, it is making the collection more accessible and increasing the use and value of the museum in the wider community. In critiquing these initiatives, it can be said that they need to be made more strategic in the long term and need to become embedded in usual museum practice through successful and sustainable funding. Furthermore, they need to be able to adapt to the forthcoming new museum space or adapt if it does not happen for any reason.

This paper has outlined the wider social context of the museum for an Egyptological audience who might not be aware of the full range of issues currently facing museums. These issues have a potential to impact upon Egyptology, and Egyptologists must become more involved in both the way that the discipline progresses and its 'management issues' in order to drive the agenda of where Egyptological practice is going. It is also necessary to be critical and reflexive about the way the discipline is practiced. There is scope for Egyptologists to engage more with other disciplines that deal with similar issues, for example, looking for lessons that can be learnt from other museums practices and within public archaeology. Public archaeology is inevitably about negotiation and conflict over meaning, and the field of public archaeology is significant because it studies the processes and outcomes whereby the discipline of archaeology becomes part of a wider public culture (Merriman 2004a, 5). By engaging more with the public through museums, Egyptologists can ensure that the discipline is presented with a good evidence base for interpretation and that aspects of the more specialised work that is done can be communicated. Moreover, by engaging with the plurality of interpretations and perspectives on ancient Egypt, academics can further challenge traditional assumptions about the past, thus ensuring the sustainability of Egyptology as an academic subject, and creating a more inclusive Egyptology. As a still relatively young discipline, Egyptology is inevitably going to undergo much change, as will the Petrie Museum, which this paper has shown to be an outward and progressive institution, with a lot to look forward to.

Postscript: Since the time of writing the proposed name – the Panopticon – for the new museum has changed. A public consultation has indicated that the name might be confusing and needs to be made more explicit about the academic focus of the new building. This change has also been important in achieving interdisciplinary support within UCL. At present, the working title for the new building is the Institute for Cultural Heritage and due to open in 2010.

Institute of Archaeology, University College London

Acknowledgements

If people are an organisation's most valuable resource, when posts come to an end, then their expertise is lost. Many of the references in this paper have been personal communications from museum practitioners and it has been important to record the views of the outreach workers before their posts end. I wish to thank the staff at the Petrie Museum for their input into this paper, commenting on draft versions and access to unpublished work, especially Okasha El Daly, Kenneth John, Sally MacDonald, Stephen Quirke and Celine West.

References

Accessing Virtual Egypt website. www.accessingvirtualegypt.ucl.ac.uk. Accessed on 1 April 2005.

Ambrose, T. and Runyard, S. (eds.) 1991, *Forward Planning: A handbook of business, corporate and development planning for museums and galleries*. Routledge, London.

Asante, M. K. 1992, *Afrocentricity*. Africa World Press, Trenton.

Asante, M. K. 1995, *Kemet, Afrocentricity and Knowledge*. Africa World Press, Trenton.

Asante, M. K. 2000, *The Egyptian Philosophers: Ancient African Voices from Imhotep to Akhenaten*. Africa World Press, Trenton.

Celenko, T. (ed.) 1996, *Egypt in Africa*. Indianapolis Museum of Art, Indianapolis.

Davis, S. 1996, *Producing a Forward Plan*. The Museum and Galleries Commission, London.

Department for Culture, Media and Sport (DCMS) 1999, *Museums for the Many: Standards for museums and galleries to use when developing access policies*. Department for Culture, Media and Sport, London.

Department for Culture, Media and Sport (DCMS) 2000, *Centres for Social Change: Museums, Galleries and Archives for All. Guidance on Social Inclusion for DCMS funded and local authority museums, galleries and archives in England*. Department for Culture, Media and Sport, London.

Department for Culture, Media and Sport (DCMS) 2001, *Libraries, Museums, Gallery and Archives for All: Co-operating Across the Sectors to Tackle Social Exclusion*. Department for Culture, Media and Sport, London.

Dodd, J. and Sandell, R. 2001, *Including Museums: Perspectives on Museums, Galleries and Social Inclusion*. University of Leicester, RCMG.

Digital Egypt for Universities website. www.digitalegypt.ucl.ac.uk. Accessed on 1 April 2005.

El Daly, O. 2003, What do tourists learn of Egypt? in S. MacDonald and M. Rice (eds.), *Consuming Ancient Egypt*, 139–150. UCL Press, London.

El Daly, O. 2005, *Egyptology: The Missing Millennium, Ancient Egypt in Medieval Arabic Writings*. UCL Press, London.

Hall, J. and Swain, H. 2000, Roman Boxes for London's Schools: An Outreach Service by the Museum of London, in P. McManus (ed.), *Archaeological Displays and the Public: Museology and interpretations*, (2nd edition), 87–95. Archetype Publications, London.

Hassan, F. A. 1998, Memorabilia: archaeological materiality and national identity in Egypt, in L. Meskell (ed.), *Archaeology Under Fire: Nationalism, Politics and Heritage in the Eastern Mediterranean and the Middle East*, 200–216. Routledge, London.

Hassan, F. A. 2003, Selling Egypt: Encounters at Khan el-Khalili, in S. MacDonald and M. Rice (eds.), *Consuming Ancient Egypt*, 111–122. UCL Press, London.

Hooper-Greenhill. E. (ed.) 1999, *The Educational Role of the Museum* (2nd edition). Leicester Museum Studies Readers, Routledge, London.

Institute of Archaeology 2004, *Strategic Plan 2004–2009*. Unpublished report, Institute of Archaeology, UCL.

MacDonald, S. 2000, University Museums and the Public: The Case of the Petrie Museum, in P. McManus (ed.), *Archaeological Displays and the Public: Museology and interpretations*, (2nd edition), 67–86. Archetype Publications, London.

MacDonald, S. 2003, Lost in Time and Space: Ancient Egypt in Museums, in S. MacDonald and M. Rice (eds.), *Consuming Ancient Egypt*, 86–99. UCL Press, London.

MacDonald, S. 2004, *Diversifying Archaeology: The Current Situation*. Unpublished report, Institute of Archaeology, UCL.

MacDonald, S. and Shaw, C. 2004, Uncovering Ancient Egypt: The Petrie Museum and its public, in N. Merriman (ed.), *Public Archaeology*, 109–131. Routledge, London.

Martin, D. 1996, Outreach, *Museum Practice* 1(3), 36–76.

Merriman, N. 2004a, Introduction: Diversity and dissonance in public archaeology, in N. Merriman (ed.), *Public Archaeology*, 1–17. Routledge, London.

Merriman, N. 2004b, Involving the Public in Museum Archaeology, in N. Merriman (ed.), *Public Archaeology*, 85–108. Routledge, London.

Mudimbe, V. W. 1988, *The Invention of Africa: Gnosis, Philosophy and the Order of Knowledge*. Bloomington: Indiana University Press.

Museums Association website. www.museumsassociation.org. Accessed 1 April 2005.

O'Connor, D. and Reid, A. 2003, *Ancient Egypt in Africa*. UCL Press, London.

Paris, S. G. 2002, *Perspectives in Object Centred Learning in Museums*. Lawrence Erlbaum Associates, London.

Reid, D. M. 1984, Indigenous Egyptology: the decolonization of a profession? *Journal of the American Oriental Society* 105, 233–246.

Reid, D. M. 2002, *Whose Pharaohs? Archaeology, Museums, and Egyptian National Identity from Napoleon to World War I*. University of California Press, Berkeley.

Sandell, R. 2002, Museums and the combating of social inequality, in R. Sandell (ed.), *Museums, Society, Inequality*, 3–23. Routledge, London.

Scott, C. 2002, Measuring Social Value, in R. Sandell (ed.), *Museums, Society, Inequality*, 41–55. Routledge, London.

Smith, L. 2004, *Archaeological Theory and the Politics of Cultural Heritage*. Routledge, London.

Stone, P. G. and MacKenzie, R. (eds.), 1994, *The Excluded Past: Archaeology in education*. Routledge, London.

Stone, P. G. and Molyneaux, B. L. (eds.), 1994, *The Presented Past: Heritage, museums and education*. Routledge, London.

UCL Museums and Collections. 2004, *Museums and Collections of University College London: 5 Year Strategic Plan 2004–2009*. University College London [available soon online at www.museum.ucl.ac.uk].

UCL Widening Participation website. www.ucl.ac.uk/prospective-students/widening-participation/. Accessed on 1 April 2005.

Virtual Kahun website. www.kahun.man.ac.uk. Accessed on 1 April 2005.

Pepi I and the Temple of Satet at Elephantine

Richard Bussmann

For fifteen years, the early provincial temples of Egypt have been viewed in light of a structural historical paradigm: the relationship between residential and provincial culture (Kemp 1989, 65–83; O'Connor 1992; Seidlmayer 1996; Wilkinson 2000, 303–320). Barry Kemp observes the difference between the 'preformal' divine temples of the 3rd millennium and the 'formal' temples of the following eras. The preformal temples are modest mud-brick constructions compared to the royal mortuary complexes made of stone. Kemp concludes: "It means that for about a third of its history, Pharaonic Egypt was a country of two cultures" (1989, 83).

This article will treat the Satet temple against this background. My central question will be how Pepi I behaved with regard to the Satet temple, considered with special reference to the royal objects found in the temple. The discussion will touch upon some archaeological problems involved. Finally, an alternative reconstruction of the 6th Dynasty temple will be proposed.

From the 6th Dynasty onwards, at the latest, Egypt was subject to a growing regionalisation. This regionalisation undermined the administrative and cultural primacy of the residence and resulted in the princedoms of the First Intermediate Period. The *ka*-house policy of the kings of the 6th Dynasty can be seen as a reaction to this regionalisation (Fischer 1958).

According to Egyptian texts, the term *ka*-house refers to a tomb or, more generally, to a cult place detached from a burial (Kaplony 1980). As far as we know, the first *ka*-houses of the latter kind were erected by the kings of the 6th Dynasty (Franke 1994, 118–127; Müller-Wollermann and Vandekerckhove 2001, 331–332). Pepi I erected *ka*-houses for his own cult throughout the country. We have evidence from Bubastis in the Delta, Memphis, Zawyet el-Meytin, Assiut, Nagada,

Figure 1. *Naos of Pepi I (after Ziegler 1990, 51.)*

Elkab and possibly Abydos and Hierakonpolis as well. The extensive list reveals an underlying programmatic strategy. One aim of Pepi I was probably to strengthen the royal presence in the province. How is the new relationship between the Crown and the provincial temples reflected in the temple of Satet?

Only a few royal objects dating before the 6th Dynasty have been found in the temple (Dreyer 1986, no. 28 and 426). At the beginning of the 6th Dynasty the number of objects with royal names increases. Among the votive material are several faience tablets with the names of Pepi I and Pepi II (Dreyer 1986, no. 428–447). Some of them mention their *Sed*-festivals. Moreover, a limestone vessel in the shape of an ape with its offspring bears the cartouche of Pepi I (Dreyer 1986, no. 455).

Stone vessels of this and other types were distributed by the residence to high ranking officials (Fischer 1993; Minault-Gout 1993; Ziegler 1997). Medunefer from Balat is one prominent example (Vallogia 1986, 105–119). Therefore, the ape vessel from the Satet temple was probably a present to a high provincial official who offered it secondarily as a votive offering in the temple. In contrast, the faience tablets are known only from the Satet temple and the temple of Abydos (Petrie 1903, pl. 21, no. 12–14) as well as from the mortuary temple of Pepi I (Leclant 1978, 279–281, pl. 27, fig. 22). It seems reasonable to conclude that the faience tablets were not presents to high officials but votives directly offered by the kings in the temples.

The most prominent royal object from the Satet temple is the red granite *naos* of Pepi I (Figure 1; Ziegler 1990, 50–53). It came to light in the debris near the late temple. It is 1.32m in height and the front side has a shallow niche. To the left and right of it, we read the name of Pepi I followed by the epithet "beloved of Satet". Obviously, Pepi I endowed the temple of Satet with this *naos*. Merenre then had his name written above the inscriptions of his predecessor. Where did the *naos* stand within the temple?

Let us turn now to the archaeology of the temple (Dreyer 1986, 11–17). It began with a natural niche formed by three granite rocks. The oldest temple layers, VIII and VII, had a skewed orientation towards the northern rock. The following layer, VI, had an orientation towards the western rock. The same is true for layers V to I where the area of the sanctuary had a rectangular plan.

Layer V is only poorly preserved and is marked by a dotted line on the drawing. That is why I refer to the plan of layer IV which is nearly identical and far better preserved (Figure 2). In the middle of the court there is the so-

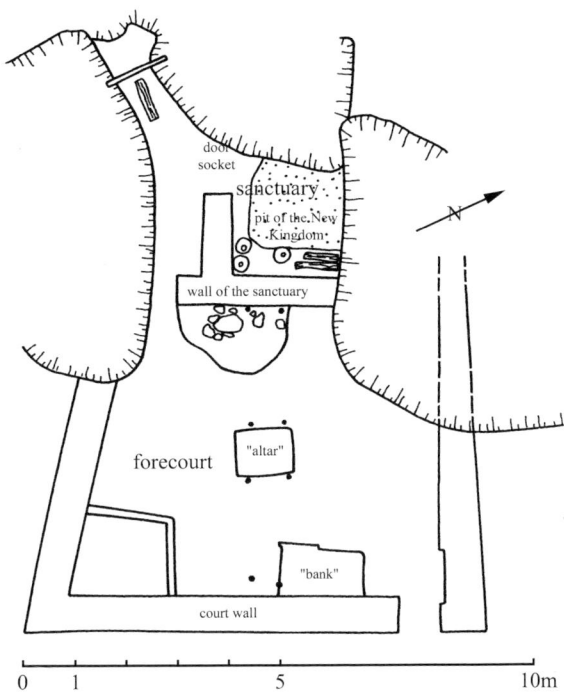

Figure 2. *Satet temple, layer IV (after Dreyer 1986, Abb. 4).*

called 'altar' (Bussmann 2006). Next to the entrance is a mud-brick structure labelled "bank" in the publication. The entrance to the sanctuary was located at a door in the rear of the rock niche. Beneath the door socket the excavators recovered a foundation deposit which will be discussed below. What remains from the original furnishing of the sanctuary, are two pots, a pottery stand and two wooden boards.

In order to avoid an anachronistic reconstruction, the date of the layers must be determined on the basis of their stratification (Figure 3; Dreyer 1986, Abb. 7–8). The designation of the layers is due to the different phases of renovation of the wall of the sanctuary. The layers VIII to I represent the brick constructions of the 3rd millennium. What follows is the stone foundation of the temples of the 11th to 18th Dynasty.

The only dating criteria currently available are stratified objects with inscriptions. Beneath the wall of the sanctuary of layer V the earliest object with an inscription has been found. It is a faience tablet with the name of Pepi I (Dreyer 1986, no. 435). On top of the layers of the brick temple, several stone slabs came to light. They probably served as the foundation for a chapel of Antef II built during the 11th Dynasty (Kaiser *et al.* 1993, 145–152). Thus layers V to I can be dated to the period between Pepi I and Antef II.

One major archaeological problem is the coherence of the layers. The floors that once connected the architectural features, such as the court wall, the so-called altar and the wall of the sanctuary, were largely disturbed and badly recorded. Consequently, and in contrast to the current interpretation, we cannot be sure of their chronological relationship to one another. On the other hand, it seems highly probable that the rebuilding of the court wall I, the altar I and the wall of the sanctuary V result from one overall reorganisation of the temple, thus making them all contemporaneous. I propose a date toward the end of the reign of Pepi I. The final publication

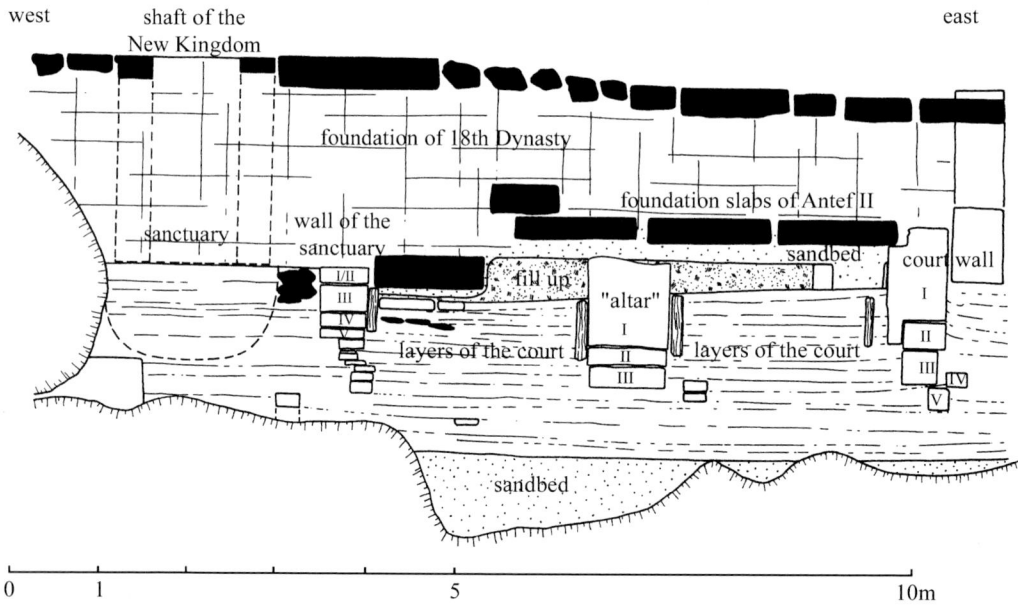

Figure 3. *Satet temple, section of early layers (after Dreyer 1986, Abb. 7)*

of the architecture and the pottery of the temple will provide further details for the dating.

The renovation of the temple is revealing in terms of my central question. The reorganisation of the temple from layer VI to V dates to the reign of Pepi I. However, there is no reason to believe that it was Pepi I who initiated it. The current interpretation of the faience tablets as foundation offerings (Dreyer 1986, 94) does not hold. The tablets were not concentrated in one deposit. They were found between different walls and in the layers of the court. The above mentioned foundation deposit beneath the door socket of the sanctuary of layer V (Dreyer 1986, findspot number 6972) contained a triangular tile, a model brick, the figure of a baboon, the figure of a boy, the lower part of a female figure, the fragment of a faience vessel, beads, gold leaf, four pebbles and fragments of an ostrich egg. Evidently, we are dealing here with old votive objects used secondarily as foundation objects. Therefore, the deposit and the reorganisation of the temple attest to a local rather than royal initiative. If it were actually a royal deposit, one would expect to find a faience tablet with a king's name, maybe the skull of an ox and pottery (Weinstein 1973).

I will now return to the location of the granite *naos*. In the present-day reconstruction of the early temple, the German Archaeological Institute has erected a copy of the *naos* within the sanctuary at the rear (Ziegler 1990, 52). According to this reconstruction, a statue of the goddess Satet had been set up in the niche of the *naos*. This reconstruction is important because it is a model for other early temples whose cult layout is otherwise unknown. The excavators of Tell Ibrahim Awad in the eastern delta reconstructed a comparable *naos* in the local temple along these lines (Eigner 2000).

In contrast, Detlef Franke (1994, 121) supposes that the *naos* was not made for a statue of Satet, but for a statue of Pepi I belonging to the cult of the royal *ka*. Bearing in mind the *ka*-house policy of Pepi I outlined above, this reconstruction makes sense. A structure that could have been the *ka*-house of Pepi I has not been excavated on Elephantine. Nor do the tomb inscriptions of the local cemeteries mention a priest of the royal *ka*. However, this missing evidence does not rule out the possibility of a royal cult within the temple enclosure.

Looking more closely at the so-called bank in the forecourt, its bricks turn out to be set up in a vertical position. This construction is characteristic of foundations made of mudbricks (Arnold 1994, 86–87). The 'bank' might therefore be interpreted as a foundation, if it is not simply a collapsed part of the wall of the court (personal communication M. Bietak to G. Dreyer). I propose that the granite *naos* of Pepi I was located here.

I have tried to visualise this arrangement more concretely and searched for statue types of Pepi I. I found two *Sed*-festival statues of Pepi I (Romano 1998). Whereas the provenance of the statue Brooklyn 39.120 (Romano, no. 3) is unknown, the other one (Romano, no.1, present location unknown) was found in Dendera. It may have functioned there in the context of the royal cult. Accordingly, the king could have sent a *Sed*-festival statue to Elephantine together with the above mentioned *Sed*-festival tablets. This is why I have considered these two statues for my reconstruction.

My reconstruction is based mainly on two observations. First, the architectural tradition of the temple points to this direction. In the forecourt of the temple of Antef III, Werner Kaiser has reconstructed a chapel for the royal cult in exactly the same location (Figure 4; Kaiser *et al.* 1993, 148–151). This cult topography can now be traced back to the 6th Dynasty. Secondly, the historical context seems to support my reconstruction. Pepi I did not dedicate a *naos* to Satet. Rather, the *naos* was erected in the forecourt to install his own cult, as in other provincial temples.

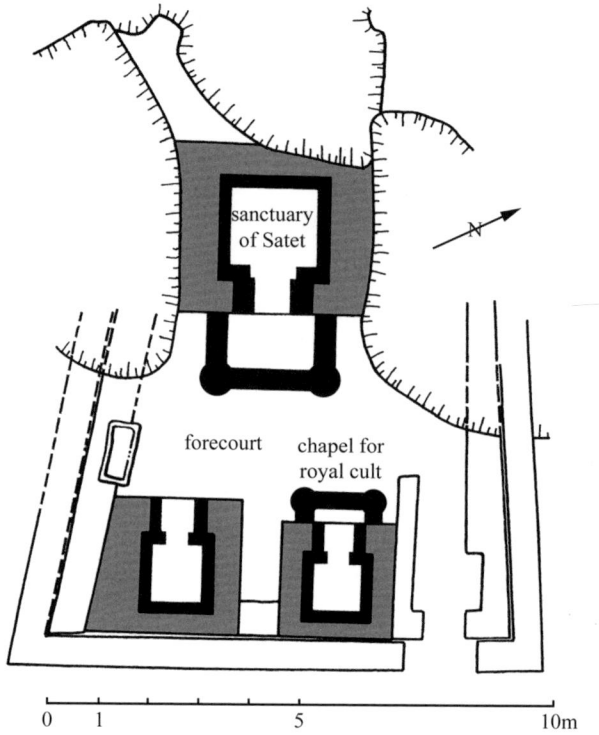

Figure 4. Reconstructed Satet temple of Antef III (after Kaiser et al. 1993, Abb. 7).

The other royal objects from the Satet temple can be explained consistently within this reconstruction. The faience tablets give the name of Pepi I and II and mention their *Sed*-festivals. Neither do the other objects refer to Satet. Merenre and Pepi II had two inscriptions written on the rocks of the sanctuary (Kaiser *et al.* 1976, 78–80). They did not include the epithet "beloved of Satet". The inscription of Merenre on the left begins with a date and mentions the visit to the temple in the context of an expedition to strike down the chiefs of the foreign land. Merenre did not visit the temple for the sake of Satet, but en route to a military mission in the south.

In conclusion, on the one hand, the royal objects reveal a royal engagement with the temple of Satet from the reign of Pepi I onwards. On the other hand, this engagement seems to have been motivated by interests of the residence rather than on behalf of the provincial goddess Satet.

I have attempted to analyse the Satet temple at the time of Pepi I in light of the discussion about the relationship between residence and provincial Egypt. The background to my considerations is a functional definition of the early provincial temples. They served as an institutionalised interface between residence and province in an Egypt of two cultures.

Freie Universität, Berlin

References

Arnold D. 1994, *Lexikon der ägyptischen Baukunst*. Artemis und Winkler, Zürich.

Bussmann, R. 2006, Der Kult im frühen Satet-Tempel von Elephantine, in J. Mylonopoulos and H. Roeder and H. Roeder (eds.), *Archäologie und Ritual. Auf der Suche nach der rituellen Handlung in den antiken Kulturen Aegyptens und Griechenlands*, Phoibos Verlag, Wien 25–36.

Dreyer, G. 1986, *Elephantine, 8: Der Tempel der Satet. Die Funde der Frühzeit und des Alten Reiches*. Philipp von Zabern, Mainz.

Eigner, D. 2000, Tell Ibrahim Awad: Divine Residence from Dynasty 0 until Dynasty 11, in *Ägypten und Levante* 10, 17–36.

Fischer, H. G. 1958, Review of L. Habachi, *Tell Basta*. Institut Français d'Archéologie Orientale du Caire, Cairo, in *American Journal of Archaeology* 62, 330–333.

Fischer, H. G. 1993, Another Pithemorphic Vessel of the Sixth Dynasty, *Journal of the American Research Center In Egypt* 30, 1–9.

Franke, D. 1994, *Das Heiligtum des Heqaib auf Elephantine. Geschichte eines Provinzheiligtums im Mittleren Reich*. Heidelberger Orientverlag, Heidelberg.

Kaiser, W., Dreyer, G., Gempeler, R., Grossmann, P., Haeny, G., Jaritz, H., and Junge, F. 1976, Stadt und Tempel von Elephantine. Sechster Grabungsbericht, *Mitteilungen des Deutschen Archäologischen Instituts, Abteilung Kairo* 32, 67–112.

Kaiser, W., Bommas, M., Jaritz, H., Krekeler, A., v. Pilgrimm, C., Schultz, M., Schmidt-Schultz, T., and Ziermann, M. 1993, Stadt und Tempel von Elephantine. 19./20. Grabungsbericht, *Mitteilungen des Deutschen Archäologischen Instituts, Abteilung Kairo* 49, 133–187.

Kaplony, P. 1980, Ka-Haus, in W. Helck and E. Otto (eds.), *Lexikon der Ägyptologie, III*, cols. 284–287. Harrassowitz, Wiesbaden.

Kemp, B. J. 1983, Old Kingdom, Middle Kingdom and Second Intermediate Period. Provincial Egypt, in: B. G. Trigger, B. J. Kemp, D. O'Connor, and A. B. Lloyd, *Ancient Egypt. A Social History*, 96–112.

Kemp, B. J. 1989, *Ancient Egypt. Anatomy of a Civilization*. Routledge, London.

Leclant, J. 1978, Fouilles et travaux en Égypte et au Soudan, 1976–1977, *Orientalia (Nova Series)* 47, 266–320.

Minault-Gout, A. 1993, Sur les vases jubilaires et leur diffusion, in C. Berger and B. Mathieu, *Études sur l'Ancien Empire et la nécropole de Saqqâra dédiées à Jean-Philippe Lauer*, 305–314. Université Paul Valéry, Montpellier 1997.

Müller-Wollermann, R. and Vandekerckhove, H. 2001, *Elkab, 6: Die Felsinschriften des Wadi Hilâl, 1*. Brepols, Turnhout.

O'Connor, D. 1992, The Status of Early Egyptian Temples: an Alternate Theory, in R. Friedman and B. Adams (eds.), *The Followers of Horus, Studies Dedicated to Michael Allen Hoffman 1944–1990*, 83–98. Oxbow Books, Oxford.

Petrie, W. M. F. 1903, *Abydos. Part II*. Egypt Exploration Fund, London.

Romano, J. F. 1998, Sixth Dynasty Royal Sculpure, in N. Grimal (ed.), *Les critères de datation stylistiques à l'Ancien Empire*, 235–303. Institut français d'archéologie orientale du Caire, Cairo.

Seidlmayer, S. J. 1996, Town and State in the Early Old Kingdom. A View from Elephantine, in J. Spencer (ed.), *Aspects of Early Egypt*, 108–127. British Museum Press, London.

Vallogia, M. 1986, *Balat, 1: Le mastaba de Medou-Nefer, 1*. Institut Français d'Archéologie Orientale du Caire, Cairo.

Weinstein, J. M. 1973, *Foundation Deposits in Ancient Egypt*. Xerox University Microfilms, Michigan.

Wilkinson, T. A. H. 2000, *Early Dynastic Egypt*. Routledge, London and New York.

Ziegler, C. 1990, *Catalogue des stèles, peintures et reliefs égyptiens de l'Ancien Empire et de la Première Période Intermédiaire vers 2686–2040 avant J.-C*. Éditions de la Réunion des musées nationaux, Paris.

Ziegler, C. 1997, Sur quelques vases inscrits de l'Ancien Empire, in C. Berger and B. Mathieu, *Études sur l'Ancien Empire et la nécropole de Saqqâra dédiées à Jean-Philippe Lauer*, 461–489. Université Paul Valéry, Montpellier 1997.

The Unique Amun-Re at Luxor Temple

András Gulyás

Introduction

This paper will present various decorative principles of the temple of Luxor, in order to understand the temple's god-concept. These principles will be then compared to contemporary solar hymns. In the following, it will be argued that in the southernmost halls of the temple proper at Luxor, Amun-Re is represented as the sole supreme solar god – unlike in the other parts of the temple, where he is represented in the company of other divinities. The religious-historical importance of this decorative pattern will also be briefly discussed.

I. Methodological remarks

If one wishes to understand the religious meaning of a given temple and its local cult statue, the inner halls provide the most vital clues. Fortunately, these halls at Luxor temple are in an excellent state of preservation. The easiest way to understand the theological meaning of Amun-Re at Luxor, as well as the god-concept of the temple proper, would be to collect the reliefs of the temple that bear the name of the local Amun-Re. However, this solution has been widely rejected by scholars as unproductive, because this name has absolutely no priority (Brunner 1977, 75) in the halls where the local cult statue of Amun-Re once resided. Considering the importance the ancient Egyptians attributed to names in general (Farkas 2003, 258–278), it is somewhat surprising that in these halls *Jpt rst* does not occur in the names of Amun-Re, even though there are plenty of representations with the local god-form *Jmn Rᶜ ḫntj ḏsr ḏsrw* in the 18th dynasty temple at Deir el Bahari (Naville 1895, pl. XIX; pl. XX; Naville 1896, pl. XXXIII; pl. XLIV; Ullmann 2002, 49).

One of the most successful approaches to the theology of Luxor temple was based on a (mis)interpretation of the temple's name, *Jpt rst*. The translation, 'southern harim', is not uncommon even today, but in earlier times it was much more widespread. This interpretation was based on the reliefs of the divine birth that can be observed in hall XIII of the temple. Consequently, according to some scholars, the temple at Luxor would be the harim of Amun (for an overview, see Pamminger 1992b).

However, several facts have challenged the interpretation of the Luxor temple as 'southern harim'. First of all, the meaning of the word *jpt* does not have much to do with 'harim', in the way this interpretation seems to suggest. For instance, Daressy – among other scholars – translated the word *jpt* simply as 'sanctuary' (Daressy 1893, 1). Comparisons with further sources increasingly clarified that the 'southern harim' theory does not reflect the theology of the temple. The story of divine birth can be found in many other temples as well, as the comparative study of H. Brunner has shown (Brunner 1964).

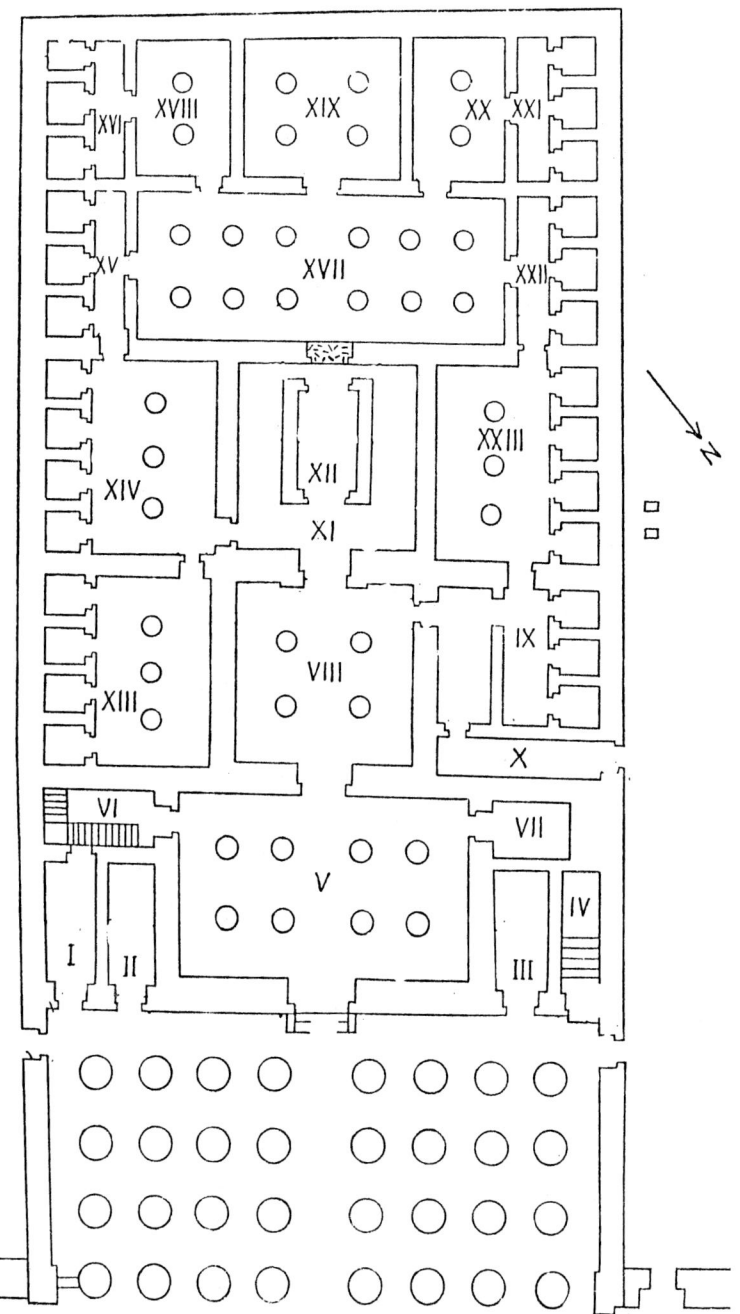

Figure 1. *The temple proper with the portico at Luxor (after Porter and Moss 1994).*

This short retrospection on the history of Egyptology will suffice to demonstrate that a single wall and its reliefs can only be taken as a representation of the theology of the temple with precautions, and all the more so since the story of divine birth is located in a hall in Luxor that does not belong to the section of the temple dedicated to the local cult statue of Amun-Re. It is not in the southernmost halls where Amun-Re at Luxor resided (Porter and Moss 1994, Plan XXXII, Hall XIX see figure 1), nor is it situated on the main axis of the temple, where Amun-Re of Karnak proceeded towards the barque sanctuary (Porter and Moss 1994, Plan XXXII, Hall V, VIII, XI).

In this paper I will follow another approach, and instead of concentrating on one specific wall or a single relief in the temple, I will focus on some general decorative principles. These principles are all the more important as they characterize the southernmost halls of the temple proper, the halls where the cult statue of Amun-Re at Luxor resided. Therefore, this approach will fulfill two methodological requirements: that of considering a relatively large number of reliefs to find an answer to such a general question as the religious meaning of Amun-Re at Luxor; and that of giving priority to reliefs found in the most relevant parts of the temple from a theological point of view.

In order to grasp the meaning of the southernmost halls and the theology of Amun-Re of/at Luxor, we must seek out those general decorative principles that characterize this section of halls as a whole. The concept of divine and/or human presence will be used in the description of the decorative pattern to denote figures depicted in a given hall or section of halls. From this point of view, roughly four different levels can be distinguished in the temple proper at Luxor.

II. Divine and human presence in the temple proper at Luxor

What we can actually observe in Luxor is the result of a more than thousand-year-long building activity (Bell 1997, 144 ff; Grallert 2001). Amenhotep III, as it is also described on his stela found in his West-Theban temple (Beylage 2002, 395; Urk. IV. 1646–1657), built a much smaller-sized temple originally, the 'temple proper' with the portico and the so-called *maru* (Cabrol 2001, 267–269; Johnson 1998, 68), the exact location of which is still unclear (Badawy 1956, 59; Cabrol 2000, 268; Gessler-Löhr 1983, 187–191; Stadelmann 1978, 179). Thus, the temple proper constitutes a section of halls that reflects the entire original religious concept. It is in the southernmost halls of this building that the cult statue of Amun-Re at Luxor resided.

1. The outermost hall

On the northern wall of the outermost hall, called the first antechamber, soldiers, priests and courtiers are depicted, who are proceeding with the king toward Amun-Re (Porter and Moss 1994, p. 320, Hall V, (118)). Although the representation of this procession does not necessarily imply that the procession actually took place in this hall, the relief is nevertheless relevant from the point of view of accessibility. Processions are frequently represented in the outermost halls of Theban temples (see for example Maher-Taha and Loyrette, 1979; one of the closest parallels to the relief in this hall can be found in TT 131: Dziobek 1994, Taf. 18, 19). In these halls a relatively large number of people could participate in the celebrations, unlike in the inner halls, to which only a limited number of individuals had access (Assmann 1969, 261, n. 61).

This hall was thus reserved for 'public' celebrations (Bell 1997, n. 146), which can also be confirmed by an observation of Murnane, as quoted by Bell (1985, 272). According to Murnane, two kinds of coronation/confirmation of royal power rituals can be distinguished in the temple

Figure 2. *Ritual of the confirmation of royal power on the southern wall of hall V at Luxor. Photo by the author.*

proper. In the inner parts of the temple, one can see rituals where the king is kneeling, facing Amun-Re, who is sitting on his throne. In the first antechamber, however, although the composition is very similar to those in the inner halls, the king is not facing the god, but is looking outward (Figure 2). The public ceremonies of the coronation/confirmation of royal power were probably celebrated in this hall (for these festivals of Amenhotep III see Cabrol 2000, 192–201). The significance of the scene where the king is facing outward, kneeling before the supreme solar god, can be captured by the fact that this scene is repeated several times on the southern wall of the hall. The hall's function is also reflected by its later use, as the place of worship for the cult of the Roman emperor (Monneret de Villard 1953).

2. The hall of processions

The hall to the south of the first antechamber, the so-called second antechamber, was defined by Arnold as an "Opfertischsaal" (Arnold 1962, 44). In fact, many different deities appear on the northern wall: on the northern wall the ennead is evoked to receive the offerings (Porter and Moss 1994, 321, Hall VIII, (125)).

Processions can be seen on the northern, eastern and western walls. In the lowest register of the eastern wall there is a procession with myrrh vessels (Figure 3); in the lowest register of the western wall a procession is taking place with the fresh water of inundation (Porter and Moss

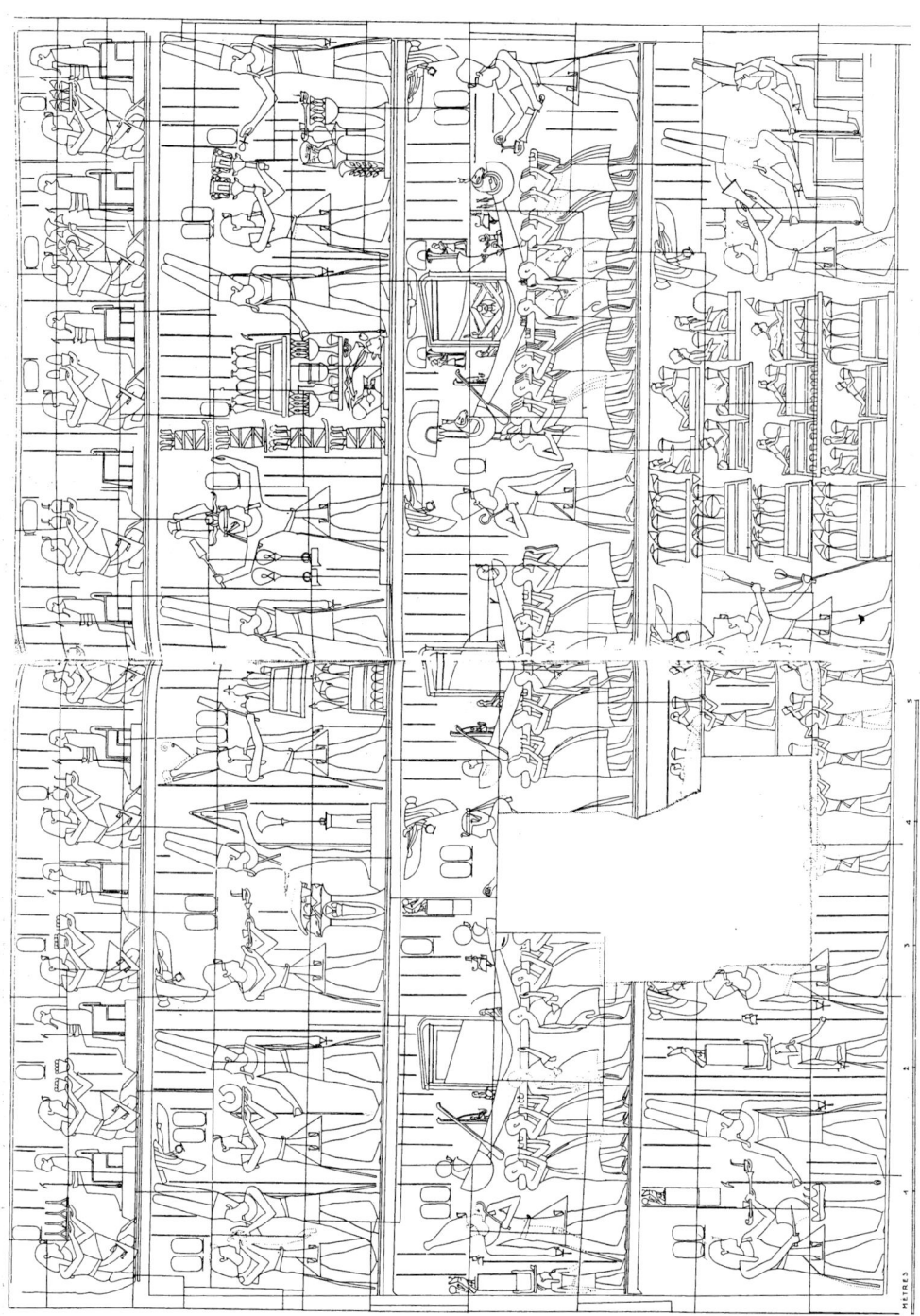

Figure 3. *The eastern wall of hall VIII, drawing by Lucy Lamie in Schwaller de Lubicz 1977, vol. II, pl. XXXI.*

1994, p. 322, Hall VIII, (128), III, 1; Gulyás forthcoming a; Schott, E. 1970). In the second register of the eastern wall, the procession of divine barques can be seen (Figure 3; Porter and Moss 1994, p. 321, Hall VIII, (126), II). Needless to say, this relief, similar to the procession of the soldiers in the first antechamber, does not necessarily imply that the divine barques reached this hall. Most probably they remained in their chapels in the outer part of the temple, except for the barque of Amun-Re (Porter and Moss 1994, 319, rooms I-III). In the same register of the western wall, the procession with the new clothes is depicted (Porter and Moss 1994; Hall VIII, (128), II, 1; Ryhiner 1995).

From the point of view of divine and human presence, this hall differs from the 'first antechamber'. The soldiers represented in the first antechamber are not present. The characteristic feature of this hall is the high number of priests who are participating in the processions. The very presence of these processions probably alludes to the transitory function of this hall, a supposition that is further confirmed by the two major functions of the door situated on the western wall. After the celebration of the rituals in the southern halls, this door was used by the king to return to the barque sanctuary (Schuller-Götzburg 1986; 1990); furthermore, the door also served as a side-entrance for the priests equipped with the accessories for the presentation of the rituals in the temple. As in other temples, and probably in Luxor as well, only a small number of priests were allowed to enter the inner halls (Kruchten 1989). Correspondingly, there are no processions in the inner halls that depict a large number of priests.

As for the gods, the souls of Pe and Nekhen are participating in the renewal of royal power on the western wall (Porter and Moss 1994, 323, Room IX, (131)). Different goddesses appear behind the supreme solar god (Porter and Moss 1994, 323, Room IX, (131)); in the upper register a series of smaller chapels is shown with various deities (see figure 3, Porter and Moss 1994, 322, Frieze).

3. The barque chapel, the hall of divine birth and the New Year's hall

The same observations hold true for halls XI, XIV and XIII, with the main difference that priestly processions, such as that of hall VIII, cannot be found here. Therefore the halls that are accessible from the processions hall (VIII) belong to another level of accessibility. This difference in accessibility is further indicated by the fact that the ritual of introducing the king is represented on the northern wall of the barque chapel (Porter and Moss 1994, 323; Hall XI, (137), III).

On the western wall of the barque sanctuary, different gods can be seen (Porter and Moss 1994, 324 (140)), and just as above, other divinities also appear beside Amun-Re on the eastern wall. The barque of Amun-Re on the lower register of the eastern and western walls, and the coronation/renewal of royal power rituals on the southern wall can be considered as the thematically important characteristics of this hall.

The orientation of the king on the reliefs gives a rough indication of the path he followed during the liturgy in the Luxor temple (Schuller-Götzburg 1986). From the barque sanctuary he first proceeded east, to hall XIV and to the hall of divine birth (Porter and Moss 1994, Plan XXXII, Hall XIII). The western wall of hall XIII is probably the best known wall of the temple, since it is occupied entirely by the story of divine birth. Needless to say, many divinities appear on this wall beside the queen, Mutemuia, Amun-Re and the king, Amenhotep III. The northern wall is dedicated entirely to the goddess, whereas the southern one, as Brunner remarks (Brunner 1964, 6), is a continuation of the story of divine birth, with the ennead, Amun-Re, the king and Iunmutef. The major theme is the confirmation of the royal power of Amenhotep

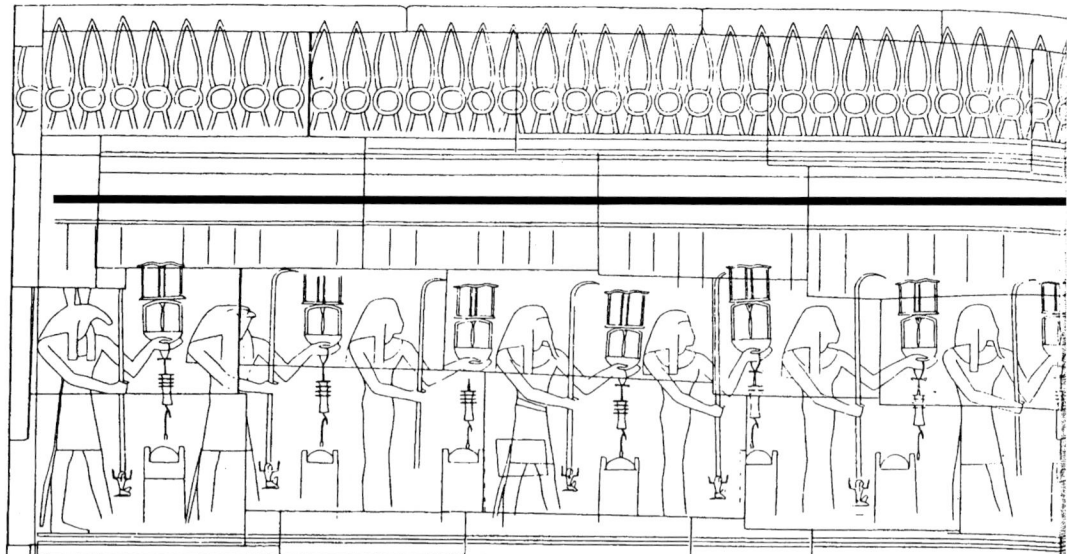

Figure 4. The procession of gods in hall XIV, after Schwaller de Lubicz 1977, vol. II, pl. XCIX.

III in the presence of the above-mentioned divinities. The eastern wall also pursues this theme: it shows the Sed-festival scenes of Amenhotep III (on his jubilees see Dorman 1994; Schiff Giorgini 2003).

The hall that is situated to the south of the hall of divine birth is less well-known and less thoroughly studied, mainly because it is almost completely unpublished. However, I had the opportunity to study its reliefs in Paris through the unpublished photographic documentation of Alexandre Moret. Many different deities appear on the walls of this hall as well. The scene in Figure 4 occupies the entire uppermost register of the western wall, and it is also repeated on the northern wall. Above the gods we find the following inscription:

As far as we can judge from the rest, a similar relief was probably carved in the uppermost register of the eastern wall as well. The repetition of the scene indicates that it plays an important role in identifying the meaning of this hall. According to the inscription, the arrival of the deities equipped with life is connected to the opening of the New Year; therefore, I suggest calling this hall the New Year's Hall. The other thematically significant feature of the hall is once again the renewal of royal power (Porter and Moss 1994, Room XIV, (157), III).

4. The halls of the solitary supreme solar god

The twelve-columned hall can be entered through room XV (Porter and Moss 1994, plan XXXII). This small-sized hall (XV) serves as a kind of antechamber, which is demonstrated by the fact that the *bsj nsw* scene is located on the eastern inner wall of the twelve-columned

hall (Brunner 1977, Tafel 74). Thus, the door between room XV and the twelve-columned hall (XVII) constitutes an important point of transition. This explains why we find the inscription about the king's secret knowledge on the western wall of hall XVII (Assmann 1970; Baines 1990; 1998; Betrò 1990; Parker *et al.* 1979), since it is exactly this knowledge that enabled the king to enter the halls (compare with Kákosy 2002, 325–329).

As for divine and human presence, the most striking decorative feature of these halls is the exclusiveness of Amun-Re. Out of the more than forty ritual scenes of the twelve-columned hall, there is no other god or goddess depicted in the company of Amun-Re (Figure 5, the only exception is a scene on the northern wall: Brunner 1977, Tafel 84). The souls of Pe and Nekhen, the Ennead, which had been represented in the previously described sections of the temple several times, are not present in the section of the solitary supreme solar god.

Apart from being represented by himself, a further feature of the reliefs – with a few exceptions – is that no other god appears on the walls of these four halls (XVII, XVIII, XIX, XX), save Amun-Re. Among the exceptions, however, there is a scene that introduces the king into this part of the temple (*bsj nsw*), where – for the sake of the composition – other gods are represented as well (Brunner 1977, Tafel 74). On the same wall, just like on the western wall of hall XVII, various gods and goddesses are travelling within the solar barque (Brunner 1977, Tafel 66). These two representations of the solar barque are accompanied by the inscription about the king's secret knowledge, which can be found in other temples as well (Assmann 1970; Brunner 1977). Although this section of halls is dedicated primarily and almost exclusively to Amun-Re as the supreme solar god, it is Re who appears in the barque. In this case, the presence of other gods can be ascribed to the tradition of the texts and the scene that belongs to it (Assmann 1970).

Unlike the other halls of the temple, rituals of the renewal of royal power, such as coronation, do not constitute an important topic in this section of halls. Apparently, whatever the exact meaning of the decoration of the temple is, the principal aim of the rituals was the renewal

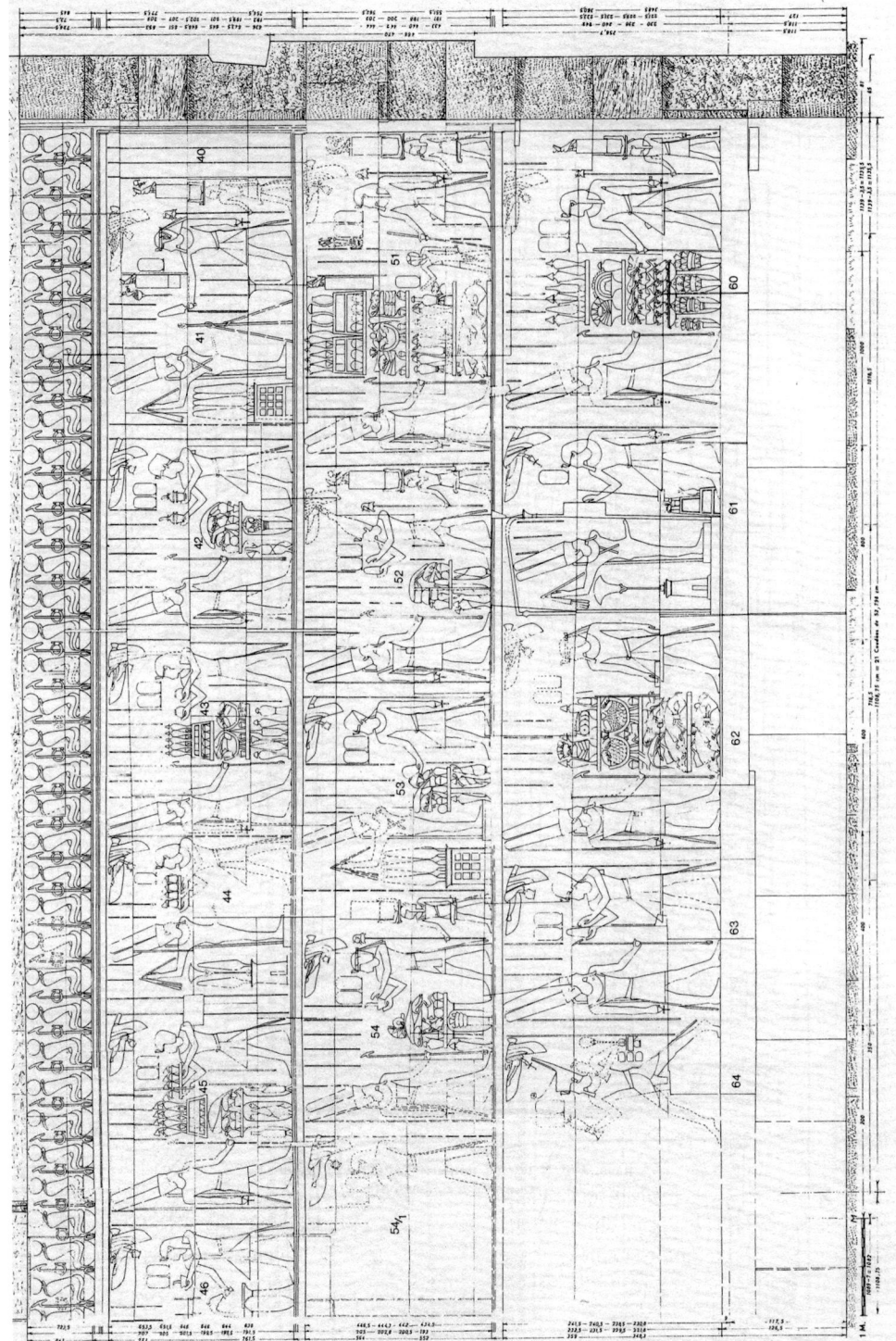

Figure 5. The eastern part of the northern wall of the twelve-columned hall (XVII) at Luxor (Brunner 1977, Tafel 9).

of Egypt/god/king, as these three concepts were interconnected in ancient Egyptian mentality. There is, however, a clear difference between the decoration of the other halls and the decoration of this southernmost section of halls. While in the northern halls entire wall surfaces (see for instance the southern wall of room XI) or entire registers were dedicated to the topic of the renewal of royal power through coronation, this is not the case in the southern halls. Two scenes above the entrance to the chapel of Amun-Re at Luxor, representing rituals of the renewal of royal power, belong to the special category of small-sized reliefs, which differ in size from the reliefs that cover the walls.

A further principle of decoration is followed consequently throughout the three southernmost halls (Porter and Moss 1994, Map XXXII, Halls XVIII, XIX, XX). Amun-Re is shown once in his ithyphallic and once in his other form. This alternation is continued on the walls where the scenes constitute sequences (on the meaning of this decoration see Gulyás forthcoming b), and is interrupted only on one relief situated on the western wall of the chapel of Amun, in the second register.

Besides the above-mentioned decorative principles, the architectural structure is also of relevance. The isolation of the southernmost halls is expressed architecturally as the main axis of the temple, which is interrupted at the southern wall of the barque sanctuary (Brunner 1977, 10; Lacau 1941; Porter and Moss 1994, Map XXXII, Hall XI). Architecturally, the twelve-columned hall roughly follows the east-west axis, while the chapel of Amun-Re at Luxor is situated on the main axis of the temple, perpendicularly to the axis of the twelve-columned hall. These two axes of the temple evoke the two axes of the ancient Egyptian world (Schott 1969, 30–4; 1970).

A further architectural feature of the chapel of Amun-Re at Luxor, corresponding to the above-mentioned principle of decoration, is the chapel's relative isolation. The cult statue of the local Amun-Re once stood in the sanctuary (XIX), where the remains of the statue base are still visible. Customarily, the chapel of the principal god, if there was enough space, was frequently flanked by the chapels of other gods. However, in this case, and quite unusually, the two neighbouring halls (XVIII, XX) could not function as the chapels of the other two members of the Theban triad, since they are divided by two columns in the middle, and no reference can be found on their walls to the Theban triad either. In this way, the chapel of Amun-Re at Luxor is a solitary structure, isolated from the much smaller chapels belonging to different gods on the eastern and western sides of the temple (Pamminger 1992a, n. 34; Arnold 1962, 20 (18), 122–123). The decoration of the walls and the architectural structure thus express the same concept, the isolation of the local Amun-form.

An inquiry into the meaning of the exclusiveness of Amun-Re in the southernmost halls leads us in two directions and two concepts. In order to understand this seemingly very simple decorative pattern, a comparison must be made with the decoration of other temples so that we can see to what extent it can be considered as a specific decoration; then, as a second step, we have to look for the meaning of this solitary god in contemporary religious literature. Since a full description of the context and meaning of this decoration would necessitate a thorough study of New Kingdom temples, the present study will be limited to one comparison.

The temple of Seti I at Abydos offers an appropriate comparison, as its inner halls are relatively well preserved. Behind the seven chapels of the temple (Porter and Moss 1991, 4.), a separate section of halls was dedicated to Osiris. These halls, which could be entered through the chapel of Osiris, have an axis that is perpendicular to the main axis of the temple, thereby emphasizing their relative independence – similarly to the southernmost halls in Luxor. Furthermore, the halls of the temple at Abydos are found in the innermost section of the temple and are dedicated to the local principal deity, once again just like in Luxor. However, Osiris is not depicted on the walls by himself, but in the company of Isis and Horus. In fact, at the northern end of this section of halls there are three chapels: the middle one is dedicated to Osiris, the western one to Isis and the eastern one to Horus. In the theology of Osiris, the succession of Horus to his father is an extremely important feature; therefore, the latter could not be represented alone, although in some 18th Dynasty texts the sole aspect of Osiris is particularly emphasized in order to describe his uniqueness as a creator god (Moret 1931).

III. The religious concept of the sole god

In order to define the meaning of the decoration of the southernmost halls at Luxor, one has to explore the context of the temple itself. The religious historical changes must also be considered, and it is also necessary, as far as possible, to define the proper place of this decoration in the context of the Theban cult-topography re-established by Amenhotep III (Bryan 1997, 270; Gundlach 1994; on his constructions see Ullmann 2002). Various levels of context must be distinguished, ranging from the religious-historical to the cult-topographical. Undoubtedly, this sketchy description cannot replace a detailed and meticulous comparison. However, all these features and aspects and the in-depth analysis of the problem go beyond the aim of the present paper.

Therefore, I will turn briefly instead to contemporary religious literature in order to explore the meaning of the sole Amun-Re in New Kingdom religious thinking on the one hand; and consequently, the meaning of the decoration of the southernmost halls of the Luxor temple on the other hand.

There was a current in religious thinking that, also because of the ancient Egyptian concept of cult statues (Luft 2000), attributed specific characteristics to each cult statue (Török 1997, 303–309). This belief is reflected to a much lesser degree in hymns and prayers where the supreme solar god is usually evoked independently of his earthly representations, *i.e.* his cult statues. Although this could be due to the loss of papyri, it is more likely that it reflects the ancient Egyptian concept of cult statues and the 'real god'. In Papyrus Harris, where Ramesses III enumerates his donations for Amun-Re and his temples, he describes the cult statue of Amun-Re of Medinet Habu as the statue of Amun-Re without making a clear-cut distinction between the local Amun-Re and the supreme solar god (Grandet 1994, Vol. 1, 227). It is probably for this reason that we know several Amun-Re forms by name, but in some cases not much can be said about their religious meaning (see Leitz 2002). The fact that religious changes observed in New Kingdom solar hymns does not seem to affect contemporary temple decoration (Assmann 1995, 16; Derchain 1988, 85) can also be explained by the bad state of preservation of the inner halls of most New Kingdom Theban temples. Thus, one cannot *a priori* exclude the possibility that originally there was a more fundamental correspondence between temple decoration and contemporary solar hymns. But even if these hymns do not immediately account for the meaning of Amun-Re at Luxor, they can be used to define the meaning of the decoration of the southernmost halls of the temple proper by comparing the decorative principles of these halls with the themes of solar hymns.

One of the central religious concepts in the theology of Amun-Re frequently found in 18th Dynasty solar hymns and also in the hymn of Suti and Hor, the architects of the temple (Fecht 1967), is the uniqueness and solitary character of the supreme solar god. Instead of describing him through his relationship to other gods or to the sun-worshippers, or instead of presenting the other gods in the assistance of the supreme solar god, the emphasis is usually laid elsewhere (Assmann 1969, 6). Quite often reference is made to the supreme solar god exclusively, and it is explicitly emphasized that he is completely alone and, thus, unique.

Assmann underlines the fact that the unique and sole creator god is a highly significant idea of Egyptian theological thought (Assmann 1983, 175; English translation by Alcock: Assmann 1995). This uniqueness and solitary aspect of the creator god might, in the first place, have a temporal meaning. In the Memphite theology for example, the creator god is unique and greater than any other god, because all the other deities came forth from him and were created by him: "Thus it is said of Ptah: He who made all and created the gods" (Lichtheim 1973, 55).

The temporal uniqueness is emphasized especially in such contexts where the creation is understood as an event that took place in ancient times. The same idea is also expressed in a Ptolemaic inscription about the theology of Amun-Re on the second pylon in Karnak. Amun-Re is alone and was created by himself, but he was associated with kingship and became the king of the gods from the moment the other deities, his creations, sprang to life (Drioton 1944, 117). Needless to say, as for the details, this hymn already reflects the Ptolemaic Amun-theology (on this view see: Doresse 1973; Sethe 1929).

The idea of continuous creation was also present in ancient Egyptian thinking (Assmann 1995, 80). In these contexts the uniqueness of the supreme solar deity could have spatial connotations: the supreme solar deity is unique also because he is unreachable and unapproachable. Although he is omnipresent, he is in the heavens, far away from the common people and the other gods (Assmann 1995; Zandee 1992). Temples and parts of the temples are frequently described as the sky and could carry similar cosmic symbolism (Arnold 1962, 3; Assmann, 1970, 54; Legrain 1917, 21 ff.). This symbolism was also represented architecturally at Luxor temple: the twelve columns of this hall probably evoke the twelve hours of the journey of the sun-god in the sky (Brunner 1977, 81).

The most characteristic expression of the uniqueness and the continuous life-giving aspect of the solar god can be found in the hymn to Aton:

> "How many are your deeds,
> Though hidden from sight,
> O Sole God beside whom there is none!
> You made the earth as you wished, you alone..."
> (trans. Lichtheim, 1976, 98)

In this hymn, as well as in the Amarna god-concept, the uniqueness of the sole supreme solar god, his characterization as the creator god and the idea of continuous creation are the principal motifs. Similar ideas can be captured in non-Amarna sun-hymns (after Zandee 1992, I. vol. 20):

"Einzigartiger (*w^c hr ḥw.f*), Herrscher der unendlichen Dauer, der im Anbeginn entstand ohne seinesgleichen." (*ḫpr m bȝḥ nn snnw.f*) (Urk. IV. 942, 12, 13)

"Einziger (*w^c*), der am Anbeginn war, Grosser, Ältester (*smsw*), Urzeitlicher, ohne seinesgleichen (*jwtj snnw.f*). Er ist der Grosse, der Menschen und Götter erschuf" (Urk. IV. 111, 9–10)

"Amun-Re, Herr der Throne der Beiden Länder, erlauchter Gott, der zufrieden ist mit der Wahrheit, Urzeitlicher, der am Anbeginn entstand, Einziger, ohne seinesgleichen" (KRI I 386, 10)

"Einzig[artiger, ohne] seinesgleichen." (Zandee 1992, pLeiden I, 344 verso I, 2)

The sole Amun-Re is often related to the idea of creation:

> "You are the One who creates all that exists, the One Alone, who creates what is" (P.Kairo 58038, VI. 2.3; Assmann 1995, 122)

In my view, the idea of the sole supreme solar god is the key to the religious meaning of Amun-Re at the southernmost halls of the temple of Luxor. The problem, however, is the question of how closely this idea is connected to the local cult statue, Amun-Re of Luxor, and to what extent can it be taken for the representation of the supreme solar deity, independently from his cult statues (Amun-Re at Luxor). Unfortunately, these questions cannot be discussed here in detail. Nevertheless, the uniqueness of the supreme solar god as the creator and life-giving god can be contrasted to his other aspect, connected to royalty. As king of the gods, the supreme solar deity is accompanied by other divinities. In the southern halls (XVII, XVIII, XIX, XX) his followers, the ennead, the souls of Pe and Nekhen who always participate in the other halls in the confirmation of royal power, are not present. Such a distinction between the life-giving aspect of Amun-Re and his royal aspect was already suggested by Otto, who relied on the work of Sethe and based his arguments on Ptolemaic texts (for a detailed discussion see Gulyás forthcoming b).

In the case of the Luxor temple, where the inner halls are preserved in excellent condition, the ideas are similar to those found in contemporary solar hymns, even if these ideas are expressed in a much more formulaic language than in the hymns (see the remarks of Cauville 1987, ix.). Thus, temples contribute to a better understanding of the original context of the religious ideas expressed in New Kingdom solar hymns (inscriptions from tombs often find their parallels/origin in temples: Assmann 1969; Gabolde 1989; Vernus 1975) and to the meaning of Amun-Re at Luxor as the sole and unique supreme solar god.

ELTE BTK – EPHE IV (Sorbonne)

References

Arnold, D. 1962, *Wandrelief und Raumfunktion in ägyptischen Tempeln des Neuen Reiches*. Verlag Bruno Hessling, Berlin.

Assmann, J. 1969, *Liturgische Lieder an den Sonnengott*. Verlag Bruno Hessling, Berlin.

Assmann, J. 1983, *Re und Amun – Die Krise des polytheistischen Weltbilds im Ägypten der 18.-20. Dynastie*. Universitätsverlag Freiburg-Schweiz – Vandenhoeck and Ruprecht, Göttingen.

Assmann, J. 1970, *Der König als Sonnenpriester*. Augustin, Glückstadt.

Assmann, J. 1995, *Egyptian Solar Religion in the New Kingdom – Re, Amun and the Crisis of Polytheism*, (trans. Anthony Alcock). Kegan Paul, London and New York.

Badawy, A. 1956, Maru Aten: Pleasure Resort or Temple? *Journal of Egyptian Archaeology* 42, 58–64.

Baines, J. 1990, Restricted Knowledge, Hierarchy, and Decorum: Modern perceptions and ancient institutions, *Journal of the American Research Center in Egypt* 27, 1–23.

Baines, J. 1998, The Dawn of the Amarna Age, in D. O'Connor and E. H. Cline (eds.), *Amenhotep III – Perspectives on his reign*, 271–312. The University of Michigan Press, Ann Arbor.

Bell, L. 1985, Luxor Temple and the Cult of the Royal Ka, *Journal of Near Eastern Studies* 44 (4), 251–294.

Bell, L. 1997, New Kingdom Royal Temple: The Example of Luxor, in B. E. Shafer (ed.), *Temples of Ancient Egypt*. Cornell University Press, Ithaca-New York.

Betrò, M. C. 1990, *I testi solari del portale di Pascerientaisu* (BN 2), Saqqara III. Giardini, Pisa.

Beylage, P. 2002, *Aufbau der königlichen Stelentexte vom Beginn der 18. Dynastie bis zur Amarnazeit 1–2.* Harrassowitz Verlag, Wiesbaden.

Bommas, M. 1999, *Die Mythisierung der Zeit.* Harrassowitz, Wiesbaden.

Brunner, H. 1964, *Die Geburt des Gottkönigs.* Harrassowitz, Wiesbaden.

Brunner, H. 1977, *Die südlichen Räume des Tempels von Luxor.* Verlag Philipp von Zabern, Mainz am Rhein.

Bryan, B. M. 1997, The Statue Program for the Mortuary Temple of Amenhotep III, in S. Quirke (ed.), *The Temple in Ancient Egypt*, 57–81. British Museum Press, London.

Cabrol, A. 2000, *Amenhotep III – le magnifique.* Éditions du Rocher, Paris.

Cabrol, A. 2001, *Les voies processionnelles de Thèbes.* Peeters, Leuven.

Cauville, S. 1987, *Essai sur la théologie du temple d' Horus à Edfou.* Institut Français d'Archéologie Orientale du Caire, Le Caire.

Daressy, G. 1893, *Notice explicative des ruines du temple de Louxor.* Imprimerie Nationale, Le Caire.

Derchain, Ph. 1988, Review of Assmann, Re und Amun, *Chronique d'Égypte* 63, Fasc. 125, 77–85.

Dorman, P. F. 1994, A Note on the Royal Repast at the Jubilee of Amenhotep III, in Berger- C. El Naggar (ed.) *Études pharaoniques, Hommages à Jean Leclant 1*, 455–470. Institut Français d'Archéologie Orientale du Caire, Le Caire.

Doresse, M. 1973, Le dieu voilé dans sa chasse et la fête du début de la décade, *Revue d'Égyptologie* 25, 92–135.

Drioton, É. 1944, Les dédicaces de Ptolémée Évergète II sur le deuxième pylône de Karnak, *Annales du Service des Antiquités de l'Égypte* 44, 111–162.

Dziobek, E. 1994, *Die Gräber des Vezirs User-Amun, TT 61, TT 131.* Verlag Philipp von Zabern, Mainz am Rhein.

Farkas, A. 2003, *Filozófia a filozófia előtt – szimbólikus gondolkodás az ókori Egyiptomban.* Typotex Kiadó, Budapest.

Fecht, G. 1967, Zur Frühform der Amarna-Theologie, *Zeitschrift für Ägyptische Sprache* 94, 25–50.

Gabolde, L. 1989 Les temples "mémoriaux" de Thoutmosis II et Toutankhamon (Un rituel destiné à des statues sur barques), *Bulletin de l'Institut Français d'Archéologie Orientale* 89, 127–178.

Gasse, A. 1984, La litanie des douze noms de Ré-Harakhty, *Bulletin de l'Institut Français d'Archéologie Orientale* 84, 89–227.

Gessler-Löhr, B. 1983, *Die heiligen Seen ägyptischer Tempel.* Gerstenberg Verlag, Hildesheim.

Grallert, S. 2001, *Bauen – Stiften – Weihen – Ägyptische Bau- und Restaurierungsinschriften von den Anfängen bis zur 30. Dynastie.* Achet Verlag, Berlin.

Grandet, P. 1994, *Le papyrus Harris I (BM 9999).* Institut Français d'Archéologie Orientale, Le Caire.

Gulyás, A. forthcoming a, A cosmic libation, *Papers of the IXe Congrès International des Égyptologues.* Grenoble.

Gulyás, A. forthcoming b, Amun-Re on the Luxor stelae of Tiberius, in H. Győry (ed.) forthcoming, *Aegyptus et Pannonia – Symposium III in memoriam László Kákosy.* Budapest.

Gundlach, R. 1994, Zum Tempelbauprogramm Amenophis' III, in R. Gundlach and M. Rochholz (eds.), *Ägyptische Tempel. Struktur, Funktion und Programm,* 89–100. Gerstenberg Verlag, Hildesheim.

Johnson, W. R. 1998, Monuments and Monumental Art under Amenhotep III: Evolution and Meaning, in D. O'Connor, and E. H. Cline (eds.), *Amenhotep III – Perspectives on his reign*, 63–94. The University of Michigan Press, Ann Arbor.

Kákosy, L. 2002 King Piye in Heliopolis, in T. A. Bács (ed.) 2002, *A Tribute to Excellence – Studies Offered in Honor of Ernő Gaál, Ulrich Luft, László Török*, 321–329. La Chaire d' Égyptologie, Budapest.

Kruchten, J.-M. 1989, *Les Annales des Prêtres de Karnak (XXI-XXIIImes Dynasties) et Autres Textes Contemporains Relatifs à l'Initiation des Prêtres d'Amon.* Peeters, Leuven.

Kuhlmann, K. P. 1996, Serif-style Architecture and the Design of the Archaic Egyptian Palace ("Königszelt"), in M. Bietak (ed.), *Haus und Palast im alten Ägypten/House and Palace in Ancient Egypt*, 117–137. Verlag der Österreichischen Akademie der Wissenschaften, Wien.

Lacau, P. 1941, *Le Plan du Temple de Louxor*. Imprimerie Nationale, Paris.

Legrain, G. 1917, Le logement et transport des barques sacrées et des statues des dieux dans quelques temples égyptiens, *Bulletin de l'Institut Français d'Archéologie Orientale* 13, 1–76.

Leitz, Chr. 2002, *Lexikon der ägyptischen Götter und Götterbezeichnungen I*. Peeters, Leuven.

Lichtheim, M. 1973, *Ancient Egyptian Literature, Vol. I: The Old and Middle Kingdoms*. University of California Press, Berkeley.

Lichtheim, M. 1976, *Ancient Egyptian Literature, Vol. I: The New Kingdom*. University of California Press, Berkeley.

Luft, U. 2000, ...Statuas dicis... NHC VI 69 (28). Anmerkungen zum Bildgedanken im hellenistischen Ägypten, *Acta Antiqua Academiae Scientiarum Hungaricae* 40, 283–310.

Maher-Taha, M. - Loyrette, A. M. 1979, *Le Ramesseum XI - Les fêtes du dieu Min*.Organisation Égyptienne des Antiquités, Le Caire.

Monneret de Villard, U. 1953, The Temple of the Imperial Cult at Luxor, *Archaeologia, or Miscellaneous Tracts Relating to Antiquity* 45, 85–105.

Moret, M. 1931, Légende d' Osiris à l'époque thébaine d'après l'hymne à Osiris au Louvre, *Bulletin de l'Institut Français d'Archéologie Orientale* 30, 725–750.

Naville, E. 1895, *The Temple of Deir el Bahari I*. Trübner, London.

Naville, E. 1896, *The Temple of Deir el Bahari II – The Ebony Shrine. Northern Half of the Middle Platform*. Trübner, London.

Pamminger, P. 1992a, Die sogenannte 'thebanische' Götterneunheit, *Studien zur Altägyptischen Kultur* 19, 249–255.

Pamminger, P. 1992b, Amun und Luxor – der Widder und das Kultbild, *Beiträge zur Sudanforschung* 5, 93–140.

Parker, R. A., Leclant, J. and Goyon, J.-Cl. 1979, *The Edifice of Taharqa by the Sacred Lake at Karnak*. Brown University Press, Providence.

Porter, B. and Moss, R. L. B. 1937, *Topographical Bibliography of Ancient Egyptian Hieroglyphic Texts, Reliefs, and Paintings – V. Upper Egypt: Sites*. Clarendon Press, Oxford.

Porter, B. and Moss, R. L. B. 1991, *Topographical Bibliography of Ancient Egyptian Hieroglyphic Texts, Reliefs, and Paintings – VI. Upper Egypt: Chief Temples (Excluding Thebes)*. Griffiths Institute, Ashmolean Museum Oxford.

Porter, B. and Moss, R. L. B. 1994, *Topographical Bibliography of Ancient Egyptian Hieroglyphic Texts, Reliefs, and Paintings – II. Theban Temples*. Griffith Institute – Ashmolean Museum, Oxford.

Ryhiner, M.-L. 1995, *La procession des étoffes et l'union avec Hathor*. Fondation Egyptologique Reine Elisabeth, Bruxelles.

Schiff Giorgini, M. 2003, en collaboration avec Clément Robichon et Jean Leclant, préparé et édité par Nathalie Beaux, *Le temple, bas-reliefs et inscriptions*, *Soleb V*. Institut Français d'Archéologie Orientale (al-Qahira), Firenze.

Schott, E. 1970, Die heilige Vase des Amon, *Zeitschrift für Ägyptische Sprache* 98, 34–50.

Schott, S. 1969, Le temple du sphinx et les deux axes du monde égyptien, *Bulletin de la Société Française d'Égyptologie* 53–54, 30–41.

Schott, S. 1970, *Ägyptische Quellen zum Plan des Sphinxtempels*. Franz Steiner Verlag, Stuttgart.

Schuller-Götzburg, T. 1986, Der Kultweg in den südlichen Räumen des Tempels von Luxor, *Varia Aegyptiaca* 2.

Schuller-Götzburg, T. 1990, *Zur Semantik der Königsikonographie – Eine Analyse des Bildprogrammes der südlichen Räume des Tempels von Luxor*. AFRO-PUB, Wien.

Schwaller de Lubicz, R. A. 1977, *Le temple de l'homme Apet du Sud à Louqsor*. Dervy-Livres, Paris.

Sethe, K. 1929, *Amun und die acht Urgötter von Hermopolis*. Verlag der Akademie der Wissenschaften, Berlin.

Stadelmann, R. 1978, Tempel und Tempelnamen in Theben-Ost und West, *Mitteilungen des Deutschen Archaeologischen Instituts Kairo* 34, 171–180.

Török, L. 1997, *The Kingdom of Kush – Handbook of the Napatan-Meroitic Civilization*. Brill, Leiden – New York – Köln.

Ullmann, M. 2002, *König für die Ewigkeit – Die Häuser der Millionen von Jahren*.Wiesbaden, Harrassowitz.

Vernus, P. 1975, Inscriptions de la troisième période intermédiaire (II), *Bulletin de l'Institut Français d'Archéologie Orientale* 75, 67–72.

Zandee, J. 1992, *Der Amunhymnus des Papyrus Leiden I 344, Verso*, 1–3. Rijksmuseum van Oudheden, Leiden.

Ostraca, Literature and Teaching at Deir el-Medina

Fredrik Hagen

The search for context for ancient Egyptian literature is one of the central concerns of Egyptology, but the evidence is fragmentary (Parkinson 2002, 45–107). The lack of archaeological provenances and contexts for manuscripts is acute, and in many cases the oldest manuscripts post-date the composition date of a text by several hundred years. Copies of Middle Kingdom compositions are frequently found only in manuscripts from the New Kingdom or later, including some of the 'classics' like *The Words of Neferti, The Words of Khakheperreseneb, The Instruction of Hordedef, The Instruction for Merikare, The Instruction of Amenemhat I, The Instruction of Khety* and *The Instruction of a Man for His Son* (Parkinson 2002, 296–319). As a consequence, the difficulty in trying to reconstruct a social context for these works is considerable, both in the Middle Kingdom and in the New Kingdom.

Most of the New Kingdom sources for literary texts are ostraca from Deir el-Medina, and they are generally seen by Egyptologists as products of activities associated with education; they are essentially thought to be student exercises (Brunner 1991 [1957]; van de Walle 1948; McDowell 1996; 2000). While this may be true for many, if not most of the ostraca, the identification of individual ostraca as the work of students remains problematic. The transmission process for literary texts at the village is poorly understood, and there are some indications that ostraca as a medium played a more diverse role than simply as cheap and accessible material for scribal students. I here review the evidence both in terms of those ostraca that are difficult to link with scribal education and those that can be said with some certainty to relate to this context. From the latter category I present a new model letter found on three ostraca in the British Museum: O.BM EA 21186, 21216 and 21284.

The ostraca from Deir el-Medina are generally classified as either figured ostraca, non-literary ostraca or literary ostraca. The painted ostraca vary from small jottings to accomplished drawings that have been described as "the work of the best draughtsmen that Egypt then had" (Davies 1917, 235). Some are examples of drafts where the finished version can be seen on tomb walls (*e.g.* Hayes 1942, 9–10), while others appear to have been more 'functional' documents. Cairo ostracon 25184 (83.5 × 14 cm), for example, contains a map of the tomb of Ramesses IX in the Valley of the Kings, and the care with which it has been drawn up and coloured suggests that it was intended to be consulted during work (Rossi 2004, 142–147). Keller has suggested that some of the larger painted ostraca deposited in royal tombs in the Valley of the Kings may have been intended as votive offerings (1995, 98). The non-literary ostraca are thought to be drafts of administrative documents, letters and 'scrap paper' for notes and records of deliveries, *etc*. In their recent study of the use of writing in the administration at the village, Haring and Donker van Heel concluded that "Some [administrative] ostraca were clearly discarded, some were used as drafts, and some were kept...one should not... attempt to force each and every [administrative] ostraca into an assumed role as a draft [but rather] allow for a number of roles" (2003, 5).

The literary ostraca are far from a homogenous group, both in terms of appearance and contents, and few are written in unpractised hieratic hands (Černý 1949, 69). Many, if not most, may have originated in an educational context, but to identify specific examples as student exercises is often problematic. Criteria that have so far been advanced as possible indicators of exercises, such as the presence of dates (McDowell 1996) or colophons mentioning an assistant and his superior (McDowell 2000), are ambiguous and their interpretation uncertain (Hagen, forthcoming a).

A considerable number of texts are attested only on ostraca at the site; no papyrus copies survive from Deir el-Medina of texts such as *Sinuhe, The Instruction of a Man for his Son, The Instruction for Merikare, The Instruction of Hordedef, The Instruction of Amenemhat I, etc.* Other texts are attested only indirectly at the site: no sources for *The Story of the Eloquent Peasant* or *The Shipwrecked Sailor* survive, but allusions to them in the 'letter' of Menna show that they were read and known in the village (Simpson 1958). The richness of the evidence notwithstanding, a considerable part is still missing; what we have is merely "the tip of a textual iceberg" (Parkinson 2004, 57).

A number of ostraca suggest that there are significant gaps in our knowledge and understanding of the transmission of literary texts at the site. That most ostraca consist of short extracts is undeniable, but there are exceptions: O.DeM 1176, for example, contains the *Hymn to the Nile* in its entirety (van der Plas 1986, table 1; Posener 1951–1952–1972, 19 and pls. 27–31). Others indicate that the extracts they contain are parts of a wider process of transmission. *The Story of Khonsemheb and the Ghost* (Beckerath 1992) survives on a number of large pottery sherds, and some of these are numbered to indicate the sequence of the sections – an organising feature that can perhaps be compared to the rare practice of numbering columns of text in papyrus manuscripts (P. Ebers, P. Butler; Posener 1975). O.DeM 1042 (with *Khety* III a–f) and O.DeM 1022 (with *Khety* X a-e) are 'signed' by the scribe Itnetjer (Helck 1970, 31, 62) and may also represent part of a more comprehensive transmission than the individual ostraca might indicate if taken in isolation. There are also examples of ostraca with only the incipits of sequential stanzas of a composition; O.DeM 1017 has the beginning only of stanzas I–VI and IX–XII of *Khety* (Helck 1970, 8–9), and O.Senmut 143 has the beginning only of stanzas I–VIII of *Amenemhat I* (Helck 1986, 6). These indicate another possibility in the organising of extracts on ostraca, where rubrics in red function as a way of structuring the text – familiarity with the start of each section allows the owner to establish the relative sequence of a series of ostraca containing parts of a single text. O.DeM 1017 and O.Senmut 143 may thus essentially be indexes; Posener suggested that the insertion of dates on ostraca may have played a similar role in organising extracts of a text (1975, 108).

The broad label 'ostraca' potentially obscures the wide range of materials and forms included under that heading. A case in point is the so-called 'ostracon' with *The Story of Sinuhe* from the tomb of Sennedjem at Deir el-Medina (Cairo CG 25216). The limestone flake, which measures 106×22 cm, has been worked into a rectangular shape and the front has been polished; it mimics the traditional form of wooden writing tablets (although the length is unparalleled). It should perhaps be classed as a limestone writing tablet rather than an ostracon (Quirke 1996, 392). Another borderline example is O.BM EA 41541 with *The Instruction of Amennakht*: the limestone flake, which measures 20×15.7 cm, has been worked into a rectangular shape, and the surface has been polished to a smooth finish to facilitate writing. There are no signs of palimpsest on it, so whether it was re-used is unknown, although the effort invested in its preparation makes this a definite possibility. It has been classified both as a writing tablet (Quirke 1996, 392) and as an ostracon (Bickel and Mathieu 1993, 32). The difficulties of categorisation illustrate the problems inherent in the traditional approach to literary ostraca, but also serve as a warning against similarly broad generalisations in regard to other classes of artefacts. Writing tablets, like ostraca, need not stem exclusively from an educational context; they were part of the scribal equipment of fully trained scribes (Parkinson and Quirke 1995, 30–36).

The most famous literary ostracon is the Ashmolean ostracon with *The Story of Sinuhe* (Barns 1952); at 88.5 × 31.5cm (inscribed on both sides) it is the largest ostracon to survive. It does not appear to have been prepared for inscription in any way, and the surface on the lower verso side is so rough as to have made writing on it difficult. It is unlikely therefore that it was used as a writing tablet, an impression that is also supported by the sheer unwieldiness of the stone – it retains an imposing and almost monumental character. The text itself is somewhat corrupt in places (Barns 1952), but not to such an extent that someone familiar with the story would not be able to understand it (Parkinson 2004, 58). The ostracon would have made an endurable medium for the storage of the text, but may also have had a less 'functional' role as a symbol of literacy and social status – in any case it is unlikely to represent a scribal exercise.

Perhaps the most interesting example of a literary 'ostracon' are the fragments which make up the pottery jar labelled O.DeM 1266 + CGC 2518 (Posener 1951–1952–1972, 43–44, pls. 74–99). The jar, of which 31 fragments survive, had a diameter of *c.* 43 cm, and is preserved to a height of approximately 36.5 cm. The sherds were found in the Great Pit to the north of the village, but unfortunately not all the fragments of the jar were recovered. Judging by the preserved portions of text certainly the upper part of the jar was complete when the text was inscribed (Posener 1951–1952–1972, 43–44), and it is possible that the jar as a whole was intact. If so, then it can hardly be classified as an ostracon, but it is still of great importance because it highlights the incompleteness of the evidence for the context of literature at Deir el-Medina. The outside of the jar is covered with the *Cairo Love Songs*, but this was not the text first inscribed on it, and enough traces remain to identify the original text as *The Instruction of a Man for his Son*. That original text was written in a hand "plus petite et plus fine ... que celle du texte qui lui a succédé" (Posener 1951–1952–1972, 44, hieratic facsimile not included), although even the later text must be said to have been written by an experienced scribe, judging by the handwriting. The re-use of the material is noteworthy and implies an original *Sitz im Leben* where the content was clearly relevant on some level – it is a rare, if unrevealing, glimpse of an ostracon's 'life' before it was eventually discarded. The owner's decision to erase an instruction text in order to inscribe love poetry may reflect the personal preferences of that individual; as a genre love poetry is the type of literary composition most readily linked to entertainment by modern Egyptologists (Guglielmi 1996, 240–242). The different handwriting of the two texts indicates an object with several different phases of existence: (1) before it was inscribed; (2) after it was inscribed with the instruction text; (3) after the first text was erased and the love poetry inscribed; and (4) its final state until it was finally discarded. How long these periods may have lasted is of course impossible to say, and the two different hands need not indicate a long period of use – they could be contemporary. The unwieldiness of a pot as opposed to a papyrus roll in terms of reading might suggest that it had more of a symbolic value than practical function, but a number of other factors may have influenced the choice of media; the social context remains inaccessible.

One argument frequently cited in support of seeing literary ostraca as products of scribal training is that many are virtually unreadable, and the Middle Kingdom compositions in particular are often so corrupt and garbled that it has been questioned whether the copyists understood what they were copying (McDowell 1992, 95–96). However, as Hoch remarks regarding the transmission of *Khety* at Deir el-Medina, most ostraca "…contain practically identical errors – suggesting that the texts were copied directly from the same papyri. In any case, the 'corruptions' seem to have been part of the received text, and to have been more or less carefully copied" (Hoch 1991–1992, 88). In other words, a corrupt manuscript tradition may account for the unintelligible state of many of the ostraca, rather than a lack of understanding of the language on the part of individual scribes (*cf.* Burkard 1977, 10–71; Spalinger 2002, 334–336). Parkinson (2002, 54), sees an historical parallel in the transmission of 'corrupt' versions of Shakespeare in Elizabethan England, which also illustrates how largely incomprehensible manuscripts can retain a cultural value as symbols of status and education.

The question of understanding on behalf of the copyists, especially in the case of those texts written in Middle Egyptian, touches on wider issues regarding the context of Middle Kingdom literature in the New Kingdom and is linked to the linguistic situation of Ramesside Deir el-Medina. McDowell (1992, 95) suggested that the linguistic gap between (literary) Middle Egyptian and the colloquial language was considerable and that it would have constituted an obstacle to the dissemination and appreciation of texts written in the older language. In this she is partly correct, but the question is complex because the 'high' language of monumental discourse and literary texts already in the Middle Kingdom differs from that found in more informal writings from the same period (Allen 1994; Junge 1984), but at this point the difference may be one of "opposition de registre" (Vernus 1996, 559). There is no doubt that knowledge of Middle Egyptian was preserved throughout most of Egyptian history: translations from Middle Egyptian into Late Egyptian survive (writing tablet Berlin 8934 with the *Instruction of Any*: Erman 1894), as do translations from Middle Egyptian into Demotic (P. Vienna D 6319 and P. BM EA 69574 in Quack 1992–1993 and 1999, respectively), and the revival of Middle Egyptian in Dynasties 25 and 26 (Der Manuelian 1994), as well as the use of ('Neo-') Middle Egyptian in the trilingual Ptolemaic decrees (Engsheden 2003), indicate a continuous transmission of linguistic knowledge. Vernus, following his study of diglossia in the New Kingdom concluded that "la langue de ces classiques [the Middle Kingdom compositions] n'est plus guère accessible à travers la seule maîtrise de la langue contemporaine" (1996, 559–560). This marks an important change in the possible context for Middle Egyptian 'classical' literature in later periods of Egyptian history: the earlier language (in addition to reading and writing skills) must be learned in order for the audience to fully access and appreciate the literature. The performative context posited for literature in the Middle Kingdom (Parkinson 2002, 78–81; Eyre 2000) may still hold, but with more restrictive and excluding parameters regarding audience (which must now be familiar with Middle Egyptian). As training in literacy appears to have gone hand in hand with training in different (textual) linguistic registers, the audience is more likely to have been elite (Parkinson 2004, 58) and the texts less accessible than in the Middle Kingdom. Despite this process the Middle Kingdom texts continue to be transmitted, albeit sometimes in less legible forms. That mastery of the classical texts was a sign of status among New Kingdom literates is well attested (*e.g.* Fischer-Elfert 2003; McDowell 1992); the most famous example is the passage from the *Satirical Letter* of P. Anastasi I where a scribe chides a colleague both for his (mis)use of a quotation from *Hordedef* and for a lack of knowledge about the original context of the quotation (Fischer-Elfert 1986, 95–97). There is no reason why the language itself should be an obstacle for enjoyment of texts written in Middle Egyptian for individuals trained in that phase of the language, *i.e.* the literati, and a high level of proficiency in the language of the classical Middle Kingdom compositions among the literate elite of the village is evident in the literary production at the site. Both the instructions of *Hori* and *Amennakht* (Bickel and Mathieu 1993; Dorn 2004) were composed by locals – they can be linked to specific historical individuals (Bickel and Mathieu 1993; Fischer-Elfert 2003, 120–123) – and at least the former of the two (*Hori*) is written in reasonably good Middle Egyptian. Another possible example is *The Prohibitions* (Hagen, forthcoming b), a wisdom text (instruction?) which is unattested elsewhere, and which despite a number of Late Egyptian influences (6 examples in 40 lines of text) generally retains Middle Egyptian syntax. The situation characterised by the diglossia of New Kingdom Egypt may be comparable to that found in the modern Arab world, where 'classical' Arabic is used in most formalised and above all literary contexts (*e.g.* R. Allen 2000, 11–16). This linguistic register is not close to any colloquial Arabic spoken today, and must be learned. As Reynolds remarks in his study of the Arabic oral epic tradition, "The stylistic and grammatical differences, along with the extensive body of vocabulary not cognate with colloquial forms or usages, render much communication in standard written Arabic almost incomprehensible for speakers of colloquial Arabic unschooled in the literary language" (1995, 30). Such schooling need not be related to literacy, as shown by Caton (1990, 186–188).

As a medium ostraca can, if only rarely, be securely linked to educational practices (a thesis on such ostraca is under preparation by Isabelle Venturini in Paris). The most likely examples include onomastic exercises based on a particular pattern (*e.g.* O.DeM 1179, 1411, 1412, 1724, 1725 and 1726), grammatical exercises (*e.g.* O.Petrie 28; Černý and Gardiner 1957, 8 n. 7), copies of *Kemit* (*e.g.* Posener 1951–1952–1972, pls. 1–21) and model letters, but here too there are problems of identification; not all are written by unpractised hands. In the case of model letters there is the additional problem that they are frequently indistinguishable from 'real' letters (Gasse 1990, viii). Examples of model letters survive from both the Middle and New Kingdom. The earliest is perhaps the collection of nine letters inscribed on a single papyrus (P. UC 32196) from Lahun (Collier and Quirke 2004, 48–49). The names in the letters are stereotypical of the period, and this has been seen as an argument in favour of a classification as model letters (Parkinson 2002, 325), but there are no duplicates and the handwriting is competent. The letters are all based on a similar pattern and would have been well suited for didactic purposes; their use of phraseology is heavily reminiscent of the Ramesside model letter of O.BM EA 21186, 21216 and 21284 (see below).

Letters found on early Middle Kingdom writing tablets are frequently thought to be model letters (*e.g.* Parkinson 2002, 325; James 1962, 97–101); examples include Cairo CG 25367 (Daressy 1901, pls. 62–63; Vernus 1984, 706 n. 5), MMA 28.9.4 (James 1962, 98–101, pl. 30; Wente 1990, 66–67) and MMA 26.3.277 AB (James 1962, 97–98, pl. 29). James's classification of MMA 28.9.4 and 26.3.277 AB as model letters rests largely on the fact that they are writing tablets, but the medium is not enough to establish an originally educational context (Parkinson and Quirke 1995, 30–36). Again the lack of duplicates and the generally competent handwriting makes the designation 'model' uncertain, and they could also represent drafts of 'real' letters which might explain the corrections on MMA 28.9.4 (James 1962, 98–99).

Three ostraca from the British Museum collections (O.BM EA 21186, 21216 and 21284) contain parallel copies of a model letter. Photographs and hieroglyphic transcriptions were published in R. J. Demarée, *Ramesside Ostraca* (2002), pages 23–24, plates 61–61 and 65, but without translations or commentaries. All three ostraca are potsherds rather than limestone flakes, and measure 12 × 9 cm, 10.5 × 8.5 cm and 17.5 × 11 cm respectively. They are written in black ink, and one of them contains traces of what may be a single versepoint (O.BM EA 21284, column 6 top); the handwriting on all three ostraca is poor and unpractised, suggesting an inexperienced copyist. The text is arranged in vertical columns divided by black lines in all the sources, and on O.BM EA 21284 there is in addition a short horizontal line at the bottom of columns 1 and 2 that seems to enclose the text above it (Figure 1). On the same ostracon, the writing in columns 1–6 stops before the lower edge of the potsherd, as do the vertical dividing lines, so that there may not be anything missing at the top or at the bottom. The top of the ostracon need not be incomplete either, as the entire opening letter-formula is preserved (*sn dd n sn=f*). The other two ostraca, O.BM EA 21184 and 21216, are incomplete.

The practice of dividing columns by inserting vertical lines between them is rare on ostraca, and with the exception of *Kemit* (see below), it seems to be restricted to hieratic imitations of inscriptional forms of writing (hieroglyphs or cursive hieroglyphs: Parkinson 2002, 323). Religious and magical (ritualistic) texts written with cursive hieroglyphs are not infrequently found employing this layout on ostraca (*e.g.* O.DeM 1227, Posener 1951–1952–1972, pl. 56; O.BM EA 29552 and 66303, Demarée 2002, pl. 82 and 205 respectively), and these are occasionally accompanied by illustrations that suggest they were copies or drafts of tomb decoration (*cf.* O.BM EA 5620, 8508, 8510, 29509 and 29510: Demarée 2002, pls. 1, 52, 53, 72 and 73). Occasionally other types of texts are found with this layout, but these are few and atypical; examples include a royal eulogy written in cursive hieroglyphs (O.BM EA 5622: Demarée 2002, pl. 4), *The Instruction of Khety* and *The Instruction of Amenemhat I*, the former written in full hieroglyphs, the latter in cursive hieroglyphs (on the recto and verso, respectively, of O.DeM 1175: Posener 1951–1952–1972, pl. 26 + 26a). Fragments of a text on O.Turin 57333 (López 1982, pl. 101) is written with a similar layout, but too little of the text is preserved to identify it – it could be a model letter.

The text most commonly written with this particular layout, however, is the 'model letter' known as *Kemit* (Parkinson 2002, 322–325). The term 'model letter' is something of a misnomer because the text, although framed by epistolographic formulae, also contains narrative sections and wisdom sayings. It is a Middle Kingdom composition, the earliest copy to survive being the 12th Dynasty papyrus UC 32271B from Lahun (Collier and Quirke 2004, 50–51), but most copies are found on ostraca and writing tablets from Ramesside Deir el-Medina. *Kemit* is almost invariably written in vertical columns, frequently in cursive hieroglyphs with lines in black ink dividing the columns (*e.g.* O.BM EA 29548: Demarée 2002, pl. 76; O.DeM 1110, 1131: Posener 1951–1952–1972, pl. 24); the only exception known to me is O.DeM 1129 with three lines of *Kemit* (§IV–V) written horizontally (Posener 1951–1952–1972, 6, pl. 25). Copies of *Kemit*, contrary to most literary texts found on ostraca, are often in poor and unpractised handwriting (*e.g.* O.BM EA 5640, 5641: Demarée 2002, pl. 35–36). A revealing example of the didactic use of the composition is provided by the writing tablet recently found at Dra Abu el-Aga and preliminarily published in *Egyptian Archaeology* (Galán and el-Bialy 2004). The tablet preserves six columns of text, where same passage is written three times (2 × 3 columns). The first two columns are written in a practiced hand, whereas columns three to four and five to six are written in a different and distinctly less practised hand. The likeliest explanation is that a teacher wrote columns one and two, and that the student then copied the same text twice to the best of his ability. Similarly, O.DeM 1143 (Posener 1951–1952–1972, 10–11) has the same passage of Kemit (§IX–XI) on the recto and the verso, but in two different handwritings; the lack of a published facsimile makes it impossible to determine which of the hands belongs to the student and which to the teacher. A different instructional method may be attested in the copy of *Kemit* found on two fragmentary ostraca in Turin 57545 and 57546 (López 1984, 39, pl. 175 + 175a). There the text is written in the customary vertical columns with dividing lines

0   5 cm

Figure 1. *Photograph of O. BM EA 21284. Copyright the British Museum.*

(in red), but the text itself was written first in red ink and then again in black ink superimposed on the first layer. Unfortunately the ostraca are too fragmentary to determine whether the two inks represent different hands, or to what extent they may differ in proficiency.

The rarity of the format of vertical columns with dividing lines, which is unattested for 'real' letters, the poor handwriting, and the existence of three copies of the same letter identifies the text on O.BM EA 21186, 21216 and 21284 as a model letter and a student exercise. A further indication of the originally didactic context of the ostraca may be the presence on two of the potsherds of sequential numbers that are not part of the text itself. The text of O.BM EA 21284 is followed by the numbers 11–20 written sequentially in the last column (Figure 1), a feature that is also shared with O.BM EA 21186, where the last column contains the numbers 26–30. The purpose of these numbers is not certain; they may simply be exercises in writing out numerals. The transcription below is based on the photographs by Demarée (2002, pls. 61, 62 and 65).

Hieroglyphs

Hieroglyphs

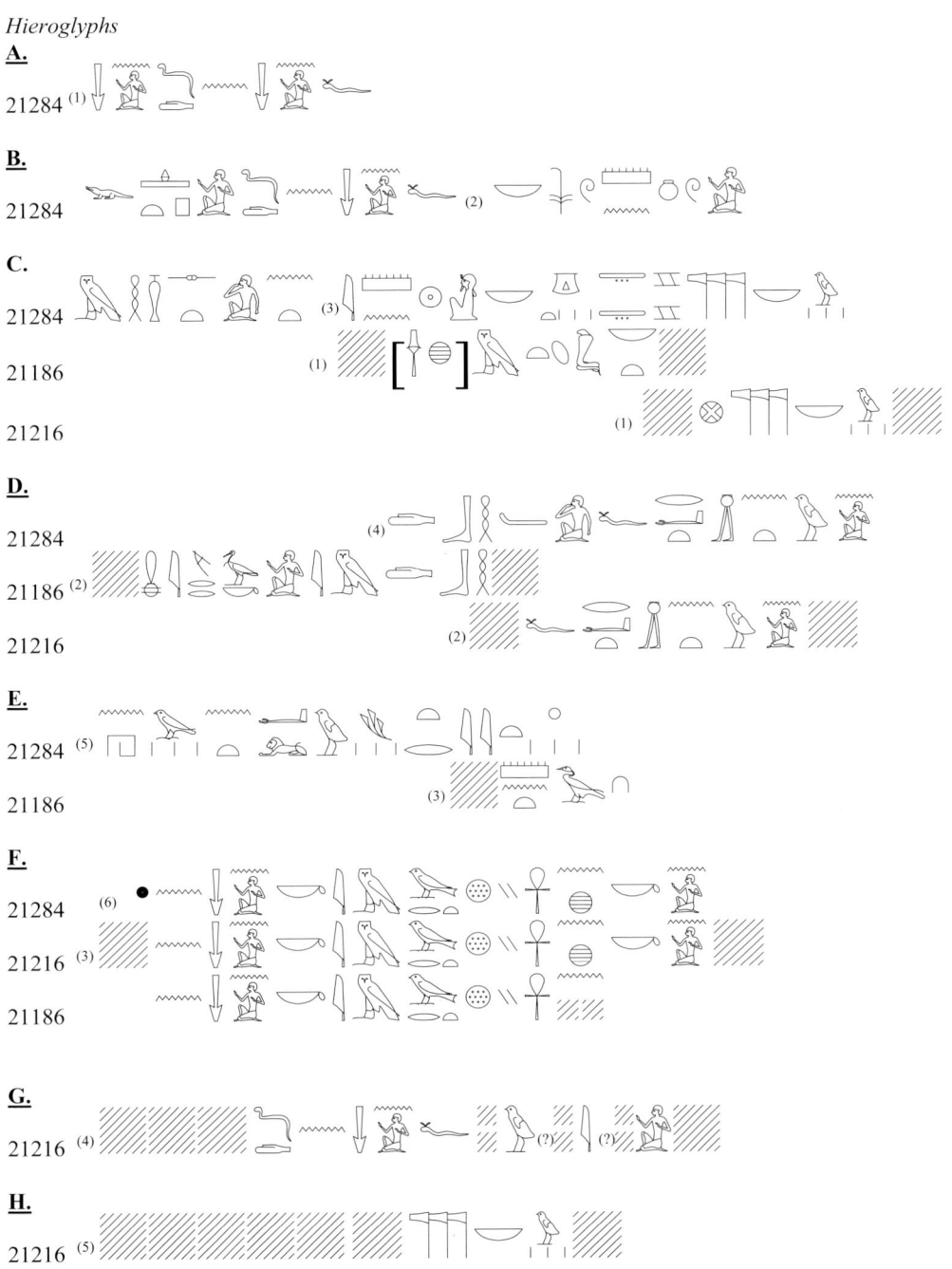

Translation

<u>**A.**</u>
21284: (It is) a brother who speaks to his brother.[a]

<u>**B.**</u>
21284: Sobekhotep [b] speaks to his brother Nebsumenu. [c]

<u>**C.**</u>
21284: In the favour of Amun-Re, Lord of the Thrones of the Two Lands, [f] and all the gods [...]
21186:   [...Sekh]met [d], Lady of [e][...]
21216:   [...] and all the gods

<u>**D.**</u>
21284:   He requests that one cause to have brought to me
21186: [...] like this servant wants [g]. He requests [...]
21216:   He [requests] that one cause to have brought to me

<u>**E.**</u>
21284: some papyrus (?) reeds
21186:   [...] 10 pigeons

<u>**F.**</u>
All sources: for your brother there, very much. As you live for me [h] [...]

<u>**G.**</u>
21186: [...] and say to my brother, [i] [...]

<u>**H.**</u>
21186: [...] all the gods [j] [...]

Commentary

(a) The introductory formula *sn ḏd n sn=f* is a variant of the standard N. *ḏd n* N. formula (Bakir 1970, 47). The grammatical form of *ḏd* here is presumably the active participle as suggested by Gardiner (1957, §450.1) *contra* Bakir (1970, 48) who analyses it, in New Kingdom letters, as the pseudo-verbal *ḥr* + infinitive construction (with *ḥr* omitted). As noted by Gardiner (1957, §450.1), Middle Kingdom examples with a female sender display a -*t* ending (add to his examples P. Hekanakhte IV, 1: Allen 2002, pl. 38–39), and there is no reason to believe that a different syntactical pattern underlies the New Kingdom formula (*cf.* Gardiner's reference to a similar practice in demotic). The use of terms denoting familial relations preceding the same formula used with titles and names is common. The closest parallel to this formula, and to certain other features of the phraseology, occurs in papyrus UC 32206 (Collier and Quirke 2002, 124–125); *sn ḏd n sn [snbw] ḏd n ʿnḫ.t(y)=f(y) ... di=k in.t(w) n=i ...[list of goods]... n sn=k im nfr sḏm=k*

"A brother speaks to a brother. Senbu speaks to Ankhtyfy...cause to have bought to me...[list of goods]...to your brother there. It is good if you will hear". Papyrus UC 32206 was classed as a 'real' letter by both Griffith (1898) and Collier and Quirke (2002), but it may in fact be a model letter: it is written in red throughout, and the handwriting is relatively poor (Griffith 1898, 78; Collier and Quirke 2003, 125).

(b) The name Sobekhotep is more common in the Middle Kingdom than in the New Kingdom, but not overwhelmingly so (Ranke 1935, 186; add to his examples P. UC 32092B, 32200 and 32284K 4, all Middle Kingdom), and it cannot be used to date the text. A letter from Deir el-Medina (O.BM EA 5627: Demarée 2002, pls. 12–13) mentions a Sobekhotep who is a *wʿb*-priest of Sekhmet (not noted by Davies 1999); the otherwise rare mention of that goddess in the letter formula of this model letter may suggest that there is a connection here – see (d) below – but the evidence is far from conclusive.

(c) The name Nebsumenu is very common from the Old Kingdom through to the New Kingdom (Ranke 1935, 305), and at least four individuals of that name are attested at Deir el-Medina (Davies 1999, 297–298). Which, if any of them, is the addressee here is unknown. The names may in any case be fictitious; the name Nebsumenu is also attested as an epithet of Sobek (Brovarski 1984, 1016; Kuentz 1929, 148–149), so the names of the sender and the addressee could be associated by their affiliation with the god Sobek.

(d) The restoration of the name Sekhmet is certain. The invocation of Sekhmet is comparatively rare in epistolographic formulae, but *cf.* the mention of "Sekhmet the Great, Beloved of Ptah" (*sḫmt ʿ3t mry ptḥ*) in a well-wishing formula in the 19th Dynasty letter P. Cairo 58056 (*KRI* III, 254, 16). The goddess is also mentioned in a list of gods (not part of the standard letter-formula) in the letter found on O.BM EA 5627 (Demarée 2002, 16, pls. 12–13), where the recipient is said to be a *wʿb*-priest of Sekhmet. The goddess is invoked in one of the model letters from the Middle Kingdom papyrus UC 32196, a letters that shares a number of aspects of its phraseology with this text. Letter six reads: "[The ser]vant of the estate Nehy [speaks to S]enebtyfy, l.p.h., in [the favour of] Sekhmet (*m [ḥst nt] sḫmt*) and Sheret, like this servant wants (*mi mrr b3k im*). It is a communication to my lord [to cause] to have brought to me some *wenesh* for [this] servant (*in.tw n=i nhw n wnš n b3k [im]*)" (Collier and Quirke 2004, 48–49; they misread *nhw n wnš* as *n prt n wnš*). The basic format and the phraseology are close to the model letter of the British Museum ostraca, but not to such an extent as to indicate an intertextual relationship.

(e) The specific epithet used here is difficult to identify, as there are no traces preserved: Hoenes (1976, 235–239) lists 67 examples of Sekhmet + *nbt* + noun (nos. 56–123).

(f) The invocation of "Amun-Re, Lord of the Thrones of the Two Lands" in the epistolographic formula is unusual, but is paralleled on O.DeM 603: *m ḥs<t> <nt> imn-rʿ nb nswt t3.wy*. An "Amun of the Thrones of the Two Lands" occurs frequently in late Ramesside letters (Černý 1939, 2.2; 2.10; 4.1–2; 4.9–11; 8.1; 11.14; 14.4–5; 17.8; 18.10–11; 27.6; 27.10; 28.4; 29.1; 30.5; 31.16; 32.4), but is occasionally found as early as the Middle Kingdom (writing tablet MMA 28.9.4 = James 1962, 98–101, pls. 30+30a; Sinuhe B206–207 = Koch 1990, 64). How "Amun of the Thrones of the Two Lands" relates to "Amun(-Re) Lord of the Thrones of the Two Lands" is not entirely clear. Wente (1961, 255–256) thought the former referred to a local cult in Western Thebes, and that "Amun, Lord of the Thrones of the Two Lands" referred to Amun of Karnak, with the latter identification being based on the association of the epithet *ḫnty* *ipt-iswt* "Foremost of Karnak" in P. Phillipps 3 (Černý 1939, 29.1). This may be correct, but "Amun of the Thrones of the Two Lands" was also worshipped elsewhere in the country – P. Wilbour mentions two temples dedicated to this aspect of Amun in the Fayum area (Gardiner 1948, §24, §30).

(g) The phrase *mi mrr b3k im* is a standard part of letter phraseology. The sender regularly speaks of himself both in the third person ("this servant", "*he* requests") and in the first person ("that one cause to be brought to *me*") as is common in Egyptian letters.

(h) This appears to the beginning of an oath formula: "As you live for me...".

(i) Alternatively "speaking to a brother": the context is obscure.

(j) The last line of O.BM 21216 contains part of another well-wishing or prayer formula, presumably directed at the "brother" mentioned in the preceding line.

The three sources display minor variations. The opening formula is only preserved in one of the sources – the other two may have had other names inserted, as is the case with the model letters found in the *Late Egyptian Miscellanies* (Erman 1925), but the same familial relationship between sender and recipient is present in all three sources. The variations occur in the letter formulas themselves, where Amun-Re and Sekhmet occur on O.BM EA 21284 and 21186 respectively, and in the contents, where the goods requested include in the one case papyrus reeds (? *ʿrw tryt,* on 21284) and in the other pigeons (21186).

The composition date of the text is difficult to establish. Its use of formulas and general phraseology is closely paralleled by the Middle Kingdom papyri UC 32196 and 32206 (Collier and Quirke 2004, 48–49; 2002, 124–125) from Lahun, as noted under (a) and (d) above, but the invocation of Amun-Re might point to a Ramesside date. As no copies from earlier periods or other sites are known, one has to assume that it was a text whose use was limited to the scribes of Ramesside Deir el-Medina.

The literary ostraca from Deir el-Medina are an invaluable resource for the study of literature and literacy in ancient Egypt, but their interpretation is rarely straightforward. As a medium ostraca, like papyrus, had a range of possible uses, and it is reductive to assume that all literary ones represent student exercises; this has important consequences for the possible social context of manuscripts and their compositions. The survival of thousands of literary ostraca is a result of the durability of the material and the location of the site (beyond the edge of the cultivated Nile valley), but the richness of the evidence obscures its incomplete nature, as indicated by the lack of papyrus manuscripts for most literary texts attested at Deir el-Medina. To focus on the possible uses of the Middle Kingdom 'classical' composition in an educational context shifts our attention away from the transmission and consumption of such texts outside this primarily didactic arena and results in a distorted view of both the literary tradition of the New Kingdom and the training of scribes in the same period. Although such training included the copying of the 'classics', it also included the copying of onomastic lists, grammatical exercises and model letters which despite their often prosaic nature reveal important aspects of the educational process.

University of Cambridge

References

Allen, J. P. 1994, Colloquial Middle Egyptian: Some observations on the language of Heqa-Nakht, *Lingua Aegyptia* 4, 1–12.

Allen, J. P. 2002, *The Heqanakht papyri*. Metropolitan Museum of Art, New York.

Allen, R. 2000, *An Introduction to Arabic Literature*. Cambridge University Press, Cambridge.

Bakir, A. M. *Egyptian epistolography from the Eighteenth to the Twenty-First Dynasty*. Institute français d'archéologie orientale, Cairo.

Barns, J. W. B. 1952, *The Ashmolean Ostracon of Sinuhe*. Oxford University Press for the Griffith Institute, Oxford.

Beckerath, J. von 1992, Zur Geschichte von Chonsuemhab und dem Geist, *Zeitschrift für ägyptische Sprache and Altertumskunde* 119, 90–107.

Bickel, S. and Mathieu, B. 1993, L'écrivain Amennakht et son *Enseignement*, in *Bulletin de l'Institute français d'archéologie orientale* 93, 31–52.

Brovarski, E. 1984, Sobek, in W. Helck and E. Otto, (eds.), *Lexikon der Ägyptologie, V*, cols. 995–1031. Harrassowitz, Wiesbaden.

Brunner, H. 1991 [1957], *Altägyptische Erziehung*. Harrasowitz, Wiesbaden.

Burkard, G. 1977, *Textkritische Untersuchungen zu ägyptischen Weisheitslehren des Alten und Mittleren Reiches*. Harrasowitz, Wiesbaden

Caton, S. C. 1990, *'Peaks of Yemen I Summon': Poetry as Cultural Practice in a North Yemeni Tribe*. University of California Press, Berkeley.

Černý, J. 1939, *Late Ramesside Letters*. Fondation égyptologique Reine Élisabeth, Brussels.

Černý, J. 1949, Review of B. van de Walle, *La transmission des textes littéraires égyptiens* in *Chronique d'Égypte* 24, 68–71.

Černý, J. and Gardiner, A. H. 1957, *Hieratic Ostraca. Volume I*. Oxford University Press, Oxford.

Collier, M. and Quirke, S. 2002, *The UCL Lahun Papyri: Letters*. Archaeopress, Oxford.

Collier, M. and Quirke, S. 2004, *The UCL Lahun Papyri: Religious, Literary, Legal, Mathematical and Medical*. Archaeopress, Oxford.

Daressy, G. *Catalogue général des antiquités égyptiennes du Musée du Caire. Nos. 25001–25385. Ostraca*. Cairo.

Davies, B. G. 1999, *Who's Who at Deir el-Medina. A Prosopographic Study of the Royal Workmen's Community*. Nederlands Instituut voor het nabjie Oosten, Leiden.

Davies, N. de G. 1917, Egyptian drawings on limestone flakes, *Journal of Egyptian Archaeology* 4, 234–240.

Demarée, R. J. 2002, *Ramesside Ostraca*. British Museum Press, London.

Der Manuelian, P. 1994, *Living in the past: Studies in archaism of the Egyptian twenty-sixth dynasty*. Kegan Paul International, London.

Dorn, A. 2004. Die Lehre Amunnachts, *Zeitschrift für ägyptische Sprache and Altertumskunde* 131, 38–55.

Engsheden, Å. 2003, *La réconstitution du verbe en égyptien de tradition 400–30 avant J.-C.* Uppsala University, Uppsala.

Erman, A. 1894, Eine ägyptische Schulübersetzung, *Zeitschrift für ägyptische Sprache und Altertumskunde* 37, 127–128.

Erman, A. 1925, *Die Altägyptische Schülerhandschriften. Aus den Abhandlungen der Preussischen Akademie der Wissenschaften. Jahrgang 1925. Phil.-Hist. Klasse.Nr. 2.* Verlag der Akademie der Wissenschaften, Berlin.

Eyre, C. J. 2000, The Performance of the Peasant, *Lingua Aegyptia* 8, 9–25.

Fischer-Elfert, H.-W. 1986, *Die satirische Streitschrift des Papyrus Anastasi I: Übersetzung und Kommentar*. Harrasowitz, Wiesbaden.

Fischer-Elfert, H.-W. 2003, Representations of the past in New Kingdom literature, in W. J. Tait (ed.), *'Never had the like occurred': Egypt's view of its own past*, 119–137. UCL Press, London.

Galán, J. M. and el-Bialy, M. 2004, An apprentice's board from Dra Abu el-Naga, *Egyptian Archaeology* 25, 38–40.

Gardiner, A. H. 1948, *The Wilbour Papyrus*. 3 vols. Oxford University Press, Oxford.

Gardiner, A. H. 1957, *Egyptian Grammar*, (3rd edition). Oxford University Press on behalf of the Griffith Institute, Oxford.

Gasse, A. 1990, *Catalogue des ostraca hiératique littéraires de Deir-el-Médina* IV *(N^{os}1676 à 1774)*. Institute français d'archéologie orientale, Cairo.

Griffith, F. Ll. 1898, *Hieratic Papyri from Kahun and Gurob*, 2 vols. Bernard Quaritch, London.

Guglielmi, W. 1996, Die ägyptische Liebespoesie, in A. Loprieno (ed.), *Ancient Egyptian Literature: History and Forms*, 335–350. E. J. Brill, Leiden.

Hagen, F. forthcoming a, Literature, Transmission, and the Late Egyptian Miscellanies, in R. Dann (ed.), *Current Research in Egyptology. Proceedings of the Fifth Annual Symposium, University of Durham 2004*. Archaeopress, Oxford.

Hagen, F. forthcoming b, The Prohibitions: A New Kingdom Didactic Text, *Journal of Egyptian Archaeology* 91 (2005).

Haring, B. J. J. and Donker van Heel, K. 2003, *Writing in a Workmen's Village: Scribal Practice in Ramesside Deir el-Medina*.Egyptologische Uitgaven 16, Nederlands Instituut voor het Nabije Oosten, Leiden.

Hayes, W. C. 1942, *Ostraka and name stones from the tomb of Sen-Mut (no. 71) at Thebes*. Publications of the Metropolitan Museum of Art 15, Metropolitan Museum of Art, New York.

Helck, W. 1970, *Die Lehre des dwȝ-ḫtii*. Harrasowitz, Wiesbaden.

Helck, W. 1986 [1969], *Der Text der 'Lehre Amenemhets I. für seinen Sohn'*. Harrasowitz, Wiesbaden.

Hoch, J. 1991 / 1992, The Teaching of Dua-Kheti: A New Look at the Satire of the Trades, *Journal of the Society for the Study of Egyptian Artifacts* 21/22, 88–100.

Hoenes, S.-E. 1976. *Untersuchungen zu Wesen und Kult der Göttin Sachmet*. Rudolf Habelt Verlag, Bonn.

James, T. G. H. 1962, *The Hekanakhte letters & other early Middle Kingdom documents*. Metropolitan Museum of Art, New York.

Junge, F. 1984, Sprache, in W. Helck and E. Otto (eds.), *Lexikon der Ägyptologie, V*, cols. 1176–1211. Harrassowitz, Wiesbaden.

Keller, C. A. 1995, Private Votives in Royal Cemeteries, in C. J. Eyre (ed.), *Abstract of Papers. Seventh International Congress of Egyptologists, Cambridge, 3–9 September 1995*. Oxbow Books, Oxford, 95–97.

Koch, R. 1990, *Die Erzählung des Sinuhe*. Fondation égyptologique Reine Élisabeth, Brussels.

Kunetz, C. 1929, Quelques monuments du culte de Sobk, in *Bulletin de l'Institute français d'archéologie orientale* 28, 113–172.

López, J. 1982, *Catalogo del Museo Egizio di Torino.Ostraca ieratici. N. 57320–57449*. La Goliardica, Milan.

McDowell, A. 1992, Awareness of the Past in Deir el-Medina, in R. J. Demarée and A. Egberts (eds.), *Village voices. Proceedings of the Symposium "Texts from Deir El-Medina and their Interpretation", Leiden, May 31 – June 1, 1991*, 95–109. Leiden University, Leiden.

McDowell, A. 1996, Student Exercises from Deir el-Medina: The Dates, in P. Der Manuelian (ed.) *Studies in honor of William Kelly Simpson*, 601–608. Museum of Fine Arts, Boston.

McDowell, A. 2000, Teachers and Students at Deir el-Medina, in R. J. Demarée and A. Egberts (eds.) *Deir el-Medina in the Third Millennium AD: A Tribute to Jac. J. Janssen*, 217–233. Egyptologische uitgaven 14, Nederlands Instituut voor het Nabije Oosten, Leiden.

Parkinson, R. B. 2002, *Poetry and Culture in Middle Kingdom Egypt. A Dark Side to Perfection*. Continuum, London and New York.

Parkinson, R. B. 2004, The History of a Poem: Middle Kingdom Literary Manuscripts and their Reception, in G. Burkard (ed.) *Kon-Texte: Akten des Symposions "Spurensuche – Altägypten im Spiegel seiner Texte", München 2. bis 4. Mai 2003*, 51–63. Harrasowitz, Wiesbaden.

Parkinson, R. B. and Quirke, S. 1995, *Papyrus*. British Museum Press, London.

Posener, G. 1951–1952–1972, *Catalogue des ostraca hiératique littéraires de Deir el Medineh* II *(N°s 1109 à 1266)*. Institute français d'archéologie orientale, Cairo.

Posener, G. 1975, Les ostraca numéroté et le conte du revenant in *Drevnii Vostok: sbornik* 1 (Festschrift Korostovstev), 105–112. 'Nauka', Moscow.

Quack, J. F. 1992–1993, P.Wien D 6319: Eine demotische Übersetzung aus dem Mittelägyptischen, *Enchoria* 19/20, 125–129.

Quack, J. F. 1999, A New Bilingual Fragment from the British Museum (Papyrus BM EA 69574), *Journal of Egyptian Arhcaeology* 85, 153–164.

Quirke, S. 1996, Archive, in A. Loprieno (ed.) *Ancient Egyptian Literature: History and Forms*, 379–401. E.J. Brill, Leiden.

Ranke, H. 1935, *Die Ägyptische Personennamen*. Verlag J. J. Augustin, Glückstadt.

Reynolds, D. F. 1995, *Heroic Poets, Poetic Heroes. The Ethnography of Performance in an Arabic Oral Epic Tradition*. Cornell University Press, Ithaca and London.

Rossi, C. 2004, *Architecture and mathematics in ancient Egypt*. Cambridge University Press, Cambridge.

Simpson, W. K. 1958, Allusions to *The Shipwrecked Sailor* and *The Eloquent Peasant* in a Ramesside Text, *Journal of the American Oriental Society* 78, 50–51.

Spalinger, A. 2002, *The Transformation of an Ancient Egyptian Narrative: P. Sallier III and the Battle of Kadesh*. Harrasowitz, Wiesbaden.

van de Walle, B. 1948, *La transmission des textes littéraires égyptiens avec une annexe de G. Posener*. Fondation égyptologique Reine Élisabeth, Brussels.

van der Plas, D. 1986, *L'Hymne à la crue du Nil*. Nederlands Instituut voor het Nabije Oosten, Leiden.

Vernus, P. 1984, Schreibtafel, in W. Helck and E. Otto (eds.), *Lexikon der Ägyptologie, V*, cols. 703–709. Harrassowitz, Wiesbaden.

Vernus, P. 1996, Langue littéraire et diglossie, in A. Loprieno (ed.) *Ancient Egyptian Literature: History and Forms*, 555–564. E. J. Brill, Leiden.

Wente, E. F. 1961, A letter to the vizier To, *Journal of Near Eastern Studies* 20, 252–257.

Wente, E. F. 1990, *Letters from ancient Egypt*. Scholars Press, Atlanta.

Children and the Dead in New Kingdom Egypt

Nicola Harrington

"Man is clay and straw,/The god is his builder./He tears down, he builds up daily/...
Happy is he who reaches the west,/When he is safe in the hand of the god"

(*Instruction of Amenemope*: trans. Lichtheim 1976, 146)

Introduction

In this paper I consider the depiction and involvement of children in the mortuary sphere, and the burial of children in contrast to adults. For the first section I have limited my study to individuals depicted as prepubescent in tomb scenes and stelae which portray mourning, funeral processions, fowling in the marshes and any scenes that do not fall into the general category of 'daily life'. While reference to other periods is inevitable, only the New Kingdom will be discussed here. My aim is to explore how far children were portrayed as being involved in the mortuary cults of their parents and grandparents, and which iconographic contexts were considered inappropriate for the young. Most New Kingdom settlement sites, particularly Deir el-Medina, have provided evidence of cults relating to the worship of deceased kin, and I will briefly assess the possibility that such cults were also devoted to children.

Children in context: the place of children in society

It is often stated that children in ancient Egypt were portrayed or treated as miniature adults, and essentially the same convention can be seen in Egypt today (Figure 1).

From the Old Kingdom onwards the size and proportion of children in relation to adults are often anatomically unrealistic. The Amarna Period, with its break with traditions and often closer attention to anatomical forms, saw children given more realistic body shapes and gestures (*e.g.* Wildung 1999, 217, cat. 47; Figure 2). In other periods relative height is used as an indicator of age, for example in the 6th Dynasty tomb of Meni, (Feucht 1995,

Figure 1. Modern Egyptian children dressed in the same way as adults. (© Nicola Harrington 2001.)

Figure 2. Damaged talatat relief depicting Nefertiti with one of her daughters displaying a sidelock. Brooklyn Museum, New York, 60.197.8. (© Nicola Harrington.)

430, fig. 47), but children are often shown fully formed yet less than the height of the major figures knees (*e.g.* in Sennedjem's tomb, TT 1, and Amennakht's, TT 218, both at Deir el-Medina). Facial expressions generally match those of the tomb owner and his family, who also do not have individual features. One exception to this pattern is the depiction of the children and grandchildren of Inherkhau in his tomb at Deir el-Medina (TT 359, 20th Dynasty), who are given expressions and gestures of their own.

In the Old Kingdom prepubescent children were depicted predominantly nude in reliefs and statuary, sometimes in the forefinger-to-mouth pose later associated in particular with Horus in infantile form (Robins 1993a, 86–87; Brovarski 1988, 89, cat. 16) and with the hieroglyphic determinative for child or orphan (Gardiner 1957, A17). Whereas nakedness in adulthood carried connotations of low status (Robins 1999, 58), the nudity of children is more an iconographic convention than a portrayal of reality: not only would constant nakedness have been impractical, particularly in winter, but some children's clothing has survived (Robins 1993a, 186). From the Old Kingdom onwards some older children were shown wearing outfits similar to those of their parents (*e.g.* Senetiti's tomb, 4th Dynasty; Feucht 1995, 427, fig. 44), but others were also depicted nude (Figure 3). However, the other characteristic marker for children, the sidelock, was more than just a pictorial convention because bodies have been found with shaved heads and this hairstyle (Meskell 2002, 81).

Figure 3. Old Kingdom tomb relief exemplifying the relative depicted dimensions of mother and daughter, named Niankhwadjet and Djefaib-sherit. False door recess from the 4th Dynasty mastaba of Mery at Saqqara. The Metropolitan Museum of Art, New York. (© Nicola Harrington.)

Figure 4 (left). *Wooden cosmetic spoon with the motif of a nude young girl. 18th Dynasty. Musée du Louvre, Paris, N 1737. (© Nicola Harrington.)*

Figure 5 (right). *Wooden cosmetic container in the form of a nude adolescent girl carrying a jar and a bag decorated with lotus petals. 18th Dynasty. Musée du Louvre, Paris, E 8025. (© Nicola Harrington.)*

The motif of the nude adolescent girl, which has no male parallel, is found on cosmetic items such as wooden spoons (Figures 4 and 5) and cosmetic jars, as well as faience drinking bowls, all objects which are often unprovenanced but from their state of preservation must derive from tombs (*e.g.* Kozloff 1992, 22). The young females, who frequently wear jewellery and a girdle around the hips, are portrayed as dancers (*e.g.* TT 38, Djeserkareseneb; Wilkinson and Hill 1983, 111), musicians, and serving girls (*e.g.* TT 52, TT 45, TT 108); along with the lotuses with which they are often adorned, their youth may have assisted symbolically in the rejuvenation of the deceased.

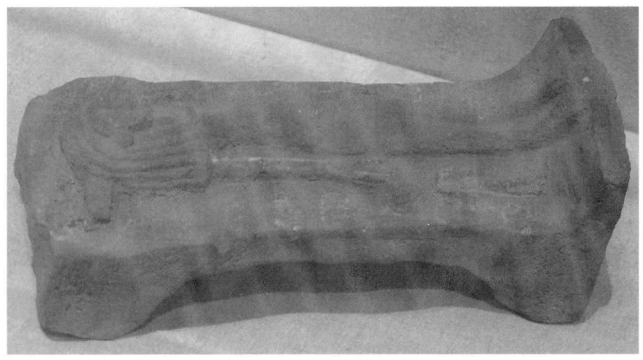

Figure 6 (above). *Terracotta figurine of a woman and child on a bed. 18th Dynasty, from Sawama. Brooklyn Museum, New York, 14.606. (© Nicola Harrington.)*

Figure 7 (right). *Limestone statuette of a nursing woman – possibly a votive object dedicated to a deity as a prayer for a healthy child. Middle Kingdom, c.12–13th Dynasty. Brooklyn Museum, New York, 51.224. (© Nicola Harrington.)*

A desire for children is apparent in such sources as letters to the dead, and votive offerings placed in tombs and temples (as at Deir el Bahri, see Pinch 1993; Figures 6 and 7).

Instructional and medico-magical texts demonstrate the importance attributed to the production of successors, as stated in the Instruction of Ani: "Happy is the man whose people are many/He is saluted on account of his progeny" (Lichtheim 1976, 136), and more euphemistically "Fill your hand with all the flowers/That your eye can see/One has need of all of them/It is good fortune not to lose them" (Lichtheim 1976, 139; *cf.* Zandee 1960, 107).

The fact that handicapped or seriously ill children were treated as full members of society is exemplified at Deir el-Medina by the burials of a severely deformed boy named Iryky, and an unnamed child who suffered from scoliosis, who were interred with jewellery and provisions within the Eastern Necropolis (Meskell 1999, 171).

The obligation of children, particularly of the eldest son, was to support their parents in old age or infirmity and to provide the mortuary cult, in order to ensure sustenance in the afterlife (*cf.* Whale 1989, 256; Lichtheim 1976, 137). If a couple were infertile, adoption was an option (Lichtheim 1976, 274; Eyre 1992, 207–221), as is stated in a 19th Dynasty letter of admonition: "You are no man for you did not make your wife pregnant as your friend did... He who has no children should get himself some orphan to bring him up. Then he will be the one who pours water upon his hands as a genuine eldest son" (Janssen and Janssen 1990, 159). Several adoptions are attested, including the case of the chief scribe Ramose and his wife Mutemwia of Deir el-Medina, who adopted Qenherkhepershef in the 19th Dynasty (Robins 1993a, 77). Respect for parents, whether natural or adoptive, was instilled from an early age: "Pay attention to your offspring/Bring him up as did your mother/Do not give her cause to blame you/Lest she raise her hands to god/And he hears her cries" (Instruction of Any, Lichtheim 1976, 141).

The transition from childhood to adulthood was marked by the end of childish gestures; the disappearance of the sidelock which was replaced by a wig, the wearing of adult, more gender-specific clothing and accessories; and relative height. Separate statues of children are rare, but an Old Kingdom example from Tomb G2009 at Giza (Freed 2003, 92) shows that adults, in this case the craftsman Ptahneferty, could be portrayed in the form of a child. Perhaps the intention here was to establish an iconographical link between the deceased and Re in his rejuvenated form, though it is possible that the statue was part of a group where Ptahneferty was shown as subordinate to an effigy his father (*cf.* Louvre E13090; a stela of Neferhotep in the pose of a child from Deir el-Medina).

Children in funerary iconography

1) Funerals

Even young children are depicted as participants in mourning rituals, for example in the 18th Dynasty tombs of Neferhotep (TT 49; Feucht 1995, 348, fig. 25) and Ramose (TT 55; Figure 8). In funerary contexts men are rarely shown displaying grief, although there are exceptions, particularly in processional boat scenes (*e.g.* TT 49; Ankhmahor, 6th Dynasty: Kanawati 2001, 47, pl.19). This gender distinction can be compared with the segregation of men and women into distinct groups at banquets. In funeral processions, even the children are divided according to gender, and girls join the women in wailing and displays of despair. A stela from Deir el-Medina dedicated by a woman and her daughter, both of whom bear the title "mourner", indicates that this was their ritual role or occupation and that it could be passed down the generations (Robins 1993a, 164; Toivari-Viitala 2001, 226).

Figure 8. *Detail of the funeral procession in the tomb of Ramose (TT 55) at Sheikh Abd el-Qurna, showing women, adolescent girls, and a child mourning. 18th Dynasty. (© Nicola Harrington.)*

Young girls are also shown carrying infants in slings during funeral processions (*e.g.* TT 4 and TT 49). In contrast, boys carry furniture such as chairs and pot stands complete with pots (*e.g.* TT 139: Wilkinson and Hill 1983, 126, fig. 35.101.3; TT C4, Manniche 1988, pl. 31, fig. 49). Statuettes of girls bearing containers were produced in large quantities in the 18th and 19th Dynasties (*e.g.* Freed 1982, 204, cat. 238); these may be later functional equivalents of the Middle Kingdom freestanding wooden models of offering bearers for the tomb. An 18th Dynasty figurine of a nude young female carrying a large linen box on her head (Russmann 2001, 170–172, cat. 80) suggests that while girls were not portrayed in this way in tombs, they may have been involved in carrying furniture as part of the funeral procession, or it might simply be an indication of their servile status.

Children could also be present at the Opening of the Mouth ceremony, as shown in the tomb of Nebenmaat, where two small nude children hold the coffins of their parents and raise their hands to their faces in a gesture of grief, while their older brother acts as *sem*-priest outside the tomb chapel (TT 219: Feucht 1995, 351, fig. 26; Gaber 2002, 42).

2) Offering scenes and processions

Sennedjem's tomb at Deir el-Medina (TT 1) includes the depiction of an offering scene, similar to the 18th Dynasty banquet scenes, with some members of the family seated before an offering table, and others carrying birds and bouquets. On the left-hand side of the doorway of the burial chamber (Figure 9), the adults are accompanied by three children, two of whom stand beneath chairs.

The children are distinguished from the rest of the family by being depicted as less than knee-height, with long sidelocks, but they are dressed as adults and carry foliage as if part of the procession. The two smallest children are identified by name and are both "true of voice", probably indicating that they are dead (*cf.* Pashedu's children: Zivie 1979, pl. 22; and Amennakht's: Gaber

Figure 9*. Processional scene in the burial chamber of Sennedjem's tomb (TT 1) at Deir el-Medina. 19th Dynasty. (© Nicola Harrington.)*

Figure 10 (left). *Stela of Humay and Senetnofret. The couple in the lower register are identified as Pahu<kh>ered and Amenhotep; their daughter Amenemope kneels beneath the chair and holds a stylised lotus blossom. Mid-18th Dynasty. The Metropolitan Museum of Art, New York, 25.184.3. (© Nicola Harrington.)*

Figure 11 (right). *Stela of four females, from Thebes. The three individuals who hold lotuses, including the two children with sidelocks, are probably deceased, although only two are explicitly labelled "justified". Late Middle Kingdom, c.1750 B.C. The Metropolitan Museum of Art, New York. (© Nicola Harrington.)*

2002, 41). The tallest of the three at the rear of the line has no text caption, but is also probably deceased along with the adults. The absence of an inscription in this context suggests that the figure may stand for several children rather than a single individual. From this and other similar examples (see Whale 1989, 254–255, 270), it seems likely that children accompanying their parents, or seated under chairs are to be understood as deceased, particularly on stelae (*e.g.* the funerary stela of Ramose and Tetpu, Robins 1993a, 167, fig. 72; see further Feucht 1995, 431, fig. 48; Martin 1991, 130, fig. 88; Figures 10, 11).

3) Fishing and fowling

The young in 18th Dynasty fishing and fowling scenes (*e.g.* Nakht TT 52, Shedid and Seidel 1996, 60–61) and in other scenes from the Old Kingdom onwards often hold a bird (including ducks, hoopoes, and lapwings) by the wing or legs, or nestled in the palm of their hands. Adults shown carrying birds outside offering processions are often identified as dead (*e.g.* three males in Sennedjem's tomb: TT 1, Figure 9), so this may also apply to children, who are sometimes untitled (*e.g.* Neferbauptah, 5th Dynasty; Harpur 1987, 485, fig. 24). The bird motif may be linked in this context to one of the many Egyptian terms for children, *ꜣ*, child, literally "fledgling"

(MacDonald 1994, 57). The function of children in these scenes was probably to emphasise the procreative potential of the tomb owner and his ability to be reborn, as well as presenting an idealised image of the family. As Robins states: "the children are concrete symbols of fertility, the result of the interaction between male and female" (1993a, 188; *cf.* Lustig 1997, 59, 61).

4) Worship of deities

With the changes in the content of decorative schemes in 19th Dynasty tombs, which saw greater emphasis on the individual's relationship with the gods and the passage to the afterlife, children are integrated more fully into depictions of the deceased with deities. Such changes in private tombs first appear near the end of the reign of Thutmose III, when ritual scenes became more common and the tomb owner's wife and children are present (Whale 1989, 241). Nineteenth Dynasty examples of children involved in worshipping deities with the tomb owner include Nakhtamun (TT 218; Feucht 1995, 365, fig. 31) praising Re, Pashedu (TT 3: Zivie 1979, pl. 15; Figure 12) before Re-Horakhty, Atum, Khepri, and Ptah, with his daughter, and Ipuy (TT 217) depicted with his wife and young daughter before Osiris and Isis. Children are also occasionally depicted in the act of adoring gods on funerary stelae (*e.g.* Turin, Museo Egizio 50051: Robins 1993a, 134, fig. 53). As with the offering scenes, it is possible that children shown with the tomb owner before gods are deceased, but this is clearly not the case for votive stelae, on which children are occasionally portrayed (*e.g.* Borla 2002, 302–303, cat. no. 253).

5) Statues

Children are largely absent from rock-cut statuary in tombs, though they occur with their parents on freestanding statues from the Old Kingdom. They are usually passive, standing with feet together, holding the leg of an adult (*e.g.* Russmann 2001, 184–186, cat. 93, EA 2319), or in a striding pose but having the finger-to-mouth gesture emblematic of infant or child status and evocative of the uncertainty and vulnerability of youth. As with tomb images, the children are often small versions of the rest of the family, for instance in the Middle Kingdom statue group of Ukhhotep, where the young girl has two sidelocks resembling the Hathoric wigs of the owner's wives (Simpson 1987, 16–17).

Figure 13. *Front, back, and right side views of an anthropoid bust with the distinctive hairstyle of a child. UC 1236, faience, New Kingdom, 4.0 cm (h) x 2.5 cm (w) x 1.5 cm (d). (Photographs by Nicola Harrington, courtesy of the Petrie Museum of Egyptian Archaeology, UCL.)*

As noted above, individual statues or figurines of children are uncommon; at least one example was part of a tomb group (Bryan 1992, 260, cat no. 51). The object originally held by Nebetya, who was identified by name only on the statuette, is likely to have been a sistrum, given that she formed part of a musician's troupe and derived from a tomb. Contrary to Bryan's statement, sidelocks are uncommon in banquet scenes, and the statue's pose is formal but unlike that of a serving girl. It most closely resembles the stance of the sistrum-bearing child god Ihy, son of Horus, as represented in a statuette from the tomb of Tutankhamun (Cairo Museum no. 423).

6) Absence of children

Children and spouses are sometimes completely absent from the decoration of a tomb. This may be due to a monument's damaged or unfinished state, or to non-marriage, remarriage, or infertility. As Whale (1989, 245) points out, although marriage and family life were the ideal, some men may have chosen not to marry or have offspring, while others may have decided not to adopt or been homosexual. It is possible that Ineni, the owner of Tomb 81 at Sheikh Abd el-Qurna, had a son who died young (Robins 1993b, 295). This child was not depicted, but while some children who predeceased their tomb owner fathers may not have been shown in the tomb, small children are represented as deceased in at least thirty tombs (Whale 1989, 254). The fact that infants were buried (see below) shows that they were considered to be social persons.

In the reign of Akhenaten unusual funerary scenes were depicted, including the king and his wife mourning one of their children; such scenes do not appear in non-royal tombs, where depictions of babies are also absent. If we accept Dorman's view that "it is necessary to regard Theban private tombs as family memorials" (2003, 41), the absence of the young in images relating to the tomb owner's afterlife is notable and suggests that representations of infants or children who were already dead may have been considered dangerous or at least inappropriate in their implications for the rebirth of the deceased. In some cases a name may have been substituted for an image.

The death and burial of children

Ancient societies experienced very high mortality rates: it has been estimated that at least 20% of all newborns died during their first year of life and most infants faced a 50% chance of reaching adulthood (Meskell 2002, 83). Although children are under-represented in the archaeological record (Meskell 1999: 158), infant mortality is reflected sometimes in Egyptian graves, for example, in a cemetery at Mirgissa, where 50% of the skeletons discovered were of children less than 2 years of age (Baines and Lacovara 2002, 14). The same percentage was found at Gurob, which had a separate children's cemetery, while at Matmar infant graves constituted 48% of burials and at Mostagedda 31% (Robins 1994–5, 28). It is therefore not surprising that death was personified as an unpredictable and terrifying force, as in the Instruction of Any: "Do not say 'I am too young to be taken'/For you do not know your own death./When death comes, he steals the infant/Who is in his mother's arms/Just like him who has reached old age" (Robins 1993a, 85; *cf.* Baines 1991, 133; Zandee 1960, 87).

The transience of life is recognised in didactic literature, as in my opening quotation from the Instruction of Amenemope, and particularly the 'harper's songs' in New Kingdom tombs: "Remember, O heart, that day of death ... because there is indeed none who passes it by, strong and weak alike" (Lichtheim 1945: 198). The tomb of Neferhotep (TT 50), from which this passage derives, contains three harpist's songs. The second song includes a section with a stark message about the unpredictability of life, when an average day terminates in sudden death: "Re reveals himself at dawn; Atum goes to rest in the western mountain; men beget; women conceive; every nose breathes air. Dawn comes and their children have gone to their places [*i.e.* graves]" (Lichtheim 1945, 178).

Infanticide, common in ancient Greece, is not known from dynastic Egypt (Filer 1998, 392); indeed suspicious deaths were a cause of concern and required investigation, as exemplified in a 19th Dynasty letter from Qenherkhepershef to a woman named Inerwau: "Why did you fail to go to the wise woman on account of the two infants who died in your care? Inquire of the wise woman about the death of the two infants, whether it was their fate or their destiny" (Ritner 2002, 205; *cf.* McDowell 1999, 115).

At Deir el Medina in the 18th Dynasty, two cemeteries were in use, the Eastern and the Western Necropolis. The Eastern Necropolis saw equality in expenditure on burials of men, women, and adolescents. While very young children were often buried more economically, they were still interred with items of jewellery and burial goods otherwise typical of adult burials; neonates, adolescents and adults were buried in age-determined zones (Meskell 2002, 82; 1999: 163). Elsewhere, the burial of children generally followed no fixed pattern and seems to have depended on the preferences and wealth of the parents and local practices. At the Middle Kingdom settlement of Kahun, Petrie found "many newborn infants… buried in the floors of the rooms and … usually in boxes made for other purposes", as well as three babies buried in a single large house in the town (Gallorini 1998, 57, 58). In the 19th Dynasty the sole known community cemetery of Deir el-Medina was the Western Necropolis with its rock-cut tombs; there, children were given comparably meagre burials (Meskell 1998, 198). A decorated pottery coffin of a child from a cemetery near Amada in Lower Nubia exemplifies the local differences in burial practice (Lacovara 1988, 60, 160, cat. 112).

In the 19th Dynasty multiple burials ensured that an entire family – twenty people in the case of Sennedjem (McDowell 1999, 13) – could all share in the afterlife that was depicted on the walls of the burial chamber, in contrast with the 18th Dynasty, when burial chambers were very rarely decorated. Multiple burials are known, including that of Neferkhawet, which included infants and young children (Dorman 2003, 34–35); perhaps deceased children could accompany their parents in order to receive offerings brought to the tomb. The fact that children, including neonates, could be buried with beer jars and ceramics indicates that the young were considered able to participate in an adult-envisaged afterlife (Meskell 1999, 170).

Cults of deceased children

Children were depicted as deceased with their parents in some Theban tombs, receiving offerings from their siblings (Whale 1989, 255). This suggests that they could benefit from ritual practices in the same manner as the tomb owner and his wife. In view of the high child mortality rate, it is perhaps surprising that such representations are so rare. Egyptologists often consider anthropoid busts to be largely genderless, generalised forms that represented the generic dead, but I have recently offered an alternative interpretation (Harrington 2005). Small busts with hairstyles characteristic of young (often male) children (*e.g.* TT 221, Horimin, and TT 359, Inherkhau; Keller 2001, pl. 28, fig. 4 and pl. 26, fig. 2) and broad collars typical of other 'ancestor busts' may well depict deceased children (Figure 13). If this is the case, the absence of the young represented on other cultic objects such as *ꜣḥ iḳr n Rˁ* stelae is noteworthy; these do not seem to be dedicated to children, while family members are rarely seen on the stelae

Figure 12. Scene from the tomb of Pashedu (TT 3) at Deir el-Medina. The daughter, whose extreme youth is indicated by the lack of a sidelock and who travels with the deceased couple on their afterlife journey to Abydos, probably predeceased the tomb owner. (© Nicola Harrington.)

(exceptions include Demarée's (1983) A21 and A26), which were largely commissioned for men. An unusual funerary stela dedicated to a young boy named Merysekhmet depicts him seated on his mother's lap and holding a lotus bouquet (Robins 1995, 83). The table before the couple is piled high with offerings, suggesting that the deceased boy was the recipient of a cult and treated as an adult after death.

In letters to the dead and other textual sources, such as the Brooklyn magical papyrus (47.218.156) and Papyrus Ebers, people seem to have feared the behaviour of deceased men and women (Ritner 2002, 200, 207–208; Robins 1993a, 86; *cf.* Robins 1995, 82), but children are not mentioned as a force for good or evil from beyond the grave. Perhaps in the case of young children, this was due to the fact that they were not considered developed or powerful enough to be a threat in that context. As Parker Pearson comments: "[in general] it is likely that the role or influence of the dead is greater the more closely they are physically integrated within society. As such, the dead may form a powerful element within the social order, as ancestors of senior status; 'without' they may have little influence on the living" (1993, 206).

Conclusions

The function of depiction as a creative act seems to have resulted in children not being shown on funerary monuments unless they were required for some aspect of the rebirth of the tomb owner. The absence of children from tomb scenes in some cases may indicate that the tomb owner was childless, but certain contexts were the preserve of the tomb owner and his spouse, while some contexts were evidently considered inappropriate for the young, in the same way that images of childbirth, pregnancy, death *etc.* seem to have been excluded. Children are not depicted at banquets in tombs of the 18th Dynasty, or in many of the Book of the Dead vignettes which decorate 19th Dynasty tombs. The focus in the latter case was on the tomb owner's (and spouse's) relationship with gods and on the individual's passage to the afterlife. An emphasis on rebirth, fertility and continuity of the family line, as symbolised by children, may not have been deemed necessary.

Many questions relating to the place of children within the funerary cult remain. For instance, is the absence of tombs or monuments dedicated to children due solely to their expense, or was it also a result of ideological conventions or constraints? At what stage of a child's life was it deemed a social person and worthy of an adult-style burial? The thematization of premature death and individual monuments for the young is a Late Period and Greco-Roman Period phenomenon, so it is probable that prior to the Third Intermediate Period there was a more communal view of the death and commemoration even of elite children (John Baines, personal communication). If the tomb was "an installation for maintaining the deceased in life, a liminal area where the dead and the living could meet and the deceased could receive the support from the living which was necessary for their survival" (Lloyd 1989, 129), then how were infants buried in pits supposed to exist beyond death? Were they assumed to have a separate afterlife, and if so, why is it not documented? These issues cannot be tackled here.

As with any study of ancient Egypt, the problems and biases of the primary sources need to be considered. "Writing about the lives of children has proved to be a difficult task for historians, who in their source material predominantly find adults' perception of children, together with a set of ideals of the concept of childhood, rather than information on the actual children themselves" (Toivari-Viitala 2001, 183). The male-oriented aspect of much of this material is a further hindrance to understanding the role of children in society, specifically in cultic rituals for deceased members of the men's families and the treatment of them after death.

In conclusion, children are depicted in a largely passive role in New Kingdom elite funerary contexts, at least until they reach puberty and lose the visual indicators of youth. This pattern fits with Janssen's contention that children in ancient Egypt were treated as "not yet complete young adults" (1997, 231). In general they were buried individually and provided with some basic grave goods, but no lasting monument. Perhaps this level of provision was all that was practicable in view of the high infant and child mortality rate, for ultimately the primary focus of Egyptian mortuary provision, as in other societies, was on the living (Baines and Lacovara 2002, 27–28).

University of Oxford

Acknowledgements

I would like to thank Professor John Baines for kindly agreeing to review the paper, Hugh Kilmister of the Petrie Museum for access to material, Alice Stevenson and Rachel Mairs for providing the opportunity to contribute to the conference and this volume, and the anonymous referees for their comments and suggestions.

References

Baines, J. 1991, Society, morality, and religious practice, in B. E. Shafer (ed.), *Religion in ancient Egypt: gods, myths, and personal practice*, 123–199. Routledge, London.

Baines, J. and Lacovara, P. 2002, Burial and the dead in ancient Egyptian society: Respect, formalism, neglect, *Journal of Social Archaeology* 2, 5–36.

Borla, M. 2002, Stèle de Neferrenpet, in G. Andreu (ed.), *Les artistes de Pharaon: Deir el-Médineh et la Vallée des Rois*, 302–303. Réunion des Musées Nationaux, Paris.

Brovarski, E. 1988, Statuette of a naked boy (cat. 16), in S. D'Auria, P. Lacovara and C. H. Roehrig (eds.), *Mummies and magic: The funerary arts of ancient Egypt*, 89. Museum of Fine Arts, Boston.

Bryan, B. 1992, Statuette of the young girl Nebetya (cat. 51), in A. P. Kozloff, B. M. Bryan and L. M. Berman, *Egypt's Dazzling Sun: Amenhotep III and his world*, 260. Cleveland Museum of Art.

Demarée, R. J. 1983, *The ꜣḫ iḳr n Rꜥ stelae: On ancestor worship in ancient Egypt*. Universiteit van Amsterdam, Leiden.

Dorman, P. 2003, Family burial and commemoration in the Theban Necropolis, in N. Strudwick and J. Taylor (eds.), *The Theban Necropolis: Past, present and future*, 30–41. British Museum Press, London.

Eyre, C. 1992, The Adoption Papyrus in social context, *Journal of Egyptian Archaeology* 78, 207–221.

Feucht, E. 1995, *Das Kind im alten Ägypten*. Campus Verlag, Frankfurt and New York.

Filer, J. M. 1998, Mother and baby burials, in C. Eyre (ed.), *Proceedings of the Seventh International Congress of Egyptologists*, 391–400. Peeters, Leuven.

Freed, R. E. 1982, Servant girl with amphora (cat. 238), in E. Brovarski, S. K. Doll, and R. E. Freed (eds.), *Egypt's Golden Age: The art of living in the New Kingdom 1558–1085 B.C.*, 204. Museum of Fine Arts, Boston.

Freed, R. E. 2003, Statuette of a young boy, in R. E. Freed, L. M. Berman and D. M. Doxey, *Arts of Ancient Egypt*, 92. Museum of Fine Arts, Boston.

Gaber, H. 2002, L'au-delà des artisans: Le décor sépultures d'Amennakht, de Nebenmaat et de Khameteri (tombes thébaines n° 218, 219, 220), in *Les Artistes de Pharaon: Deir el-Médineh au Nouvel Empire; Exposition au Louvre*, 38–47. Dossiers d'Archéologie n° 272; Editions Faton S.A, Dijon.

Gallorini, C. 1998, A reconstruction of Petrie's excavation at the Middle Kingdom settlement of Kahun, in S. Quirke (ed.), *Lahun Studies*, 42–59. Sia Publishing, New Malden.

Gardiner, A. 1957, *Egyptian Grammar: Being an introduction to the study of hieroglyphs,* (3rd edition). Griffith Institute, Ashmolean Museum, Oxford.

Harpur, Y. 1987, *Decoration in Egyptian Tombs of the Old Kingdom: Studies in orientation and scene content*. KPI, London and New York.

Harrington, N. 2005, Anthropoid busts and ancestor cults at Deir el Medina, in K. Piquette and S. Love (eds.), *Current Research in Egyptology 2003: Proceedings of the Fourth Annual Symposium*, 71–88. Oxbow Books, Oxford.

Janssen, J. J. 1997, Review of Erika Feucht, *Das Kind im alten Ägypten*, *Journal of Egyptian Archaeology* 83, 228–231.

Janssen, R. and Janssen, J. J. 1990, *Growing Up in Ancient Egypt*. Rubicon Press, London.

Kanawati, N. 2001, *The Tomb and Beyond: Burial customs of Egyptian officials*. Aris and Phillips, Warminster.

Keller, C. A. 2001, A family affair: The decoration of Theban Tomb 359, in W. V. Davies (ed.), *Colour and Painting in Ancient Egypt*, 71–93. British Museum Press, London.

Kozloff, A. 1992, Egypt's Dazzling Sun: Amenhotep III and his world, *Egyptian Archaeology* 2, 18–22.

Lacovara, P. 1988, Coffin (cat. 112), in S. D'Auria, P. Lacovara and C. H. Roehrig (eds.), *Mummies and Magic: The funerary arts of ancient Egypt*, 66, 160. Museum of Fine Arts, Boston.

Lichtheim, M. 1945, The songs of the harpers, *Journal of Near Eastern Studies* 4, 178–212.

Lichtheim, M. 1976, *Ancient Egyptian Literature* 2: *The New Kingdom*. University of California Press, Berkeley.

Lloyd, A. B. 1989, Psychology and society in the Egyptian cult of the dead, in W. K. Simpson (ed.), *Religion and Philosophy in Ancient Egypt,* 117–133. Yale Egyptological Studies 3, New Haven.

Lustig, J. 1997, Kinship, gender and age in Middle Kingdom tomb scenes and texts, in J. Lustig (ed.), *Anthropology and Egyptology: A developing dialogue*, 43–65. Monographs in Mediterranean Archaeology 8, Sheffield Academic Press, Sheffield.

MacDonald, D. N. 1994, Terms for "children" in Middle Egyptian: A sociolinguistic view, *Bulletin of the Australian Centre in Egypt* 5, 53–59.

Manniche, L. 1988, *Lost Tombs*. Rubicon Press, London.

Martin, G. T. 1991, *The Hidden Tombs of Memphis: New discoveries from the time of Tutankhamun and Ramesses the Great*. Thames & Hudson, London.

McDowell, A. 1999, *Village Life in Ancient Egypt: Laundry lists and love songs*. Oxford University Press, Oxford.

Meskell, L. 1998, An archaeology of social relations in an Egyptian village, *Journal of Archaeological Method and Theory* 5, 209–243.

Meskell, L. 1999, *Archaeologies of Social Life*. Blackwell, Oxford and Malden, Massachusetts.

Meskell, L. 2002, *Private Life in New Kingdom Egypt*. Princeton University Press, Princeton and Oxford.

Parker Pearson, M. 1993, The powerful dead: Archaeological relationships between the living and the dead, *Cambridge Archaeological Journal* 3, 203–229.

Pinch, G. 1993, *Votive Offerings to Hathor*. Griffith Institute, Oxford.

Ritner, R. K. 2002, Magic, in D. B. Redford (ed.), *The Ancient Gods Speak: A guide to Egyptian religion*, 191–214. Oxford University Press, Oxford.

Robins, G. 1993a, *Women in Ancient Egypt*. British Museum Press, London.

Robins, G. 1993b, Review of Sheila Whale, *The family in the Eighteenth Dynasty of Egypt: A study of the representation of the family in the private tombs*, *Journal of Egyptian Archaeology* 79, 294–297.

Robins, G. 1994–5, Women and children in peril: Pregnancy, birth and infant mortality in ancient Egypt, *KMT* 5 (4), 24–35.

Robins, G. 1995, *Reflections of women in the New Kingdom: Ancient Egyptian Art from the British Museum*. Exhibition catalogue, Michael C Carlos Museum, Atlanta. Van Siclen, San Antonio, Texas.

Robins, G. 1999, Hair and the construction of identity in ancient Egypt, *Journal of the American Research Center in Egypt* 36, 55–69.

Russmann, E. R. 2001, *Eternal Egypt: Masterworks of ancient art from the British Museum*. Exhibition catalogue. British Museum Press, London.

Shedid, A. G. and Seidel, M. 1996, *The Tomb of Nakht: The art and history of an Eighteenth Dynasty official's tomb at Western Thebes*. Philipp von Zabern, Mainz.

Simpson, W. K. 1987, *A Table of Offerings: 17 years of acquisitions of Egyptian and Ancient Near Eastern art*. Museum of Fine Arts, Boston.

Toivari-Viitala, J. 2001, *Women at Deir el Medina: A study of the status and roles of the female inhabitants in the workmen's community during the Ramesside period*. Nederlands Instituut voor het Nabije Oosten, Leiden.

Whale, S. 1989, *The Family in the Eighteenth Dynasty of Egypt: A study of the representation of the family in the private tombs*. Australian Centre for Egyptology, Sydney.

Wildung, D. 1999, Statuette of a princess (cat. 47), in R. E. Freed, Y. J. Markowicz, S. H. D'Auria (eds.), *Pharaohs of the Sun: Akhenaten, Nefertiti, Tutankhamun*, 217. Thames & Hudson, London.

Wilkinson, C. K. and Hill, M. 1983, *Egyptian Wall Paintings: The Metropolitan Museum of Art's collection of facsimiles*. Metropolitan Museum of Art, New York.

Zandee, J. 1960, *Death as an Enemy According to Ancient Egyptian Conceptions*. E. J. Brill, Leiden.

Zivie, A. 1979, *La Tombe de Pached à Deir el-Médineh [N° 3]*. Institut Français d'Archéologie Orientale, Cairo.

'It is better to be silent than speak in vain': The Challenge of Producing Proverbs in Demotic and Greek

Nikolaos Lazaridis

Introduction

Proverb production was a common phenomenon in ancient Egyptian and Greek cultures. In Hellenistic and Roman Egypt, proverbs (by 'proverb' here I conventionally refer to all the freestanding sentences in the texts I examine, the majority of which, as is the case with the Greek proverb in the title of this paper, were short statements or precepts discussing general truths or practical matters of life) were collected in texts that continued the tradition of earlier Instructions (Jasnow 1999; Houser-Wegner 2001). These texts were often attributed to a sage and their wisdom material was presented as an instruction from a father to a son (Shupak 1989).

The Greek counterpart to the Egyptian Instructions were sapiential genres like the *gnomologium* and the *gnomic poem* (Wilson 1991, 56ff.). These were collections of wisdom material attributed to famous Greek intellectuals. Although some of these texts, as is the case with the Μοσχίωνος Γνῶμαι listed below, were only preserved in Byzantine manuscripts, the papyrological evidence suggests that the largest part of their material originally circulated within the educational milieu of the Hellenistic and Roman worlds (Morgan 1998, 120ff; Cribiore 2001, 178–180, 200).

The proverbs that are investigated in this paper come from Demotic Instructions (for a list of these texts and their publications, see Smith 1986) and Hellenistic or Roman collections of Greek proverbs. Specifically, the sample of Greek works selected for analysis includes the following texts: the Γνῶμαι Μονόστιχοι (Jäkel 1964, 33–83), *The Sentences of Sextus*, *The Sentences of Clitarchus* (Chadwick 1959, 12–63 and 76–83), *The Sentences of Pseudo-Phocylides* (Young 1971, 95–112), the Μοσχίωνος Γνῶμαι (Schenkl 1894, 481–485), and the Φιλοσόφων Λόγοι (Boissonade 1962 [1829], 120–126), all dating from the 2nd century B.C. onwards.

The main characteristic that is shared by the Demotic and Greek texts selected is the fact that the majority of their proverbs were short, single sentences that were grouped loosely together, in most of the cases making sense without the help of an immediate context. In fact, all that was needed for them to make sense was their proverbial status, which called for: (a) brevity of form; (b) great thematic range; and (c) wide applicability.

On this basis, the Demotic and Greek proverbs studied can be divided into: (1) proverbs of the statement and instructional type; and (2) monopartite, bipartite, and multipartite ones. The monopartite proverbs consist of one independent clause, the bipartite ones consist of two independent clauses or one independent and one subordinate clause, while the multipartite ones consist of three or four independent or independent and subordinate clauses.

The comparative investigation of this material has produced numerous results on all levels. As a sample of this, this paper will briefly touch on the structural comparison between the monopartite proverbs, the use of metaphor and simile, and the thematic variation observed in these proverbs.

(1) Monopartite Proverbs in Demotic and Greek

The monopartite proverb, common in both Demotic and Greek collections, was the shortest form of proverbial expression. Therefore, the challenge of conveying wisdom in brevity was here at its peak. This challenge can be explained as the task of the author of proverbs to express a general observation or give a piece of general advice, relating it to one or more circumstances, reasons, intentions, or effects (all of which I will call here 'condition') in relation to which what the proverb observed or advised on is valid. In other words, the author of such material had to describe a bipartite relationship (namely, the relationship between a 'condition' and an observation or a piece of advice) in a monopartite structure.

In general, in the face of this task, Egyptian and Greek authors reacted in the same way. Specifically, they focused on the observation or the piece of advice (that is, the main body of the proverb), rendering it through the main verbal or nominal construction of the proverb, and described the condition only in the cases when was needed to clarify the circumstances under which the main message of the proverb could be valid. In this case, the description of the condition was undertaken by an elliptical construction, namely, an incomplete construction that could be developed into a full clause.

Such a construction could be a unit in anticipation, some adverbials (that is, mainly prepositional phrases, adverbs, or nouns used adverbially – the last only in the case of Greek), or a participial phrase (employed also only in Greek), all of which qualified the whole proverb rather than simply one of its units. The different ways of describing the condition in a monopartite Demotic or Greek proverb are illustrated in the following examples:

> *p3 nt iw=f d̠ bn iw=y rh̠ ir t3 wp.t my wšd=f p3-Rᶜ* "The one who will say: 'I will not be able to do the task', let him pray to Pre" (*Pap. Louvre 2377* 9) (phrase in anticipation);
>
> ὁ προνοῶν ἀνθρώπων εὐχόμενός τε ὑπὲρ πάντων οὗτος ἀληθείᾳ θεοῦ νομιζέσθω "The man who is considerate of people and prays for everyone's sake, let him be considered as truly (a man) of God" (*Sextus* 372) (phrase in anticipation);
>
> *m-ir in ḥt r ms.t r ir ᶜnḫ ᶜ3 n-im=f* "Do not borrow money at interest in order to have a good life by it" (*Ankhsheshonqy* 16/12) (prepositional phrase);
>
> ἀγαθὸν μέγιστον ἡ φρόνησίς ἐστ̓ ἀεί "Prudence is always the greatest good" (*Menander* 14) (adverb); and
>
> πρὸ δὲ παντὸς ἔργου καὶ λόγου τὸν θεὸν σέβου, καθαρὸς ὢν ἀπὸ πάσις κακίας "Above all word and deed honour God, (so) being free from all evil" (*Philosophon Logoi* 4–5) (participle).

The conditions of these exemplary monopartite proverbs can be analyzed respectively as follows: 'when one says that he will not be able to do the task', 'when the man takes care of people and prays for everyone's sake', 'when one has the intention to have a good life by the money he will borrow', 'under all circumstances', and 'when one is free from all evil'. The first, second, fourth, and fifth are circumstances, while the third is an intention. It was with these conditions that what the main body of the proverb observed or advised on was true.

Dealing with the description of such a condition, the Greek author of proverbs could make use of a greater variety of grammatical and syntactic units than those available to the Egyptian author. Units exclusively employed in Greek were the participles or the nouns used as adverbs, both of which could be elliptical but at the same time clear, since they could be easily developed into real clauses. On the other hand, his Egyptian workmate had to deal with the rigidity of Demotic word order and the lack of similar tools of ellipsis. However, on the latter's side was the phenomenon of anticipation, a pure device of emphasis which was not commonly used in the Greek proverbs but which could create a logical interplay with the members of the main body of the proverb as effectively as the Greek participles did.

In addition to the specific condition described in participles or in anticipatory units, all Demotic and Greek proverbs were also linked to an overall condition, associated with the very proverbial status of these sentences. This overall condition considered that all these proverbs were valid in any given society or culture, since their observations concerned general matters that were involved in the life of mankind, at all times and places. Thus, even if the specific condition of a Greek proverb was the time one planned to get married, as is the case with one of the aforementioned proverbs, this applied to all humans that planned (and were planning) to get married. The fact that no subject is specified meant that all members of the audience could identify with it.

In contrast to the proverbs including a specific condition, there were some examples where there was no need for this condition to be mentioned, as the main message of the proverb was directly related to the overall condition. For example, this is the case with the proverbs:

> *hmy iw ḥr ḫpr šp p3 mwt* "Would that existence [lit. becoming or happening] succeed death!" (*Ankhsheshonqy* 10/18); and

> πατρίδα τὸν κόσμον ἡγοῦ "Consider the (whole) world as (your) homeland" (Clitarchus 3).

These two proverbial statements did make sense under all circumstances: the Demotic one expressed a universal wish made by Man facing the mystery of Death and the Greek one advised its anonymous everyman to move on and not get stuck with past misfortunes.

(2) Use of Metaphor and Simile

Turning to the issue of the use of metaphor and simile in Demotic and Greek proverbs, since the main challenge of proverb production was to convey as many important ideas in as few words, metaphors and similes were a favourite tool for both the Egyptian and Greek authors of proverbs. Although, with regard to the basic morphological or functional principles, the two types of material seem to have had much in common, in the realm of metaphor differences were more apparent. This was mainly due to the fact that the employed metaphors drew imagery from a cultural reservoir linked to the experience of landscape and everyday life in Egypt and Greece; thus the imagery was different as much as the landscape of the two countries and the *vie quotidienne* of the two societies were different.

Such images might have alluded to other texts of the same corpus of literature they belonged to or could have been pieces of common experience. In either case, their allusions were to be comprehensible to the majority of their contemporary readers and therefore the objects of their allusions should have been part of common knowledge.

In the Demotic proverbs such images alluded to myths or other aspects of Egyptian religion and they were most often used to elucidate the message of proverbial statements. An instance of this is the proverb:

> *nʒ-ḥrš pʒy=f btw r pʒ btw 4ḥmy iw=s ḥʿr.w* (*sic*) "Its punishment [*i.e.* the punishment of retribution] is heavier than the punishment (of) Sekhmet when she is enraged" (*P. Insinger* 34/4).

Here the punishment of the enraged Sekhmet was a metaphor for the harshest possible punishment (this metaphor being popular from earlier works of Egyptian literature as, for instance, in the *Story of Sinuhe* (*Sinuhe* B45) and was compared to the degree of harshness that characterized the way retribution punishes.

Concerning the Greek proverbs, there were a small number of examples that employed metaphors with mythological connotations, as is the case with the proverb:

> ἐν πλησμονῇ μέγιστον ἡ Κύπρις κράτος "In satiety the greatest power (is) Aphrodite [lit. the Cypriot]" (Menander 263).

Here the highlighted popular epithet of Aphrodite stood as a metaphor for love, alluding to the popular attributes of and stories about the Greek goddess (Breitenberger 2004).

An example of a Demotic metaphor alluding to common experience, on the other hand, is found in the proverb:

> *rmt iw=f mr tʒy=f ḥm.t n lby m-bʒḥ=f* "A man, when he is suffering, his wife is a lioness before him" (*Ankhsheshonqy* 15/12).

Here the meaning of the equation between 'the wife' and 'the lioness' depended on the common knowledge of the features of the latter. A similar Greek example, where common experience was eluded by an image used metaphorically, is the proverb:

> λιμὴν νεὼς ὅρμος, βίου δ̓ ἀλυπία "The refuge of a ship (is) a port, while (the refuge) of life (is) freedom from worry" (Menander 436).

In this example, the metaphorical play involved the equation of freedom of worry with a port, an image common to a naval power like ancient Greece.

In general, metaphors were used to the same extent and in the same way in Demotic and Greek proverbs, but the imagery they employed was a remnant of a cultural reservoir exclusive to each of the nations in question. With respect to the relationship between the modern reader and this material, metaphors often become points of obscurity by their very value as pieces of a cultural reservoir the biggest part of which has not survived to the modern times. Such is the case with the proverb:

> *ẖe.t sḥm.t ḥʒt ḥte* "Belly (of) a woman, heart (of) a horse" (*Ankhsheshonqy* 23/24).

Before one interprets such a proverb, one needs, firstly, to examine whether each part of the equation was meant metaphorically or whether the very equation of two literally meant phrases was what constituted the metaphor here and, secondly, to identify what the metaphor in this case stood for.

Kindred to metaphor and simile was personification, another common stylistic phenomenon that stressed the value of proverbial wisdom as a human property communicated by humans to humans. In the material examined personified appear to have been not only entities traditionally treated in anthropomorphic terms, like gods or divine forces, but also anything that may have an impact on the lives of men. For instance, this is the case with the proverbs:

ḥr ṯ nkt pꜣy=f nb "**Wealth** seizes its owner" (*Ankhsheshonqy* 9/22); and

Θυμὸς ὑπερχόμενος μανίην ὀλοόφρονα τεύχει "**Anger** that steals over one gives birth to baleful madness" (Pseudo-Phoclides 63).

Here the highlighted words denoted personified entities. Practically speaking, the personification of non-human entities enabled actions to be described in a vivid way, offering more liberties for tone manipulation and conveyance of emotions.

Finally, one must note that figures like metaphor, simile, and personification were employed only in proverbs of the statement type and never in admonitions of any sort. This, I believe, is due to the fact that proverbs of the instructional type were to be directly addressed to an anonymous audience and therefore needed to be more straightforward and clearer in their language than the proverbs of the statement type. Given thus that stylistic devices like the ones discussed here conveyed messages in an indirect way (that is, illustrating what they wanted to say rather than directly expressing it), the ancient authors avoided their use in proverbs that needed to give straightforward commands or warnings.

(3) Themes in Demotic and Greek Proverbs

Turning to observations about the thematic aspect of these proverbs, given that the identification of a theme presupposes that a number of sentences discuss the same topic (see discussion in Seitel 1999, 4–5), one may observe that in the texts investigated thematically associated proverbs were found more frequently scattered around and less frequently gathered together and forming thematically coherent passages (as, for instance, in *The Instruction of P. Insinger*). In other words, it was not very common in these collections of wisdom material to use a theme as an organizational device. Therefore, what is left to the student of this material is to interpret on his own the proverbial messages and group together those that seem to have discussed the same theme.

This has been done before by Egyptologists and classicists who skimmed through the translation of the material and produced an overview or list of the matters it discussed (for instance, Lichtheim 1983, 52–56 on *The Instruction of Ankhsheshonqy* or Chadwick 1959, 97–106 on *The Sentences of Sextus*). This, however, is a risky job as it results at treating collections of wisdom material as philosophical treatises that self-consciously presented the ideology of one or more authoritative sources. My opinion is that when the text itself did not show signs of 'thematic consciousness', making an effort, that is, to identify themes and focus on them, this indicates that theme was not a significant feature of the text and so it should not be used to characterize the text *per se*. What the study of themes indicates is the choice of the producers of proverbs to discuss some matters and ignore other ones. Before discussing this choice of the ancient authors, one ought to touch on the nature and typology of the themes the proverbs treated.

A simple glance at the themes discussed by the Demotic and Greek proverbs studied reveals that similarities are predominant. Thus, for instance, the Demotic and Greek proverbs discussed 'death', 'the features of a wise man versus those of a fool', 'god(s)', 'life', and so on. However, the similarity in themes should not be a surprise, since ancient (and modern) proverbs, by definition, were concerned with general matters that touched on universal norms of human society and that were bound to be common in works from different cultures. The main trend running in the heart of these themes was the morality of human action; how humans should behave, that is, in a multitude of circumstances, what makes them good men or bad men, and so on.

What are more interesting in a comparative study of themes discussed in Demotic and Greek proverbs are the differences observed. Thematic differences were fewer than similarities and might have represented differences either in the ideologies and activities involved in the two cultures that gave birth to the proverbial material or simply in the mentality of proverb production, that is, what themes the producers of these proverbs considered as appropriate to be discussed in such material. With regard to the first, it should be noted that this material gives only a limited insight into its parent culture and therefore does not allow its modern student to jump to conclusions.

Thematic difference was identified only in minor themes, such as the differences between body and soul and how one should treat them, treated only in the Greek material. Proverbs that discussed this theme instructed their audience, among other things, that the body is the carrier of the soul and how one should take care of his soul rather than his body. These are illustrated by the following examples:

> ἐκμαγεῖον τὸ σῶμά σου νόμιζε τῆς ψυχῆς· καθαρὸν οὖν τήρει "Consider that your body bears the imprint of the soul; therefore keep it pure" (*Sextus* 346); and

> οἱ μὲν ἄλλοι ἄνθρωποι τῆς τοῦ σώματος εὐεξίας φροντίζουσιν· ὁ δὲ σοφὸς τὴν τῆς ψυχῆς ἀπάθειαν "While the other men take care of the good health of the body, the wise man (takes care of) the immunity of the soul" (*Philosophon Logoi* 101–2).

In this case, the difference in theme could be explained in relation to what we know about the two cultures. In other words, Greek culture and its philosophy did recognize an entity that it called the 'soul' and this entity greatly affected human ethics (see, for example, the discussion in Plato, *Phaedo* 64 *cf.* Fowler 1914, 200ff.), making it, in this way, an appropriate topic for proverbs like those studied here to discuss. On the contrary, the demotic proverbs analyzed did not discuss this issue probably because the Egyptian culture, with its essentially unitarian concept of the human being (see Ikram 2003, 23–31), had no concept corresponding to the concrete Greek notion of the soul.

Furthermore, although major themes were common in both bodies of proverbs, they were sometimes approached in a different way. In other words, each body of proverbs chose to discuss different aspects of the same theme, revealing in this way what each culture thought of being significant and what insignificant. For example, within the boundaries of the theme of 'death', discussed by both the Demotic and the Greek material studied, the Demotic proverbs referred to the process of mummification and the actual burial in association to the judgement of the deceased, funerary practices that were never treated in the Greek proverbs. Examples of Demotic proverbs discussing these themes are:

> *p3 wr iyḥ p3 nt ir ḫrp r ir btw m-s3 p3 ṯ nfe / syf snṯ.t ḥsmn ḥm3 pẖr.t ḥm.t pẖr n3y=f šhy.w / bne iw bw-ir=f n⁽ /...t3 ḥ⁽3.t p3 rmt-ntr tms=f ḥr p3 tw irm t3y=f ḳes3.t* "The chief spirit is the one that gives the first (blow) so to punish after the taking (of) breath / Cedar oil, incense, natron, and salt are a small remedy (for) healing his wounds /…The end (of) the man of god is to be buried on the mountain with his burial equipment" (*P. Insinger* 18/8, 18/9, and 18/12) (for a discussion of these examples, see Quack 1999; Stadler 2001).

If this preference of the demotic proverb literature to discuss the importance of funerary practices is to be explained in cultural terms, one could observe that, in general, the process of mummification in Egypt was considered as a divinizing medium for the mortal deceased and thus as a significant preparatory stage for a happy afterlife, while, in the case of Greece, funerary preparations were not thought to play such a significant role for the post-mortem survival of the deceased (contrast the overviews of Egyptian and Greek funerary ideas and practices in Quirke 1992, 141–144; Burkert 1996, 190–194).

Moreover, some proverbs from one body of texts referred, in some cases, to concepts that did not exist in the culture of the other body of texts. Thus, similar to Demotic examples discussing the Egyptian idea of mummification which was not part of Greek culture, there are a few instances of Greek proverbs that referred to concepts that did not exist in Egyptian culture, as, for instance, in the proverb:

> ὅμοια πόρνη δάκρυ<α> καὶ ῥήτωρ ἔχει "The same kind of tears shed a prostitute and a rhetorician [or advocate]" (*Menander* 584).

This proverb implied that one should mistrust the rhetorician/advocate who becomes emotional, as he is professional and his job is to make people be moved by what he says. The concept of a public speaker was central in the culture of classical Greece (Kennedy 1980), while it was absent from any phase of the Egyptian culture.

Conclusions

As shown above, the comparison between the Demotic and Greek proverbs examined involves a balanced mixture of similarities and differences. Specifically, we have seen, first that both types of monopartite proverbs were based upon the model of expression 'condition + main body' with the former being sometimes described in elliptical constructions whose variety and frequency of use differed between the two kinds of material; secondly, that both types of proverb showed the same degree of preference for metaphors, similes, and personification that employed images drawn from different cultural reservoirs, appealing to different elements of natural environment or social life; and thirdly, that although most themes discussed by the Demotic and Greek proverbs were common matters of human concern, there were a number of minor differences involving allusions to specific traditions and norms exclusive to one of the cultures in question.

Therefore, one may remark that, on the one hand, the similarities observed were linked to the proverbial status of the sentences investigated, confirming the elements of a universal definition of proverbs or similar wisdom material, while the differences, on the other hand, were related to the national character of each of the two types of material, seen as pieces of wisdom rooted in the heart of each culture.

Merton College, University of Oxford

References

Boissonade, J. F. 1962, *Anecdota Graeca e Codicibus Regiis*, 1. (Reprint of first edition 1826.) Olms, Hildesheim.

Breitenberger, B. 2004, *Aphrodite and Eros: the Development of Greek Erotic Mythology*. Routledge, New York.

Burkert, W. 1996, *Greek Religion*, (trans. J. Raffan). Blackwell, Oxford.

Chadwick, H. 1959, *The Sentences of Sextus. A Contribution to the History of Early Christian Ethics*. Texts and Studies: Contributions to Biblical and Patristic Literature NS 5. Cambridge University Press, Cambridge.

Cribiore, R. 2001, *Gymnastics of the Mind. Greek Education in Hellenistic and Roman Egypt*. Princeton University Press, Princeton, NJ.

Fowler, H. N. 1914, *Plato: Euthyphro, Apology, Crito, Phaedo, Phaedrus*. (Reprinted 2001.) The Loeb Classical Library 36. Harvard University Press, Cambridge, Massachusetts and London.

Houser-Wegner, J. R. 2001, *Cultural and Literary Continuity in the Demotic Instructions*. Unpublished Ph. D. thesis, Yale University.

Ikram, S. 2003, *Death and Burial in Ancient Egypt*. Longman, Harlow.

Jåkel, S. 1964, *Menandri Sententiae / Comparation Menandri et Philistionis*. Teubner, Leipzig.

Jasnow, R. 1999, Remarks on Continuity in Egyptian Literary Tradition, in E. Teeter and J. A. Larson (eds.), *Gold of Praise: Studies on Ancient Egypt in Honor of Edward F. Wente*. SAOC 58. Oriental Institute of the University of Chicago, Chicago, 193–210.

Kennedy, G. A. 1980, *Classical Rhetoric and its Christian and Secular Tradition from Ancient to Modern Times*, Croom Helm, London.

Lichtheim, M. 1983, *Late Egyptian Wisdom Literature in the International Context: a Study of Demotic Instructions*. Vandenhoeck and Ruprecht, Freiburg, Schweiz and Göttingen.

Morgan, T. 1998, *Literate Education in the Hellenistic and Roman Worlds*. Cambridge Classical Studies. Cambridge University Press, Cambridge.

Quack, J. F. 1999, Balsamierung und Totengericht im Papyrus Insinger, *Enchoria* 25, 27–38.

Quirke, S. 1992, *Egyptian Religion*. British Museum Press, London.

Schenkl, H. 1894, *Epicteti dissertationes ab Arriano digestae*. Teubner, Leipzig.

Seitel, P. 1999, *The Powers of Genre: Interpreting Haya Oral Literature*. Oxford Studies in Anthropological Linguistics. Oxford University Press, Oxford.

Shupak, N. 1989, Instruction and Teaching Appellations in Egyptian Wisdom Literature (and their Biblical Counterparts), in S. Schoske (ed.), *Akten des Vierten Internationalen Ägyptologen Kongresses – München 1985*, 3, 193–200. Studien zur altägyptischen Kultur Beihefte 3. Buske, Hamburg.

Smith, M. 1986, Demotische Weisheit, in W. Helck and E. Otto (eds.), *Lexikon der Ägyptologie*, VI, cols. 1192–1204. Harrassowitz, Wiesbaden.

Stadler, M. A. 2001, War eine dramatische Aufführung eines Totenriten?, *Studien zur altägyptische Kultur* 29, 331–348.

Wilson, W. T. 1991, *Love without Pretense: Romans 12.9–21 and Hellenistic-Jewish Wisdom Literature*. Wissenschaftliche Untersuchungen zum Neuen Testament 2, Reihe 46. Mohr, Tübingen.

Young, D. 1971, *Theognis*, (2nd edition). Teubner, Leipzig.

Egyptian Artefacts from Central and South Asia

Rachel R. Mairs

Historical Note

Bactria (modern northern Afghanistan / southern Central Asia) was settled by Greeks under Alexander the Great in the late 4th century B.C. The Graeco-Bactrian state survived until its destruction by nomadic incursions in the mid-2nd century B.C. Campaigns by the Graeco-Bactrians had, however, established a number of kingdoms (conventionally referred to as 'Indo-Greek') in the north-west of the Indian Subcontinent, at least one of which survived into the 1st century A.D. The Kushan Empire, founded by a dynasty of Central Asian origin, succeeded that of the Graeco-Bactrians in Central Asia, and later spread into South Asia.

A number of important works on the history and archaeology of Hellenistic (c. 3rd century B.C. – 1st century B.C.) and Kushan (c. 2nd century B.C. – A.D. 2nd century) South and Central Asia are available in western European languages. On the Graeco-Bactrian and Indo-Greek states, see Tarn 1951, Narain 1957, Holt 1988; 1999 (in English). On the Kushans, see Staviskij 1986 (in French). Gorbunova 1986 (in English translation) covers the archaeology of the Ferghana Valley.

Introduction

"When his majesty was in Nahrin according to his annual custom, the princes of every foreign land came bowing in peace to the might of his majesty from as far as the farthest marshlands. Their gifts of gold, silver, lapis lazuli, turquoise and every kind of plant of god's land were on their backs, and each was outdoing his fellow. The prince of Bakhtan had also sent his gifts and had placed his eldest daughter in front of them, worshiping his majesty and begging life from him."

The Bakhtan (Bentresh) Stele, Louvre C284, trans. Lichtheim 1980, 91.

"The Great King Ptolemy [III] … inherited from his father kingship over Egypt, Libya, Syria, Phoenicia, Cyprus, Lycia, Caria and the Cyclades islands. He invaded Asia with his infantry, cavalry, fleet, and elephants from Troglodytike and Ethiopia. . . [H]e crossed the Euphrates River and subdued Mesopotamia, Babylonia, Susiana, Persis, Media, and everything else as far as Bactria . . ."

The Adulis Inscription, Orientis Graeci Inscriptiones Selectae (OGIS) 54, trans. Holt 1999, 176. (See also Austin 1981, 365; Burstein 1985, 125–126.)

The theme of the king as triumphant over his enemies, receiving the tribute of foreign lands, is one familiar to the point of banality in Egyptian royal inscriptions. The Bakhtan Stele and the Adulis Inscription, despite being dated to the reigns of Ramesses II and Ptolemy III respectively, and written in two different languages, Middle Egyptian and Greek, share this common theme, presenting the king of Egypt as militarily dominant over the lands of the Near East and North Africa.

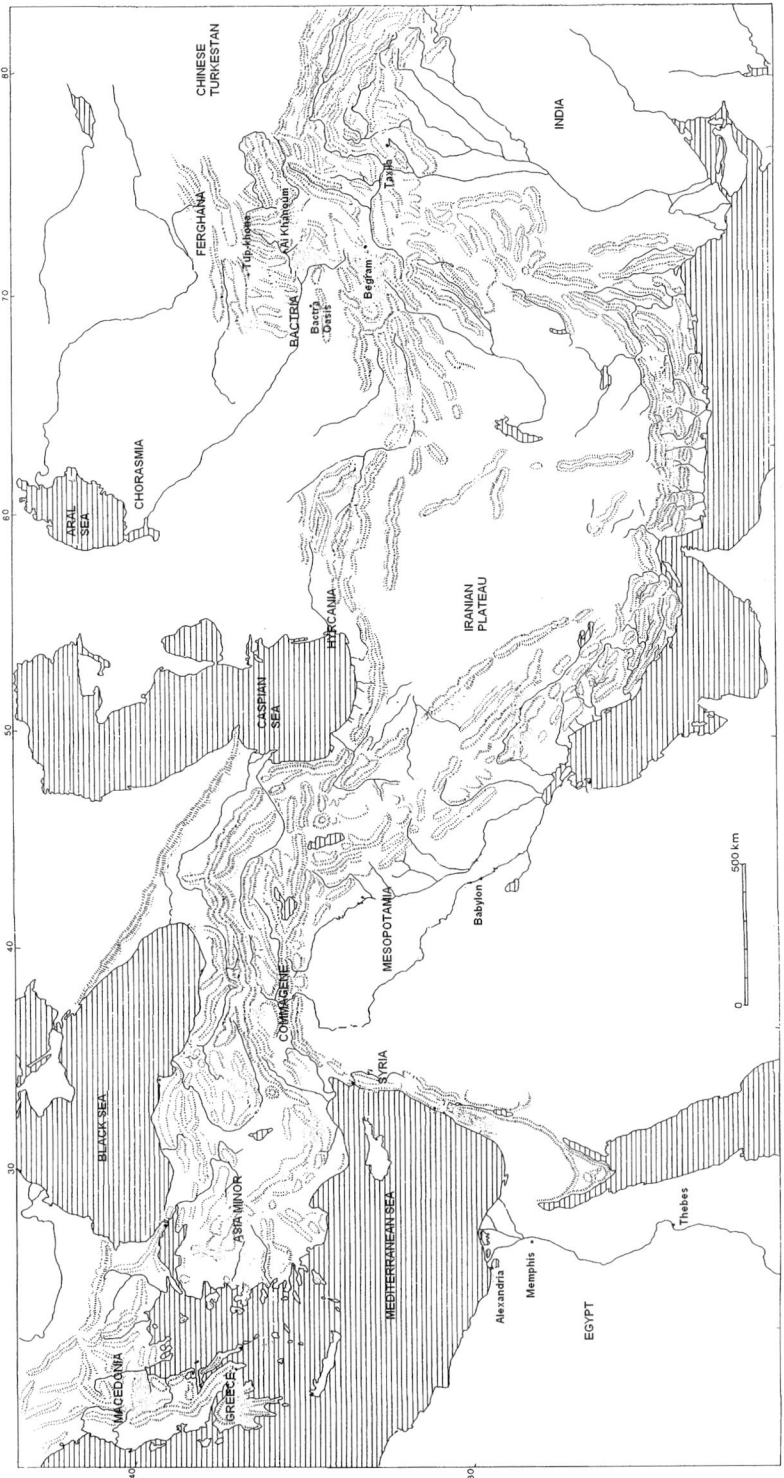

Figure 1. From the Eastern Mediterranean to the borders of India and Central Asia.

What these two inscriptions also have in common is that they are not quite what they claim to be. The Bakhtan Stele, from a small Ptolemaic sanctuary (no longer extant) at Karnak, is in fact Persian or Ptolemaic in date (Lichtheim 1980, 90). The Adulis Inscription, purportedly from the Red Sea coast of modern Eritrea, is known only from the Christian Topography (2.58–59) of Cosmas Indicopleustes (A.D. 6th century), and its authenticity is therefore open to question. Both misrepresent the historical circumstances on which they are based. Ramesses II's supposed marriage to the princess of Bakhtan is apparently based on his historical marriage with a Hittite princess (Lichtheim 1980, 93). In the Third Syrian War, Ptolemy III may have advanced as far as Babylon, but he did not reach Bactria (Austin 1981, 365). The use of such hyperbole to glorify the king is hardly unusual. What is noteworthy in both cases is the use of Bactria to mark the limits of the king's power (on the identification of Bakhtan with Bactria, see Breasted 1906–7, 189; Posener 1934, 77; Lefebvre 1949, 222; Lichtheim 1980, 93).

Although lapis lazuli from Bactria is attested in Egypt from the Predynastic period (Bavay 1997), it is significant that our only two, highly-dubious, Egyptian textual references to Bactria date to the Persian or Ptolemaic periods. From the time of the Persian conquest in 525 B.C., Egypt became part of a wider geopolitical unit, which reached from the Eastern Mediterranean to the borders of India and Central Asia. In the Hellenistic Period, the centuries following the conquests of Alexander the Great, this region was fragmented under a number of Greek dynasties – such as the Ptolemies in Egypt and the Seleucids in West Asia – but in many ways it can still be considered as an organic whole, with networks of diplomatic, cultural and economic relationships between the constituent states.

Bactria lay on the north-eastern marches of the Persian Empire and, to the Greeks, was the proverbial 'ends of the earth'. Although archaeological discoveries, for example at the Greek city of Ai Khanoum in northern Afghanistan, and revisionist histories have revealed that Bactria was a fertile, wealthy country, supporting a thriving Greek and local Iranian culture (Holt 1988), from the perspective of the Greeks of the Mediterranean littoral it was doubtless still regarded as a remote place of exile – the "Siberia of the Hellenistic world" (Rawlinson 1909, 23). It is possible that some Egyptians came to have knowledge of the wide reaches of the Persian Empire and Hellenistic states, whether through encountering soldiers from these regions in Egypt, or travelling there themselves as mercenaries or traders (Fraser 1967, 31; Posener 1934, 78), but these will probably only ever have been few in number. The genealogical connections of the Ptolemaic dynasty with Bactria through Artakama wife of Ptolemy I and Apama wife of Seleucus I (genealogical tables in Green 1990, 734–737) are of passing interest, but no great historical or cultural significance. The mentions of Bactria in the Adulis Inscription and the Bakhtan Stele, on balance, presuppose no familiarity with the region. 'Bactria' is a rhetorical device: an exotic, faraway place, within the reach only of great kings, which provides a suitable setting for a romantic tale or exaggerated boasts of conquest (Briant 1984, 32). Whatever its basis in the real events of the Third Syrian War, the Adulis Inscription is not a record of an actual campaign, but a standard claim that a powerful ruler has extended his control to the mythical 'ends of the earth'.

In this article, I intend to examine the more tangible, material connections between Egypt and the 'Far East' (Schmitt 1990, 42) of the Hellenistic world. The maritime trade between India and Egypt has been dramatically illuminated by the excavations at ports such as Arikamedu in southern India (Begley (ed.) 1996) and Berenike on Egypt's Red Sea coast (Sidebotham and Wendrich (eds.) 1995, and subsequent reports). There was, however, also an overland route between the Mediterranean and the Hellenistic East, as a result of which a number of items of Egyptian manufacture have been found in archaeological sites in Central and South Asia. I will discuss two groups of such artefacts. The first group – images of the gods Sarapis and Harpocrates, of Hellenistic or Roman date – derive for the most part from urban contexts, at cities such as Taxila and Begram. These may be considered alongside other evidence for the spread of the cults of Sarapis and Harpocrates throughout the Mediterranean world and beyond. The second group encompasses pendants and amulets made of Egyptian faience and conforming to attested Egyptian types. These have been excavated at sites across Central Asia, and fit into a wider pattern of the diffusion of such objects.

It is not my intention to provide a comprehensive discussion of these artefacts, their archaeological context and the many complex issues which surround them; limitations of space, if nothing else, place that beyond the scope of the present study. My aim is simply to draw attention to this body of material and suggest what we might productively do with it. The vast majority of archaeological reports from Central Asia are published solely in Russian, which is generally sufficient to ensure limited exposure in Western Europe and North America. (The collaborative projects and Russian-language skills of many French archaeologists of Central Asia are a notable exception to this general rule.) South Asian archaeological publications are for the most part in English, but may be difficult to access outside India or Pakistan. Key sites such as Begram (Hackin 1939; 1954) and Taxila (Marshall 1951; 1960) received masterful publication according to the standards of the first part of the twentieth century, but require modern readers to exercise considerable critical judgement (Allchin 1993, 69–70). There is therefore much to be said for providing a concise account of the material available and relevant bibliography, and a discussion of some theoretical issues likely to be productive in its analysis. Although the two groups of artefacts – images of Sarapis and Harpocrates and Egyptian faience amulets – will be discussed separately, there is inevitably a great deal of potential overlap, both geographically and in terms of the general issues to be considered. My aim in the present study is to set these rarely-discussed artefacts into wider frameworks of contemporary theory on the movement and transformation in meaning of objects, and into the context of the wider Hellenistic world.

Sarapis and Harpocrates in South and Central Asia

Sarapis (*Wsir-Hp*, 'Osiris-Apis') and Harpocrates (*Ḥr pꜣ ḫrd*, 'Horus the Child') are characteristically Hellenistic developments of Egyptian gods. Both had a strong connection with the cult of Isis (Fraser 1960, 5), which spread throughout the Hellenistic world and the Roman empire. The cult of Isis is indirectly attested in Hellenistic Central Asia, for example in the theophoric name Isidora in a funerary inscription from Ai Khanoum (Bernard 1972, 618–619), but my concentration here will be on Sarapis and Harpocrates, and their occurrence as statuettes or on coins and seals. Both gods are readily identifiable by their iconography: Sarapis is commonly depicted as a bearded man, from the Roman period onwards with a *kalathos* ('grain-measure') on his head (Ashton 2003, 13), Harpocrates as a naked child with one finger raised to his lips, sometimes wearing the dual crown of Upper and Lower Egypt. Ten figures or engraved images of the gods Harpocrates and Sarapis from South and Central Asia have so far been published, a number always subject to augmentation by new discoveries or publications. These are described in the Appendix, and are referred to by number in the following discussion.

Most of the items (particularly those which have appeared on the antiquities market) can only be given a broad date, but the concentration in the first two centuries A.D. is notable. By this period, commercial and cultural contacts between the eastern Mediterranean and South and

Central Asia had long been in operation, first under the Graeco-Bactrian and western Hellenistic dynasties, and from the 1st century B.C. onwards under the Kushan and Roman empires.

Communication between South and Central Asia and the Mediterranean could be a laborious and lengthy process, but transport links were reasonably efficient and well-maintained in the last centuries B.C. under the Achaemenids and Seleucids; the later rise of Parthia and the Kushans did not greatly disrupt long-distance contact and trade (Sherwin-White and Kuhrt 1993, 61–62; 66–67). Regular contact between Bactria and the Mediterranean world, for example, has been attested by excavations at the Graeco-Bactrian city of Ai Khanoum, which revealed Greek commodities such as olive oil (Bernard 1980, 442), pottery (Gardin 1990) and even dramatic and philosophical works on papyrus (Lerner 2003). Rapin (1990, 341), plays down the level of trade between Bactria and the Mediterranean, stressing the proportionally small volume of western imported goods at Ai Khanoum. The importance of contact, however, as Rapin concedes, lay in quality not quantity. The trade of articles between the Mediterranean world and Central Asia was nothing unusual in this period, and there is therefore no need to view the presence of Egyptian artefacts in the East as especially problematic.

The question of what meaning and significance images of Sarapis and Harpocrates held in South and Central Asia is, however, not so open to clear-cut resolution. They may be seen in the context of the diffusion of the cults of these gods beyond Egypt, and of the widespread syncretism and acceptance of 'foreign' cults in the Graeco-Bactrian/Indo-Greek and Kushan states. On the other hand, images of Harpocrates and Sarapis occur in the East within a general – and even sometimes specific archaeological – context of the trade in Graeco-Roman *objets d'art* and transmission of Graeco-Roman artistic and architectural styles (see Appendix, items **(1)**, **(3)** and **(4)**). Should we consider these images as cult objects, or as high-prestige art?

Although Harpocrates is, essentially, the Greek form of the long-standing Egyptian god 'Horus the Child', Sarapis, a fusion of Osiris and the Apis bull, underwent significant development under the Ptolemies (Ashton 2003, 10–11). His appeal within Egypt itself seems always to have been restricted: greater in the 3rd century B.C. than in later periods, largely confined to Alexandria, and with his attested dedicants almost all Greeks (Fraser 1960, 9). The cult was, however, disseminated throughout the Mediterranean world (Fraser 1960, 32ff), often via private initiative and the movements of traders and mercenaries rather than exclusively because of its political connection with the Ptolemaic dynasty (Fraser 1960, 42; 1967, 31). Certainly, evidence for the presence of the cult of Sarapis occurs from well beyond the limits of any direct Ptolemaic control, in Meroë (Seguenny and Desanges 1986), and also in Hyrcania, where a Greek inscription of c. 281–261 B.C. records the manumission of a slave and his consecration to Sarapis (Robert 1960, 85–91).

The evidence for religious practice in the Graeco-Bactrian, Indo-Greek and Kushan states suggests official tolerance of, and general receptiveness to, western cults such as those of Sarapis and Harpocrates. Elements of Greek, Iranian and Indian religious iconography appear on coins. Complex syncretisms of gods occur, which are often difficult to identify by iconography or artistic style alone (Grenet 1991 on Zeus-Mithra at Ai Khanoum; Grenet 1987 on Athena-Arštāt at Dil'berdzhin). This is in many ways comparable to the picture which emerges from elsewhere in the Hellenistic world, for example in Commagene (Sanders (ed.) 1996), and may productively be considered alongside it.

Although there is at present no evidence for any temple cult of Sarapis in Central or South Asia, a few rare coins of the Kushan emperor Huvishka (A.D. 2nd century) bear the legend 'SARAPO' (Grenet 1982, 156; 1987, 41–42). The occurrence of images of Sarapis at sites across the Kushan Empire and adjacent regions suggests that the god enjoyed some popular appeal, connected with the diffusion of his cult in Hellenistic world. Harpocrates is unattested in any official context but, like Sarapis, appears in the form of statues and figurines and on seals.

The images of Harpocrates and Sarapis from the East may, however, also be viewed within a wider framework of the diffusion of artistic motifs and luxury goods throughout the Hellenistic world. Maillard (1975, 229) asks whether we should consider these items as 'cult statues' or simply as 'trade goods'. Grenet is apparently also of two minds about how to interpret the images of Harpocrates and Sarapis in the East:

> "Les conditions de leur découverte ne permettent pas de décider s'ils avaient été acquis pour leur seule valeur artistique, ou bien pour servir aux besoins cultuels d'adeptes locaux de la religion sérapéenne; l'existence de tels adeptes à l'époque et sur le territoire de l'empire kouchan est en tout cas assurée par les monnaies de Huviška figurant Sérapis" (Grenet 1982, 230).

By the time of its deposition in a cache underneath a house, the Harpocrates statuette from Taxila **(1)** was evidently considered to be of some value, perhaps quite apart from any religious association it may have had. This hoard contained other items imported from the Hellenistic or Roman Mediterranean. Commercial connections specifically with Hellenistic and Roman Egypt are also well-attested in the region. The site of Begram, the source of items **(3)** and **(4)**, yielded a large number of plaster reliefs depicting Graeco-Roman gods or mythological figures, some of likely Egyptian origin (Hackin 1954, 127–128, pls. 303 and 422), and two porphyry bowls of Egyptian provenance (Hackin 1954, 150, nos. 95 and 119, figs. 354 and 354bis). The most remarkable Egyptian object from Begram is a glass vase depicting the *pharos* (lighthouse) of Alexandria (identified by Seyrig 1941, 262, n2; see also Hackin 1939, 42, pl. 16; Kurz 1954, 101–102). The vase is part of a large group of glassware from Begram (Kurz 1954, 93), which conforms to well-known Graeco-Roman types and can be dated to around the 1st century A.D. (Kurz 1954, 108). The Periplus of the Erythraean Sea mentions the export of Egyptian glass to India via the sea route (Casson 1989, 53): the finds at Begram show that glass was a valued commodity on the northern land route as well. Like the other glassware from Begram, the pharos vase is most likely an Egyptian import, a 'souvenir from Alexandria' (Kurz 1954, 108; Brill 1972; Thompson 1984, 8). The statuettes of Harpocrates and Sarapis from Begram therefore form part of a much larger body of imported Graeco-Roman material, which went on to influence local artistic styles (Taddei 1969, 366–367; see also examples in Errington and Cribb (eds.) 1992).

The distinction between 'religious' and 'artistic' reasons for the use and transportation of images of Harpocrates and Sarapis in South and Central Asia is perhaps somewhat of an artificial one, and we should remain open to the possibility that the significance attached to them varied, both chronologically and geographically. They clearly demand to be considered within a wider context, taking account of the contemporary South and Central Asian cultural milieu, and of the relations of these regions with the Graeco-Roman Mediterranean.

This wider question of the cultural relationship between the Graeco-Bactrian/Indo-Greek and Kushan states and their neighbours in the Graeco-Roman Mediterranean has long been a contentious one. Tarn's (1951) thesis was that the Graeco-Bactrian and Indo-Greek states should be viewed as strongholds of Hellenistic Greek culture; Narain made the oft-quoted assertion that the history of the Indo-Greeks "is part of the history of India and not of the Hellenistic states; they came, they saw, but India conquered" (Narain 1957, 18). In line with current scholarship on Hellenistic Egypt (e.g. Goudriaan 1988; Thompson 2001), this debate is now best viewed as "an unfortunate quarrel waged on two sides of an imaginary fence" (Holt 1984, 6). Central Asia and the north-western part of the Indian Subcontinent, under the Graeco-Bactrian and Indo-Greek dynasties of the Hellenistic period, and under the subsequent Kushan Empire, had ethnically and linguistically varied populations, with a correspondingly complex material culture. These states, with their constant negotiation of ethnic boundaries and fusion of different artistic styles, provide the context for the presence of images of the Graeco-Egyptian gods Harpocrates and Sarapis in the East.

Central Asia in the late centuries B.C. and early centuries A.D. lay at the ill-defined borders of the Graeco-Roman, Iranian and Indian worlds. The culture of such a periphery or 'frontier zone' can often seem to defy reasonable analysis and categorisation. Centre-periphery models must be used with caution (Alcock 1993, 162), and often fail to provide an adequate explanation of the complexities of interaction at the fringes of a major cultural or political unit. The dividing line between 'influence', 'control' or 'acculturation' (see e.g. Woolf 1997 on Romanisation) is seldom well-defined, either in what can be gleaned from archaeological material, or in scholarly analysis.

Burstein's (1993) and Holt's (1993) discussions of the frontier zones of the Hellenistic world, in Meroë and Bactria respectively, highlight this complexity. In Meroë, finds of Greek ceramics and evidence of Egyptian or Graeco-Egyptian influence in religion do not correspond to any degree of direct control or colonisation (Burstein 1993, 52–53). Holt's (1993, 58–59) concept of Meroë and Bactria as 'resource frontiers' is a useful one, and should be viewed as a two-way process: while the Ptolemaic and Seleucid empires used these regions as sources of raw materials, local peoples acquired goods and commodities from the Mediterranean world. In Hellenistic Meroë, just as in New Kingdom Nubia (Smith 2003), evidence of cultural interaction with Egypt must be interpreted with caution, particularly in deciding what the presence of any particular object in the archaeological record means in terms of how this object and its source culture were perceived. The same is true of the regions of South and Central Asia at the eastern fringes of the Hellenistic world, and the goods of Mediterranean origin excavated there. Images of gods such as Harpocrates and Sarapis doubtless bore many different associations, religious and cultural, and their western origin may not always have been key in dictating how they were conceptualised by the people who used them. A rather different example of the changes in meaning objects of Egyptian provenance might undergo when traded over long distances is provided by my second case study.

Egyptian Faience Amulets from Central Asia

With the exception of a few anomalous finds, such as an alabaster jar from the Urals inscribed with the name of the Achaemenid king Artaxerxes in Egyptian, Babylonian, Elamite and Persian (Berlev and Hodjash 1998, 238), Egyptian artefacts from Central Asia for the most part consist of beads, amulets and pendants made of faience. Piotrovskii (1958) presented the first major discussion of Egyptian faience amulets in the former Soviet Union. Important syntheses of this material have been produced by Litvinskii and Sedov (1984, 58–64) and Bulygina (1986). Although there is still scope for more in-depth analysis of the evidence than that of previous studies, it should be emphasised that the Egyptian faience pendants and amulets of Central Asia are a scattered and rather sparse body of material. A full treatment of them would require a much more detailed discussion of their regional archaeological context than is either within my expertise, or practicable in the space available in the present discussion. Detailed and well-referenced compendia of the artefacts are already available in the sources cited above. It is my intention here simply to highlight some key features in the immediate archaeological context and chronological range of the Egyptian faience amulets from Central Asia, and use these points as the basis for a wider discussion of their possible use and significance.

Amulets and pendants of Egyptian faience have been excavated at archaeological sites across Central Asia, from Bactria (Rtveladze 1977) in the south to Ferghana and Chorasmia (Bulygina 1986, 250) in the north and east. The types which occur at the site of Tup-khona (Grenet 1984, 51–52, 102–104, 130–132), in southern Tajikistan, provide an illustrative selection: fist-, amphora-, and phallus-shaped pendants, amulets in the form of frogs, and scarabs (Litvinskii and Sedov 1984, 58–64, pls. 19–20). More unusually, the finds from the site also include a small figure identified as Ptah-Sokar; (Sherkova 1981; Litvinskii and Sedov 1984, 62). The archaeological contexts in which these pendants and amulets are found date from the 1st century B.C. until roughly the 3rd century A.D., although there is some difficulty in determining the upper chronological limit since the amulets may have remained in use and been handed down over more than one generation (Bulygina 1986, 252). This broad dating is further confirmed by comparison with similar items excavated in Egypt (Litvinskii and Sedov 1984). As Bulygina (1986, 251) notes, Egyptian faience amulets in Central Asia occur almost exclusively in female burials, strung on necklaces worn on the body of the deceased. In the cemetery at Tup-khona, there is also some concentration of Egyptian artefacts within particular graves. Grave 262, for example, yielded one fist-shaped amulet, two pendants in the shape of amphorae, a frog amulet and two phallus pendants (Litvinskii and Sedov 1984, 63). Insufficient comparative data is available to make much of this small-scale but notable concentration: it may simply owe something to the individual's status or personal preference.

The identification of some of these artefacts as Egyptian – especially the figurines discussed by Berlev and Hodjash 1998, 237ff – is, to my mind, questionable. In the case of the majority of the amulets, however, an ultimate Egyptian provenance is reasonably certain, and is supported both by their form and by evidence of contemporary trade routes (see further below). The possibility that some of these items are in fact of local manufacture must also be borne in mind, as also, for example, suggested by Lilyquist (1999) for the faience fragments with the name of Amenhotep III found at Mycenae, in Greece. Faience was produced in Central Asia from an early date (Abdourazakov 2001, 399) and the fist-shaped pendants, in particular, continued to be reproduced in the region through into the Middle Ages (Bulygina 1986, 251). To ask whether these constitute 'local imitations' of Egyptian originals is perhaps the wrong question. The popularity – and simplicity – of the fist amulet, for example, suggests a rather different kind of interplay between local and foreign motifs, perhaps with little importance being attached to their ultimate derivation.

Especially in the Hellenistic and Roman periods, as noted above, commodities and *objets d'art* from the Mediterranean world were frequently traded over relatively long distances. It was similarly not unusual for items such as amulets to travel outside Egypt (Sherkova 1981). The overland trade via the Iranian plateau was, however, only one of the routes by which goods might reach South and Central Asia. Analogous finds in the region north of the Black Sea suggest that the Egyptian amulets excavated in Central Asia may also have been transported across the steppes (Bulygina 1986, 252; Staviskij 1986, 192, with references). The establishment of Greek colonies or emporia at sites such as Naucratis in northern Egypt, and along the Black Sea littoral, from the middle of the 1st millennium B.C., demonstrates the potential of north-south trade across the eastern Mediterranean basin. It is quite possible that this is the route by which the

Egyptian faience amulets reached Central Asia, although in the absence of any firm evidence such a suggestion must, of course, remain highly speculative.

The importance and meaning which Egyptian faience amulets held in their new, Central Asian context is a more fraught question. The danger here is in tracing a direct line of continuity between the Egyptian amulets in Egypt, these same amulets in Central Asia and later, local imitations. We should not, for example, on the basis of the discovery of these amulets, postulate the presence of any formal Egyptian religion in either the Black Sea region or Central Asia (Bulygina 1986, 252). There are indications, however, that the amulets were something more than simply jewellery to their new Central Asian owners. As already noted, Egyptian amulets tend to occur in very specific archaeological contexts in Central Asia. Whereas in the Black Sea region they occur almost exclusively in the graves of children, in Central Asia they are found in female burials (Bulygina 1986, 251). It is a straightforward – if hardly radical – suggestion that these amulets carried some association with fertility, sexual power and the warding-off of danger from vulnerable groups (Bulygina 1986, 252). What is remarkable is the strong regional differentiation in the use of these amulets outside Egypt. More remarkable still is the fact that, given the context of the finds, the amulets apparently retained something of their original protective function, even when removed from Egypt and placed into a new social and geographical context. If we were to take a more active view of the processes by which they reached Central Asia from Egypt, we might even tentatively surmise that their retention of meaning suggests that they were traded or exported not 'just as objects', but specifically because they had this particular protective function.

Recent studies on the 'cultural biographies' of objects (Kopytoff 1986), and the different meanings and associations they may acquire in new contexts, provide us with some useful theoretical constructs and repertoires of comparison for the Central Asian Egyptian amulets. Significantly, many of these lead us to question the simple models of 'influence' or '-isation' so often projected onto items of material culture:

> "Biographies of things can make salient what might otherwise remain obscure. For example, in situations of culture contact, they can show what anthropologists have so often stressed: that what is significant about the adoption of alien objects – as of alien ideas – is not the fact that they are adopted, but the way they are culturally redefined and put to use" (Kopytoff 1986, 67).

Not enough is known about the separate stages in the life histories of the Egyptian faience amulets from Central Asia to construct meaningful cultural biographies for them, but the issues highlighted by Kopytoff, and now often applied to the interpretation of archaeological remains (Gosden and Marshall 1999), are still of relevance and utility here. A number of recent archaeological cultural biographies focus on objects which were produced and transformed in meaning in colonial contexts, and on the meanings of these objects in modern museum collections (e.g. Peers 1999). The very specific situations of close cultural contact, conflict and intermarriage, and the range of shifting meanings an object may acquire in such contexts, are, however, quite different from the case of the Central Asian Egyptian faience amulets, which were eventually used in a society well beyond the reaches of any direct Egyptian (or even Hellenistic) control or influence. These amulets will have passed through many sets of hands between their manufacture in Egypt and their final resting place in a Central Asian tomb (and later museum collection), with perhaps little concept or awareness of their origins being transported along with them. The amulets retained and lost very specific elements of their original meanings: while they retained a ritual value as protective symbols, to be worn on the bodies of vulnerable groups (women and children), I would argue that they lost any perceived 'Egyptianness' or specific association with Egyptian culture or religion.

This selective retention of meaning is a common phenomenon when objects are transferred from one social or cultural context to another: "the biographies of artefacts over the long term can be expected to be modified in ways that take some aspects of their life history with them while discarding others" (Rainbird 1999, 214). What is retained and what is left behind can vary dramatically from one individual case to another. Beck, for example, argues that "the movement of the material item and its meaning or ideal is not a single event" (Beck 1995, 170), and in particular that, while material culture may sometimes remain uniform across ethnic boundaries, ritual and symbolism are less readily transferred. Although this may be a valid analysis of the material from Beck's case study, this is clearly not the case with the Egyptian amulets from Central Asia, where it is specifically the object's ritual function which is retained.

Arafat and Morgan's (1994) study of the Attic (Athenian) pottery from Hallstatt (Early Iron Age) sites in western Europe presents another case where, as with the Egyptian amulets in Central Asia, items were transferred from one locality to another not by direct contact, but through intermediaries (Arafat and Morgan 1994, 121 ff). They conclude that, being insufficient in quantity to be linked to any widespread pattern of élite emulation of or enthusiasm for Greek culture, imports of commodities such as Greek wine (in Greek wine jars) must be considered in the context of existing local practices of communal drinking and feasting.

When an artefact moves from one geographical area to another, it may also be moving between different social and cultural systems. The integration of such an artefact into its new context will therefore, to whatever extent, involve the shedding or retention of various aspects of its former meanings, and the acquisition of new ones (Arafat and Morgan 1994, 108). The analysis of 'foreign' artefacts found in particular archaeological contexts must take this into account. In particular, where possible, attention should be paid to intermediate processes and societies, not just the start and end points of a long exchange train (Arafat and Morgan 1994, 133). In the case of the Egyptian amulets from Central Asia, we are fortunate to have the evidence of their presence and use in the Black Sea region, which enables us to go some way towards tracing some of the subtle changes in meaning they underwent.

The usefulness of the metaphor of biography lies in its ability to make us consider the possibility of shifts in an object's meaning and examine the processes by which these took place (Gosden and Marshall 1999, 17). Parallel case studies can only take us so far, and much of the cultural biography of the Central Asian amulets remains, in the current state of the evidence, frustratingly beyond our reach. Aside from the retention of an apotropaic function, it would be interesting to know what other meanings these amulets retained, and what they left behind, in the stages of their journey from Egypt to Central Asia. I would suggest that, in the absence of any direct and frequent contact between the two regions, one of the aspects which was lost was any significance held by their being specifically Egyptian. They were doubtless regarded as unusual or exotic – hence their incorporation into necklaces composed of beads and stones sometimes traded over long distances – but we should question whether the name 'Egyptian' is ever one their owners applied to them, despite the repertoire of parallels which enable us to identify them as such today. The question of how their Central Asian owners used these amulets and conceptualised them within the framework of their own religious beliefs must also remain a matter of conjecture. Any distinction we might be tempted to make between the occasional occurrence of an Egyptian amulet and the everyday toolkit of local religious practice is probably an artificial one: to those who wore and used them, the form and origin of these amulets most probably presented no conflict at all.

Concluding Remarks

The presence of both these groups of objects – images of Sarapis and Harpocrates and faience amulets – in South and Central Asia testifies to the strong commercial and cultural links maintained between even the most distant parts of the Hellenistic world, links which persisted despite later political fragmentation under Roman, Parthian and Kushan rule. Some religious ideas or cultural associations might be transported in association with the objects themselves, although this process was subject to levels of variation and is difficult to trace securely. Different forms of value and symbolism might remain in interplay within the same object, as in the case of statuettes of Sarapis and Harpocrates as religious images and as works of high-prestige Graeco-Roman art. Ritual function might – perhaps unexpectedly – continue to be attached to Egyptian amulets, but other meanings could also fall away from them.

Although these amulets and statuettes might be considered 'Egyptian' in a modern academic, classificatory sense, and in terms of their ultimate origin or source of their artistic or iconographical inspiration, we should guard against defining them by this term alone. Any 'ethnic' affiliation which may have originally been attached to these objects and images did not necessarily travel along with them, or remain their primary distinguishing feature to the people who owned and used them. Cultural and ethnic identity is, in any case, something which people express in how they use and conceptualise objects, and may have a varying correlation with the style of the object itself.

Faculty of Classics, University of Cambridge

Acknowledgements

I am grateful to my supervisor, Dr. Dorothy J. Thompson for reading and commenting on an earlier draft of this article, and also to Current Research in Egyptology's anonymous referees. Thanks are also due to the staff of the Délégation archéologique française en Afghanistan, the Society for the Preservation of Afghanistan's Cultural Heritage and the National Museum of Afghanistan, for their assistance and hospitality during research in Kabul in August 2005. My visit to Afghanistan was made possible by a generous grant from the Committee for Central and Inner Asia, and conducted with the logistical support of the Minaret of Jam Archaeological Project.

Appendix: Representations of Sarapis and Harpocrates from South and Central Asia

A bronze statuette of Harpocrates (1) was found in a cache under the courtyard of a house at Sirkap, Taxila (Marshall 1951; 1960). The cache contained a number of other items of Graeco-Roman manufacture or artistic style, and may have been buried around A.D. 60 (Marshall 1960, 76), although Marshall's interpretation of the stratigraphy remains open to considerable doubt. This *terminus ante quem*, as well as artistic comparison, gives us a date for the statuette of the first half of the 1st century A.D., or thereabouts (Marshall 1951, 605). The statuette is made of cast bronze, around 12.5 cm in height and depicts Harpocrates in his typical pose with double crown and finger raised to lips. Marshall (1960, 76) was of the opinion that it was an import from Alexandria, although he did not rule out an origin elsewhere in the Graeco-Roman world (Marshall 1951, 159; 605).

A ring bezel with the image of Harpocrates **(2)** (Bivar 1961, 319, pl. VII.9) occurs in a collection of uncertain provenance, probably acquired in Pakistan (Bivar 1961, 309–310). Harpocrates again appears in his typical attitude with finger raised to lips, but wearing a *kalathos*, more often associated with Sarapis, on his head. Bivar (1961, 319) found no firm evidence as to whether it was of local or Egyptian manufacture, but it is comparable to Graeco-Roman work of the 1st century A.D.

The site of Begram (Hackin 1939; 1954), north of modern Kabul, yielded two bronze statuettes of Harpocrates and Sarapis. The statuette of Harpocrates **(3)** (Hackin 1954, no. 153, figs. 322 and 324) is around 12 cm in height and depicts the child-god with finger raised to lips and wearing the double crown. The other figure **(4)** (Hackin 1954, 147, figs. 323 and 325) is 22.5 cm in height and has the head of Sarapis, with his *kalathos*, but the body and stance of the Greek hero Heracles. Both are to be dated to around the 1st century A.D.

An engraved seal with a profile bust of Sarapis **(5)** (Grenet 1982), skilfully worked and encorporating all the traditional Hellenistic iconography of the god, emerged on the antiquities market, but is said to have been found at the Graeco-Bactrian/Kushan site of Dil'berdzhin, in the Bactra oasis (Kruglikova 1974; 1977; 1986; Kruglikova and Pugachenkova 1977). On stylistic grounds, Grenet (1982, 156) is inclined to consider it an import from Alexandria. The seal is, however, made of jade, which was known in contemporary Central Asia but apparently not further west. This suggests that the seal, despite its clear resemblance to work from Alexandria, may have been of local manufacture (Grenet 1982, 156). Grenet (1982, 157) dates it to the 3rd or 2nd century B.C.

Two further figures of Harpocrates are known from Afghanistan, neither, unfortunately, with a secure provenance. A steatite statuette of Harpocrates **(6)**, with finger to mouth but a somewhat unusual stance, in the collection of the Metropolitan Museum in New York, is dated by Parlasca (1983, 102) to the late 2nd century A.D. A bronze statuette of Harpocrates **(7)**, again probably of the 2nd century A.D. but of more 'standard' iconography and artistic style, is published by Lecuyot (1998).

Figures of Sarapis and Harpocrates occur even well outside the boundaries of the Graeco-Bactrian or Kushan empires proper. Some terracottas of Harpocrates are known from Kushan period Chorasmia (Lecuyot 1998, 117, n6). A Harpocrates figure **(8)** from the Ferghana Valley, sculpted in a dark blue mineral, was excavated in a grave of the 1st or 2nd century A.D., the furnishings of which showed close ties to the culture of the Kushan Empire (Brentjes 1971). The figure is not particularly 'Classical' in appearance, but it has its finger clearly raised to its lips. Of more certain identification are two terracotta figures from Chinese Turkestan (Maillard 1975). The first **(9)**, of Sarapis on a throne with Harpocrates by his side (Maillard 1975, fig. 1) is so similar to an example from the Fayum (Maillard 1975, fig. 2) that Grenet (1982, 230) suggests that they may even have been made from the same mould. The association of Harpocrates with Sarapis, also to be seen on the ring bezel from Pakistan, is to be noted. The second figure **(10)** (Maillard 1975, fig. 3) is of Harpocrates on horseback, and is again similar to examples from Egypt (e.g. UC 8758, UC 8759, UC 8761, Petrie Museum of Egyptian Archaeology). Although these artefacts serve to demonstrate the links between the Kushan Empire and Ferghana and Chinese Turkestan (Maillard 1975, 228), they are too isolated to allow us to realistically posit any influence of the cults of Harpocrates or Sarapis in these regions.

References

Abdourazakov, A. 2001, La production artisanale en Bactriane-Tokharistan (Résultats des études chimiques et restauration), in P. Leriche, C. Pidaev, M. Gelin and K. Abdoullaev (eds.), *La Bactriane au carrefour des routes et des civilisations de l'Asie centrale*, 399–403. Maisonneuve et Larose and IFÉAC, Paris.

Alcock, S. E. 1993, Surveying the Peripheries of the Hellenistic World, in P. Bilde, T. Engberg-Pedersen, L. Hannestad, J. Zahle and K. Randsborg (eds.), *Centre and Periphery in the Hellenistic World*, 162–173. Aarhus University Press, Aarhus.

Allchin, F. R. 1993, The Urban Position of Taxila and its Place in Northwest India-Pakistan, in H. Spodek and D. M. Srinivasan (eds.), *Urban Form and Meaning in South Asia: The Shaping of Cities from Prehistoric to Precolonial Times*, 69–81. National Gallery of Art, Washington, D. C.

Arafat, K. and Morgan, C. 1994, Athens, Etruria and the Heuneberg: Mutual Misconceptions in the Study of Greek-Barbarian Relations, in I. Morris (ed.), *Classical Greece: Ancient Histories and Modern Archaeologies*, 108–134. Cambridge University Press, Cambridge.

Ashton, S.-A. 2003, *Petrie's Ptolemaic and Roman Memphis*. Institute of Archaeology, University College London, London.

Austin, M. M. 1981, *The Hellenistic World from Alexander to the Roman Conquest: A Selection of Ancient Sources in Translation*. Cambridge University Press, Cambridge.

Bavay, L. 1997, Matière première et commerce à longue distance: le lapis-lazuli et l'Égypte predynastique, *Archéo-Nil* 7, 79–100.

Beck, L. A. 1995, Regional Cults and Ethnic Boundaries in "Southern Hopewell", in L. A. Beck (ed.), *Regional Approaches to Mortuary Analysis*, 167–187. Plenum Press, New York and London.

Begley, V. (ed.) 1996, *The Ancient Port of Arikamedu: New Excavations and Researches 1989–1992*. Centre d'histoire et d'archéologie, École française d'Extrême-Orient, Pondichéry.

Berlev, O. D. and Hodjash, S. I. 1998, *Catalogue of the Monuments of Ancient Egypt from the Museums of the Russian Federation, Ukraine, Bielorussia, Caucasus, Middle Asia and the Baltic States*. University Press, Fribourg and Vandenhoeck & Ruprecht, Göttingen.

Bernard, P. 1972, Campagne de fouilles à Aï Khanoum (Afghanistan), *Comptes rendus de l'Académie des inscriptions et belles-lettres*, 605–632.

Bernard, P. 1980, Campagne de fouilles 1978 à Aï Khanoum (Afghanistan), *Comptes rendus de l'Académie des inscriptions et belles-lettres*, 435–459.

Bivar, A. D. H. 1961, An Unknown Punjab Seal-Collector, *Journal of the Numismatic Society of India* 23, 309–327.

Breasted, J. H. 1906–7, *Ancient Records of Egypt: Historical Documents from the Earliest Times to the Persian Conquest*. 5 vols. University of Chicago Press, Chicago.

Brentjes, B. 1971, A Figure of Harpocrates from the Farghāna Valley, *East and West* 21(2), 75.

Briant, P. 1984, *L'Asie centrale et les royaumes proche-Orientaux du premier millénaire (c. VIIIe – IVe siècles avant notre ère)*. Éditions Recherche sur les Civilisations, Paris.

Brill, R. H. 1972, A Laboratory Study of a Fragment of Painted Glass from Begram, *Afghanistan Historical and Cultural Quarterly* 25(2), 75–81.

Bulygina, T. N. 1986, Новые Находки Египетских Изделий в Фергане, *Советская Археология*, 247–253. ['New Discoveries of Egyptian Artefacts in Ferghana', *Sovyetskaya Arkheologiya*.]

Burstein, S. M. 1985, *The Hellenistic Age from the Battle of Ipsos to the Death of Kleopatra VII*. Cambridge University Press, Cambridge.

Burstein, S. M. 1993, The Hellenistic Fringe: The Case of Meroë, in P. Green (ed.), *Hellenistic History and Culture*, 38–54. University of California Press, Berkeley.

Casson, L. 1989, *The Periplus Maris Erythraei*. Princeton University Press, Princeton.

Errington, E. A. and Cribb, J. E. with Claringbull, M. A. (eds.) 1992, *The Crossroads of Asia: Transformation in Image and Symbol in the Art of Ancient Afghanistan and Pakistan*. Ancient Iran and India Trust, Cambridge.

Fraser, P. M. 1960, Two Studies on the Cult of Sarapis in the Hellenistic World, *Opuscula Atheniensia* 3, 1–54.

Fraser, P. M. 1967, Current Problems Concerning the Early History of the Cult of Sarapis, *Opuscula Atheniensia* 7, 23–45.

Gardin, J.-C. 1990, La céramique hellénistique en Asie centrale. Problèmes d'interpretation, in *Akten des XIII Internationalen Kongresses für Klassische Archäologie, Berlin 1988*, 187–193. Verlag Philipp von Zabern, Mainz am Rhein.

Gorbunova, N. G. 1986, *The Culture of Ancient Ferghana: VI Century B.C. – VI Century A.D.*, (trans. A. P. Andryushkin). British Archaeological Reports, Oxford.

Gosden, C. and Marshall, Y. 1999, The Cultural Biography of Objects, *World Archaeology* 33(1), 169–178.

Goudriaan, K. 1988, *Ethnicity in Ptolemaic Egypt*. J. C. Gieben, Amsterdam.

Green, P. 1990, *Alexander To Actium: The Hellenistic Age*. University of California Press, Berkeley.

Grenet, F. 1982, Trois documents religieux de Bactriane Afghane, *Studia Iranica* 11, 155–162.

Grenet, F. 1984, *Les pratiques funéraires dans l'Asie centrale sédentaire: de la conquête grecque à l'Islamisation*. Éditions du CNRS, Paris.

Grenet, F. 1987, L'Athéna de Dil'berdžin, in F. Grenet (ed.), *Cultes et monuments religieux dans l'Asie centrale préislamique*, 41–45. Éditions du CNRS, Paris.

Grenet, F. 1991, Mithra au temple principal d'Aï Khanoum? in P. Bernard and F. Grenet (eds.), *Histoire et cultes de l'Asie centrale préislamique: Sources écrites et documents archéologiques*, 147–151. Éditions du CNRS, Paris.

Hackin, J. 1939, *Recherches archéologiques à Begram*. 2 vols. Les Éditions d'Art et d'Histoire, Paris.

Hackin, J. 1954, *Nouvelles recherches archéologiques à Begram*. 2 vols. Imprimerie Nationale-Presses Universitaires, Paris.

Holt, F. L. 1984, Discovering the Lost History of Ancient Afghanistan: Hellenistic Bactria in Light of Recent Archaeological and Historical Research, *Ancient World* 9, 3–11.

Holt, F. L. 1988, *Alexander the Great and Bactria: The Formation of a Greek Frontier in Central Asia*. E. J. Brill, Leiden.

Holt, F. L. 1993, Response to S. M. Burstein, in P. Green (ed.), *Hellenistic History and Culture,* 54–64. University of California Press, Berkeley.

Holt, F. L. 1999, *Thundering Zeus: The Making of Hellenistic Bactria*. University of California Press, Berkeley.

Kopytoff, I. 1986, The Cultural Biography of Things: Commoditization as Process, in A. Appadurai (ed.), *The Social Life of Things: Commodities in Cultural Perspective*, 64–91. Cambridge University Press, Cambridge.

Kruglikova, I. T. 1974, *Дильберджин (раскопки 1970 – 1972 гг). Часть 1*. Moscow, Nauka. ['*Dil'berdzhin (Finds 1970 – 1972).*']

Kruglikova, I. T. 1977, Les fouilles de la mission archéologique Soviéto-Afghane sur le site gréco-kushan de Dilberdjin en Bactriane (Afghanistan), *Comptes rendus de l'Académie des inscriptions et belles-lettres*, 407–427.

Kruglikova, I. T. 1986, *Дильберджин, Храм Диоскуров: Материалы советско-афганской археологической экспедиции*. Moscow, Nauka. ['*Dil'berdzhin, Temple of the Dioscuri: Material from the Soviet-Afghan Archaeological Expedition.*']

Kruglikova, I. T. and Pugachenkova, G. A. 1977, *Дильберджин (раскопки 1970 – 1973 гг). Часть 2*. Moscow: Nauka. ['*Dil'berdzhin (Finds 1970 – 1973).*']

Kurz, O. 1954, Begram et l'Occident Gréco-Romain, in J. Hackin, *Nouvelles Recherches Archéologiques à Begram*, vol. 1, 93–146. Imprimerie Nationale-Presses Universitaires, Paris.

Lecuyot, G. 1998, Un Harpocrate Bactrien, *Bulletin of the Asia Institute* 12, 113–119.

Lefebvre, G. 1949, *Romans et contes égyptiens de l'époque pharaonique*. Maisonneuve, Paris.

Lerner, J. D. 2003, The Aï Khanoum Philosophical Papyrus, *Zeitschrift für Papyrologie und Epigraphik* 142, 45–51.

Lichtheim, M. 1980, *Ancient Egyptian Literature, 3: The Late Period*. University of California Press, Berkeley and London.

Lilyquist, C. 1999, On the Amenhotep III Inscribed Faience Fragments from Mycenae, *Journal of the American Oriental Society* 119(2), 303–308.

Litvinskii, B. A. and Sedov, A. V. 1984, *Культы и Ритуалы Кушанской Бактрии: Погребалный Обряд*. Moscow: Nauka. ['*Cults and Rituals of Kushan Bactria: Funerary Ritual.*']

Maillard, M. 1975, À propos de deux statuettes en terre rapportées par la mission Ōtani: Sarapis et Harpocrates en Asie Centrale, *Journal Asiatique* 263, 223–230.

Marshall, J. H. 1951, *Taxila*. 3 vols. Cambridge University Press, Cambridge.

Marshall, J. H. 1960, *A Guide to Taxila*. (4th edition.) Cambridge University Press, Cambridge.

Narain, A. K. 1957, *The Indo-Greeks*. Clarendon Press, Oxford.

Parlasca, K. 1983, Eine Harpocrates-Statuette aus Afghanistan, in H. de Meulenaere and L. Limme (eds.), *Artibus Aegypti: Studia in Honorem Bernardi V. Bothmer*, 101–108. Musées royaux d'art et d'histoire, Bruxelles.

Peers, L. 1999, 'Many Tender Ties': The Shifting Contexts and Meanings of the S BLACK Bag, *World Archaeology* 31(2), 288–302.

Piotrovskii, B. B. 1958, Древнеегипетские Предметы, Найденные на Террнтории Советского Союза, *Советская Археология*, 20–27. ['Ancient Egyptian Objects Found in the Territory of the Soviet Union,' *Sovyetskaya Arkheologiya*.]

Posener, G. 1934, A propos de la Stèle de Bentresh, *Bulletin de l'Institut français d'archéologie orientale* 34, 75–81.

Rainbird, P. 1999, Entangled Biographies: Western Pacific Ceramics and the Tombs of Pohnpei, *World Archaeology* 31(2), 214–224.

Rapin, C. 1990, Greeks in Afghanistan: Aï Khanum, in J.-P. Descœudres (ed.), *Greek Colonists and Native Populations, Proceedings of the First Australian Congress of Classical Archaeology*, 329–342. Humanities Research Centre, Canberra and Clarendon Press, Oxford.

Rawlinson, H. G. 1909, *Bactria: From the Earliest Times to the Extinction of Bactrio-Greek Rule in the Punjab*. The "Times of India" Office, Bombay.

Robert, L. 1960, *Hellenica: Recueil d'épigraphie, de numismatique et d'antiquités grecques*, XI–XII. Librairie d'Amerique et d'Orient, Adrien-Maisonneuve, Paris.

Rtveladze, E. V. 1977, Несколько Древнеегипетских Предметов из Северной Бактрии, *Советская Археология*, 235–238. ['Some Ancient Egyptian Objects from Northern Bactria,' *Sovyetskaya Arkheologiya*.]

Sanders, D. H. (ed.) 1996, *Nemrud Dagi: The hierothesion of Antiochus I of Commagene*. Eisenbrauns, Winona Lake, Ind.

Schmitt, R. 1990, Ex Occidente Lux: Griechen und griechische Sprache im hellenistischen Fernen Osten, in P. Steinmetz (ed.), *Beiträge zur Hellenistischen Literatur und ihrer Rezeption in Rom*, 41–58. Franz Steiner, Stuttgart.

Seguenny, E. and Desanges, J. 1986, Sarapis dans le royaume de Kouch, *Chronique d'Égypte* 61, 324–329.

Seyrig, H. 1941, Antiquités syriennes, *Syria* 22, 223–270.

Sherkova, T. A. 1981, Скульптурка Египетского Божества из Могильника Туп-Хона (Южный Таджикистан), *Вестник Древней Истории*, 73–80. ['A Statuette of an Egyptian God from the Cemetery of Tup-Khona (Southern Tadjikistan),' *Vestnik Drevnei Istorii*.]

Sherwin-White, S. and Kuhrt, A. 1993, *From Samarkhand to Sardis: A New Approach to the Seleucid Empire*. Duckworth, London.

Sidebotham, S. E. and Wendrich, W. Z. (eds.) 1995, *Berenike 1994: Preliminary Report of the 1994*

Excavations at Berenike (Egyptian Red Sea Coast) and the Survey of the Eastern Desert. Research School CNWS, Leiden.

Smith, S. T. 2003, *Wretched Kush: Ethnic Identities and Boundaries in Egypt's Nubian Empire.* Routledge, London.

Staviskij, B. Ja. 1986, *La Bactriane sous les Kushans: Problèmes d'histoire et de culture.* Maisonneuve, Paris.

Taddei, M. 1969, Harpocrates-Brahma-Maitreya: A Tentative Interpretation of a Gandharan Relief from Swat, *Dialoghi di Archeologia* 3, 364–390.

Tarn, W. W. 1951, *The Greeks in Bactria and India.* (Second edition.) Cambridge University Press, Cambridge.

Thapar, R. 2002, *Early India: From the Origins to AD 1300.* Allen Lane, London.

Thompson, D. J. 1984, The Ptolemaic Kingdom, in R. Ling (ed.), *The Cambridge Ancient History: Plates to Volume VII Part I*, 3–16. (Second edition.) Cambridge University Press, Cambridge.

Thompson, D. J. 2001, Hellenistic Hellenes: The Case of Ptolemaic Egypt, in I. Malkin (ed.), *Ancient Perceptions of Greek Ethnicity*, 301–322. Center for Hellenic Studies and Trustees for Harvard University, Washington D. C.

Woolf, G. 1997, Beyond Romans and Natives, *World Archaeology* 28(3), 339–350.

Investigating Ancient Egyptian Towns:
A Case Study of Itj-tawy

Claire Malleson

Introduction

The Middle Kingdom town of Itj-tawy has long been accepted as having been the principal royal residence and capital of the 12th and 13th Dynasties (Griffith 1898). Little research has been done on this issue, most probably due to the fact that there is (to date) no direct archaeological evidence for the town. The lack of physical evidence for the vast majority of ancient Egyptian towns has inhibited discussion about the nature and character of settlements. However, it is possible to address these issues if a strong holistic, theoretical framework is applied to the evidence. The socio-economic and political status of Itj-tawy, combined with this apparent lack of information make it highly suitable as a case study.

By utilising all available relevant source material and adopting an empirical approach to the data this paper will address this issue in a fully holistic framework. Throughout, it will refer to the character of the town as being the focus of the research question. The character of a town may be determined by the following: who lived there; what the inhabitants' occupations were; where the inhabitants were buried; the social structure of the town; the physical appearance of the town; and the nature of the surrounding landscape.

In the first publication of part of the Petrie Museum Lahun Papyri archive in 1898, Griffith made the following statement: "The Turin papyrus, as we have seen, calls the XIIth dynasty that of the Residence Ath-taui… That the city of Ath-taui was founded by Amenemhat I is shown by the inscription of Hetep (CG20516)… It is therefore quite clear that Ath-taui was originally the Royal Residence (*ẖnw*)... In later times the locality reappears on the stela of Piankhy as in between Meidum and Memphis. It was then a garrisoned fortress…It may be placed with all probability at Lisht, which name may even retain a reminiscence of the old one. The position was doubtless chosen as central, and to all appearance Ath-taiu lay actually on the boundary between upper and lower Egypt" (1898, 87).

This statement sums up what was known in the nineteenth century about Itj-tawy, and scholars have added little more since (e.g. Hayes 1953, 1980; Helck 1958; Simpson 1963; Von Beckerath 1965, 78–81; Arnold 1991, 16; Kuhrt 1995, 164; Callender 2000, 159). It has continued to be generally accepted that Itj-tawy was in the vicinity of Lisht, and it is still viewed as the new capital of the country, but what role the town played in the administration of the country has not fully been examined. Since the revolution in archaeological methods in Egypt brought about by the Aswan dam projects of the 1970s and the adoption of more functional-processual (e.g. Butzer 1976; 1982) or empirical comparative (e.g. Eyre 1999) approaches in Egyptology there has been little discussion about Itj-tawy.

It must be borne in mind that the nature of the evidence for this issue means that no indisputable conclusions can be reached. This paper will re-evaluate previous discussions using the primary evidence, and where possible, suggest new theories.

Principal Textual Sources for Itj-tawy

The two principal sources for the study of Itj-tawy are the Turin Royal Canon and the Victory Stela of Piankhy. The Turin Royal Canon is reputed to have been almost intact when it was discovered by Drovetti in the nineteenth century and although its current fragmentary condition has led to a variety of reconstructions, its structure is now generally agreed upon. The list begins with the names of deities and the kings of Dynasties 1 to 2 and breaks off after the end of the Hyksos and Theban rulers of the Second Intermediate Period.

According to Malek's reconstruction of the Turin Canon (Malek 1982) the start of the 11th Dynasty (marked in red) is at the top of column nine (Gardiner 1959, V, 11); halfway down this column is the start of the 12th Dynasty in which the kings are named as being 'of the residence of Itj-tawy'.

[ ] Residence of Itj-tawy (Gardiner 1959, V, 19)

A list of the 12th Dynasty rulers follows, and is concluded with an affirmation of the location of this Dynasty:-

Kings of the Residence [ ] (Gardiner 1959, VI, 3)

The 12th Dynasty is the only dynasty in the papyrus to be specifically linked to a named residence. However, in all other instances where the location of the dynasty might have been noted (Herakleopolis or Thebes of the 9–11th Dynasties), the papyrus is broken. It is impossible to know if the 12th Dynasty was marked out as being unique in having a named residence or if it was usual. What must be noted about this source is that it was compiled approximately seven hundred years after the 12th Dynasty and the agenda of the author is unknown. The apparent prominence of the 12th Dynasty residence should not be taken as evidence of any actual importance of this establishment in the Egyptians' understanding of their own history.

What this document does tell us is that in the 19th Dynasty, the kings of the 12th Dynasty were thought to have ruled from a residence named Itj-tawy. The Turin Canon is the only piece of evidence linking the name Itj-tawy to the residence of the Middle Kingdom. This is very important, as much of the discussion of Itj-tawy has to be based on occurrences of the *ḥnw*. Written examples of the name Itj-tawy are very sparse (see later discussion). The Wörterbuch (Erman and Grapow 1926, 150) lists [ ] as a variant for [ ] and vice versa (Erman and Grapow 1929, 369); the 'residence' is generally taken to mean Itj-tawy in the Middle Kingdom (e.g. Stadelmann 1996, 226).

The Piankhy Victory Stela (Cairo Museum JE48862 and 47086–47089) was discovered in 1862 by Mariette in the Amun temple at Napata in Nubia (Lichtheim 1980, 66). It records the conquest of Egypt by the Nubian king Piankhy who founded the 25th Dynasty. Although

Gardiner (1935) did express some doubts, it is very detailed and is generally thought to be an accurate historical account (Lichtheim 1980, 67).

According to the text of the stela, it was reported to Piankhy that the northern ruler Tefnakht had conquered all of the western Delta and southwards as far as Itj-tawy (Lichtheim 1980, 68; Grimal 1981, line 4). After resolving to prevent the domination of Tefnakht, Piankhy set off into Egypt, and the towns he passed through surrendered to him and his troops as they travelled northwards. He arrived at Meidum, which he found to be barricaded (Lichtheim 1980, 74; Grimal 1981, line 81). He then travelled north and discovered Itj-tawy with its rampart closed and filled with Lower Egyptian troops (Lichtheim 1980, 74; Grimal 1981, line 83) who surrendered immediately. He moved northwards again and arrived in Memphis (Lichtheim 1980, 74; Grimal 1981, line 85).

The inscription clearly places Itj-tawy somewhere between Meidum and Memphis during the 25th Dynasty. Whether or not this is the same place as the original town of Itj-tawy, however, should be questioned. Quirke (2004, 10) states that Itj-tawy 'survived as a fortress'. It is possible that if Itj-tawy had originally been surrounded by a large fortified mud-brick enclosure wall, the site could have survived over one thousand years and been re-used/still in use during the Late Period. It is also possible that the locality of the Middle Kingdom town Itj-tawy retained this name throughout history and thus the newer Late Period fortress/town became known as Itj-tawy.

Writing of the Name Itj-tawy

As an aside, it is important to know that the writing of the name of Itj-tawy changed throughout its history. The earliest examples name the town as Amenemhat Itj-tawy (e.g. Stela of Intef, CG 20516).

There is one example in which the town is named Sehetepibre Itj-tawy, suggesting that the inscription dates to the reign of Amenemhat II or later (false door of Ihy, Firth and Gunn 1926 pl. 83).

After that, in inscriptions the town is named simply Itj-tawy, (i.e. Stela of Djedu-sobek, BM EA 830) and in hieratic writings as Itj-tawy without the crenelated wall surround).

The Location of Itj-tawy

In order to fully address the contentious issue of the exact location of Itj-tawy it is helpful to examine the motives that led Amenemhat I to re-locate his principal royal residence and admistrative capital away from Thebes (where the victorius southern rulers of the First Intermediate Period had established their capital).

As seen above, Griffith (1898, 87) suggests that the location of Itj-tawy was Lisht, based principally on the similarity in pronunciation of these two names. Simpson (1963) argues that the relationship between Memphis and Saqqara in the Old Kingdom is an indicator that there would be a similar relationship between the Middle Kingdom necropolis at Lisht and the Middle Kingdom residence Itj-tawy, placing Itj-tawy to the east of Lisht. Von Beckerath (1965, 78–81) proposes that Dahshur was the most likely location for Itj-tawy, based on a theory that Amenemhat I seems to have been keen to associate himself with the Old Kingdom Pharaoh Sneferu, and may have achieved this by locating his new town close to the 4th Dynasty pyramids. Michałowski (1968) suggests Hawara as a potential location based on its proximity to the symbolically and politically important boundary between upper and lower Egypt, the old Herakleopolitan centre and Memphis.

Based on Middle Kingdom texts (The Prophecy of Neferti (Parkinson 1997, 131–143), The Tale of Sinuhe (Parkinson 1997, 21–53), Papyrus Westcar (Parkinson 1997, 102–130), the inscriptions of Nesumontu (Breasted 1906, 469–471) and Khnumhotep I (Breasted 1906, 463–465)), the reasons why Amenemhat may have chosen to establish a new capital in the north become apparent. There was the need to be closer to the 'Asiatic' threat in the north-east and also the 'Libyans' in the north-west as well as the desire to develop links between Amenemhat I's reign and the Old Kingdom Pharaohs (legitimising his place on the throne). Finally, there was a desire to symbolically re-unite the two lands after the political divison of the First Intermediate Period.

The two problems with Egypt's neighbours to the north-east and north-west do seem to have been addressed by the construction of fortresses in the Wadi Natrun (Fakhry 1940) and the north-east Delta ('Walls of the Ruler' – Parkinson 1997, 44, note 11). It is highly unlikely that either of these locations was Itj-tawy. The north-eastern fortress is named, and the north-western fortress is far away from the Nile and the majority of the population. However, by re-locating north from Thebes Amenemhat I (and perhaps more importantly, his advisors) would have been closer to these sources of trouble and would have been able to deal with any real threats without delay.

There is no non-textual evidence to back up Amenemhat I's apparent desire to link himself to the Old Kingdom rulers. The most obvious way to associate himself with the ancient pharaohs would have been to locate his mortuary complex as close to theirs as possible, but Lisht is some way south of the Old Kingdom Saqqara-Dahshur necropolis. It is possible that he may have chosen to re-locate the capital back to the Old Kingdom capital at Memphis. If that were the case it is odd that he did not simply re-locate directly back to Memphis, and herald the return to the old power-base.

Amenemhat's symbolic re-unification of Upper and Lower Egypt is most apparent in the name of the new capital – Itj-tawy translates literally as 'Seizing of the two lands'. The Memphite region, at the Nile-Delta transition is the area in which a Pharaoh is best placed to 'seize' the two lands. Although, as discussed above, there is no evidence to suggest that Amenemhat I moved back to Memphis, he may have chosen a new site in the region in which to establish his new capital.

By continuing to have a major group of elite officials placed in Thebes, as well as establishing a new administrative capital in the north, Amenemhat I would have been very clearly seizing political control of both Upper and Lower Egypt. If he chose a location which was near to the crucial Nile-Delta divide he would have been continuing the tradition of controlling Egypt from the very distinct physical divide between the 'two lands' of the Nile and the Delta.

One other motive for locating the capital in the north might be to be close to the old Herakleopolitan capital just south of the Fayum. Amenemhat I may have felt the need to clearly take control over the area in which the 'enemy' Herakleopolitan dynasty had ruled during the First Intermediate Period. Given the evidence in the Piankhy stela it is not likely that Itj-tawy was a new name for a new town at Herakleopolis (Herakleopolis is south of Meidum, not north). Itj-tawy may have been located somewhere in-between the crucial Memphite and Herakleopolitan regions – a theory which places Itj-tawy in the Lisht region. However, there is no evidence to support this.

There is one further hypothesis which supports the (long-standing) theory that Itj-tawy was close to modern Lisht. The tradition of building a planned settlement to house workers and officials affiliated to state projects (i.e. Pyramid construction) began in the Old Kingdom; demonstrated by the settlements at Giza (Bussman 2004). This continued and was well established by the 12th Dynasty; there is both textual (Gomaà 1986b, 49–51) and archaeological evidence (Borchardt 1905; Petrie 1890; 1891, Bussman 2004) of state planned workers towns associated with the pyramids of Senwosret II at Kahun, and Amenemhat II and III, and Senwosret III at Dahshur.

However, in contrast to the evidence from the Old Kingdom or 12th Dynasty, there is an almost total absence of evidence for a planned workers town at Lisht. The existence of an 'Overseer of the Pyramid Town' at Lisht (Intefoker, Porter and Moss 1934, 79) is the only suggestion that there was a specific state built town to support the workers, officials and priests associated with the construction and cults of the pyramids of Amenemhat I and Senwosret I.

It is highly unlikely that there would not have been a planned workers settlement at Lisht; this absence of evidence could be taken as evidence of absence. The lack of a pyramid builders' town suggests that there was a major town nearby which provided accomodation and offices for the craftsmen and officials associated with the pyramid construction. It is therefore possible that one role of Itj-tawy was to house the pyramid building workforce, and that Itj-tawy was located at Lisht, close to the pyramids.

All the evidence does seem to uphold the theory that Itj-tawy was located somewhere adjacent to modern Lisht/Bamha. The only archaeological evidence for a settlement at Lisht is housing excavated near the pyramids. This has proven to be of a much later date (late 12th or 13th Dynasties (Arnold 1996)) than the probable founding of Itj-tawy (Year 20 of Amenemhat I (Arnold 1991, 16)). However, the Metropolitan Museum of Art expedition to Lisht have noted that there are extensive settlement remains evident in the neraby Mahit canal and around the village of Bamha to the north-east of Lisht (Arnold 1988, 14; Arnold 1996, 14). As they conclude, this ephemeral settlement evidence combined with the presence of a large Middle Kingdom cemetery surrounding the pyramids does strongly suggest that there was indeed a large town or a city close to the Lisht necropolis.

The Physical Appearance of Itj-tawy

Having established that Lisht is indeed the most likely location for Itj-tawy, it is now possible to examine the physical character of the town, its appearance and position in the landscape. As was the case with most settlements in ancient Egypt (Bietak 1979, 101) Itj-tawy was probably built on a levée in the Nile floodplain. The location of the Bahr Libeni channel along the western side of the floodplain rules out the possibility that Itj-tawy was located on the border between the desert and the floodplain, it was therefore likely to have been in-between the two water-courses.

The Bahr Libeni would have provided a second route to the north from Lisht/Itj-tawy. Lisht is at the narrowest point of the Nile valley in this region. Locating a settlement here would be an effective way to ensure absolute control over river traffic (movement of goods and people) between the north and south. A reference to a harbour at Itj-tawy in the Tale of Sinhue confirms the idea that the town was located adjacent to a watercourse (Blackman 1972, line B247; Parkinson 1997, 39).

Architecture of the Town

The lack of any physical evidence for Itj-tawy or the residence means that discussion of the character of the settlement must be based on a comparative study of other Middle Kingdom settlement sites, and analysis of the developments from the Old Kingdom.

In general, from the Old Kingdom onwards the only settlements sufficiently preserved to allow discussion of their character are those associated with major state building, quarrying or military projects (i.e. Giza, Kahun, Abydos, Qasr-es-Sagha, Deir el-Medina); all carefully-planned towns, not the more organic settlements that would have lined the banks of the Nile. Because of their location in the desert margins these settlements have not suffered the adverse taphonomy that can have such detrimental effects on the majority of ancient Egyptian settlement evidence. As Itj-tawy was almost certainly a state-planned settlement, built in a relatively short space of time and designed to fulfill specific purposes, it can be expected to have shared characteristics with these towns.

Based on examination of excavation results from Giza (Saleh 1974; 1996, Lehner 2000), Kahun (Petrie 1890; 1891, O'Connor 1987; Quirke 1998), Tell el-Dab'a (Bietak 1996, Czerny 1999), Abydos (Wegner 1998; 2001), Qasr es-Sagha (Śliwa 1986; 1992) and Abu Ghalib (Larsen 1936, Bagh 2002), it is possible to summarise the characteristics of a Middle Kingdom planned town thus:

- Walled.
- Square or rectangular unless restricted by the geography of the location.
- One notably large dwelling for the mayor.
- A series of virtually identical large dwellings for the principal officials. (each would contain sets of rooms for administrative duties, male, female and servant living quarters, at least one large open courtyard).
- Containing a series of virtually identical smaller dwellings for the lower ranking inhabitants.
- Each dwelling having its own domestic installations.
- The larger dwellings containing (and probably also administering) granaries (Kemp 1986).
- Even the lower class inhabitants are likely to be skilled stone-masons and craftsmen, the more elite members being scribes and head officials.
- An associated settlement built for the lowest class workers and/or the men who built the planned town.

In all probability Itj-tawy could also have been described in the same terms.

Walling of the Town

The writing of the name Itj-tawy within a crenellated wall symbol (⧇) could suggest that the town was a fortress. The wall surrounding Itj-tawy is refered to once, in the 'Tale of the Sporting King' (Caminos 1956, 32), but in no instance is this settlement referred to as a fortress. However, the writing does strongly imply that the town was fortified more extensively than other Middle Kingdom planned towns.

There are other examples of town names that include the ⧇ sign, most notably Memphis (*inb ḥd*), but in all cases the sign is part of the name, as opposed to enclosing the name as is the case with Itj-tawy. There are much earlier parallels for the writing of a town name within a crenellated wall on the Libyan and Narmer palettes (Baines 2003). In both instances these towns represent traditional enemies of Egypt in Western Asia (Baines 2003). Egyptians had engaged in trade with these countries by the start of the Middle Kingdom (as is shown by evidence from Tell el-Dab'a, Bietak 1996), and would have seen their walled towns. Fortification of settlements became standard in Palestine during the Old Kingdom (Kempinski 1992, 68–81). It is possible that Itj-tawy may to some extent have been modelled on Western Asiatic fortified towns, and was seen as a fortified settlement as opposed to a walled settlement. It might have been in order to convey this difference that the name of the town was written in a crenellated wall.

There is one other possibility to consider that could explain this issue. Walling of towns during the Middle Kingdom was not an unusual phenomenon (e.g. evidence from Edfu, Elephantine, Hierakonpolis and Abydos (Moeller 2004, 264)), and there has been a suggestion (Moeller 2004, 265) that these walls may not have played a defensive role, but served a symbolic purpose – sending out an impressive message of power and strength. By walling Itj-tawy, and reinforcing the idea through the name of the town, Amenemhat I may well have been intending to convey these ideas in an attempt to fully establish his legitimacy as ruler.

Given that Itj-tawy was probably one of the most important settlements in Egypt during the Middle Kingdom there are two establishments, in addition to those discussed above, that should have been built within the town: a royal palace and a temple.

There are three inscriptions that name a temple of Amenemhat I that may have been in or near Itj-tawy (*ḥwt sḥtpibrᶜ*, Gomaà 1986b, 39), and there is further evidence for the existence of a temple in Itj-tawy on two Abydene stelae; Hotep (Lange and Schafer 1902, 108–111, CG20516) and Nakht (the younger) (Lange and Schafer 1902, 105–108, CG20515) were both priests who worked in Itj-tawy. Other evidence that does indicate the presence of a temple in Itj-tawy are offering tables discovered in a canal near Lisht (el-Khouly 1978; Arnold 1988, 14).

There are four Middle Kingdom texts that include references to the existence of a palace that was probably in Itj-tawy; The Tale of Sinuhe (Blackman 1972, line B249; Parkinson 1997, 40), Papyrus Westcar (Blackman 1988, line 8.10; Parkinson 1997, 114) Papyrus Brooklyn 35.1446 insert C (Wente 1990,12) and The Sporting King (Caminos 1956, 29, 32). Further evidence of the existence of a royal palace in Itj-tawy has survived at Saqqara in the form of a false door in the chapel of Ihy (Firth and Gunn 1926, pl. 83). Ihy's most prominent title is *imy-r pr nsw sḥtp-ib-rᶜ it-tȝwy*, 'Overseer of the Royal Palace of Amenemhat-Itj-tawy'. The text of 'The Sporting King' is very damaged (Caminos 1956, 22) but it is apparent not only that the Palace is on the edge of a body of water, reached by boat (Caminos 1956, 29) but also that it is home to the King's family. It may well be that this palace is the central royal palace within Itj-tawy and is reached via the harbour referred to in The Tale of Sinuhe, but it could also be a 'pleasure palace' on the edge of Lake Moeris, unconnected to Itj-tawy.

Textual evidence of the probable inhabitants of Itj-tawy

Evidence for the inhabitants of the town can be gleaned from inscriptions. By examining the titles these people held it is possible to establish their probable social and economic status and then infer further detail about the true nature and functions of both the residence and Itj-tawy. Given that there are just eleven occurrences of the name Itj-tawy in Middle Kingdom inscriptions it is first important to discuss these in some detail and then examine the evidence derived from the Lisht necropolis. The following list is compiled from Gauthier (1925, 124), Simpson (1963) and Gomaà (1986). Dating is based on Simpson (1963) and prosopographical observations. Translation of the stelae was by the author, with reference where possible to published translations.

a) The stela of Intef. CG 20516. (Lange and Schafer 1902, 108–111.)

This large, high quality stela from Abydos is often quoted in discussions regarding the co-regency of Amenemhat I and Senwosret I (Obsomer 1995, 45). It is dated to year ten of Senwosret I and year thirty of Amenemhat I and is the earliest dated evidence for Itj-tawy. The inscription behind Intef's son Hotep, shows that the latter is *ḥry-ḥbt imn-m-ḥ3t ʿnḫ ḏt it-t3wy*. No more information is given about this individual – what is important is that Hotep is a lector priest, therefore he must have either worked in a local mortuary complex or the temple of the local deity of Itj-tawy.

b) The stela of Nakht. CG 20515. (Lange and Schafer 1902, 105–108.)

This stela was inscribed for Nakht, 'Overseer of Goldsmiths' by his son Nakht, who was *sš ḳdwt m imn-m-ḥ3t it-t3wy*: 'Draughtsman in Amenemhat Itj-tawy', and a lector priest during the reigns of Senwosret I and possibly also Amenemhat I (the stela is dated year ten Senwosret I). This is evidence that there was a body of highly trained craftsmen based in Itj-tawy.

c) Stela of Shen. Los Angeles A5141.80–876. (Faulkner 1952, includes translation.)

At some point in his career (during the reign of Amenemhat I or Senwosret I) Shen moved to Abydos, where this stela was found. He had previously worked as a sculptor in Amenemhat Itj-tawy (*iw ir.n(=i) gnwty m imn-m-ḥ3t it-t3wy di ʿnḫ ḏt*). This is further evidence of craftsmen's workshops in Itj-tawy.

d) False door of Ihy. Saqqara. (Firth and Gunn 1926, pl. 83, includes translation.)

The tomb of Ihy probably dates to the reign of Amenemhat II (Simpson 1963; Aldred 1950, 43–44) and is a simple shaft tomb with an adjoining chapel that contained an intact false door on which his numerous official titles are listed. The second and most frequent title he lists is *imy-r pr nsw sḥtp-ib-rʿ it-t3wy*, 'Overseer of the Palace of Sehetepibre-Itj-tawy'. This false door is the principal piece of evidence for the existence of a royal palace in Itj-tawy.

e) Stela of Djedu-sobek. B.M EA 830. (British Museum 1913, 136; Franke 1984, 440/763.)

Djedu-sobek's title *imy-r ḥwt wrt 6 m it-t3wy*, 'Overseer of the Six Law Courts in Itj-tawy' is very interesting in this context. Throughout the Old Kingdom this title was almost without exception assigned to viziers in Memphis (Strudwick 1985, 176–178), this is a rare Middle Kingdom example of the title. His numerous titles suggest that Djedu-sobek was a man of some importance in Itj-tawy. This inscription provides evidence of the existence of a judicial establishment within Itj-tawy.

f) Fragments from tomb of Ameny-sonebu. Hawara. (Petrie 1890, pl. XI, 2, 3, 4.)

When first published by Petrie (1890) these fragments were attributed to the tomb of Ameny Seneb Nebau (the correct translation is Ameny-sonebu), owner of a tomb at Hawara, probably dating to the reign of Amenemhat III (Simpson 1963). From translation of the fragments it is apparent that Ameny-sonebu was the 'Controller of a Phyle' (of wab priests) (*mty n s3 imnysnbw*), 'Head of the Builders' (*tp gnwty*) and 'Govenor' (*ḥᶜty-ᶜ*). It is possible that Itj-tawy was the location of his employment as one fragment bears the name of the town, but the inscription is damaged so it is impossible to be certain. Franke (1984, 108, 125) suggests that this is the Ameny-soneb of the well known ankh-shaped Stela, Liverpool E30.

g) Stela of Amenemhat-Soneb. CG 20100. (Mariette 1880; Lange and Schafer 1902, 121–122; Franke 1984, 217, 326.)

This poor quality stela was discovered at Abydos. The owner was *rpᶜ ḥ3ty-ᶜ smr ᶜ3 n mrwt im3ḥy m it-t3wy ḥtmty bity imy-r pr smsw nmty m wsḫt*, 'Count and Great Companion beloved and revered in Itj-tawy, Seal Bearer and Elder Overseer of the House of Nemtyemweskhet,'. Amenemhat-Soneb states that he was 'beloved in Itj-tawy' which raises the possibility that he lived and worked there. He may also have been buried in Lisht, but like so many Middle Kingdom officials he also chose to erect a cenotaph at Abydos.

h) Stela of Waswy – hotep. CG 20149. (Lange and Schafer 1902, 175–177.)

This is a very standard Middle Kingdom offering stela. The owner states that he is 'revered in Itj-tawy', indicating that he may have been buried in Lisht but also had a cenotaph in Abydos. The title *iḥms n 3ḫt* is listed in Ward (1982, 562) as 'Attendant of the Still-room', however Hannig (1995, 97) translates this as 'Servant of the Butchery'; essentially the title implies that he worked in a food storage area. This places him among the workers in Itj-tawy, possibly in the palace.

i) Stela of Hor-aa. Virginia Museum 63–29. (De Meulenaere 1971.)

This statue entered the museum via the antiquities market in New York in 1960 and has been dated to the reign of Amenemhat II on artistic grounds (De Meulenaere 1971). The inscriptions name the statue as that of *sr ḥyt ḥr-ᶜ3, Hor-aa*, 'Official of the Portal', according to Quirke (2004, 31, 33) this places him in the Outer Palace. One of the offering formulae asks for a good old age in Itj-tawy and it is therefore probable that this individual lived and worked in the town.

j) Stela of Ptah-wer. Berlin 8808. (Berlin 1913,146; possibly Franke 1984, 172, 240.)

Simpson (1963) lists the owner of this Middle Kingdom stela simply as Ptah-wer, Chief Steward. However, the full translation shows that Ptah-wer held many other interesting titles. The slightly ambiguous title *hry sšt3 n sdmt wᶜ* 'Master of Secrets which One Person Hears' is accompanied by other titles that place him in the court. It can be suggested that he was buried in Lisht because he states that he was revered and justified in Itj-tawy. Ptah-wer held a variety of very important titles suggesting that he, like Ihy, Djedu-sobek and Amenemhat-soneb was amongst the high elite.

k) Stela of Horemkauef. Metropolitan Museum 35.7.55. (Hayes 1947, Lichtheim 1975, 129–130, including translations.)

This stela was discovered in March 1935 by Ambrose Lansing and the Egyptian Expedition of the Metropolitan Museum of Art in an appropriated tomb north-west of the fort at Hierakonpolis, and has been dated to the late 13th dynasty (Hayes 1947). In the context of this paper it is of great interest, since although Horemkauef had no personal connection to Itj-tawy, the text clearly places the king in Itj-tawy. The fact that Horemkauef travelled to Itj-tawy in order to collect a statue of the god for the temple at Nekhen strongly implies that there was an important body of highly skilled craftsmen in Itj-tawy.

The Lisht Cemeteries

Given the earlier conclusion that Itj-tawy was located adjacent to the pyramids at Lisht, it is important to discuss the texts from the surrounding cemeteries. On account of gaps in publication (Arnold 1988, 14–16) due to be rectified to a large degree in the future (Bourriau 2003, note 1) this examination of the Lisht cemetery is not as detailed as would be desirable for a full analysis, but it does give a basic introduction to some of the individuals buried there. As is to be expected, the burials containing inscribed material are of only the highest elite officials.

Dating evidence indicates that of the many burials at Lisht these elite burials are more certainly attributed to the reigns of Amenemhat I and Senwosret I than the lower class burials (Bourriau 2003). Including this evidence in the present discussion is therefore relatively 'safe'. The titles found in the cemeteries at Lisht which belong to individuals who probably lived and worked in Itj-tawy include 'Vizier' and 'Overseer of a Pyramid Town' (Gauthier and Jéquier 1902, 98–99), 'Chief Steward' (Gauthier and Jéquier 1902, 100) 'Overseer of the Granary' (Porter and Moss 1934, 81), 'Chief Lector Priest' (Gauthier and Jéquier 1902, 77), 'Overseer of the Cabinet' (Gauthier and Jéquier 1902, 83–85), 'Steward' (Lansing 1933) and 'Official' (Porter and Moss 1934, 85).

These inscriptions strengthen the theories about the character of the town already apparent from analysis of the eleven 'Itj-tawy' stelae: that it was home to a body of officials and priests.

Other Written Evidence

Examination of non-mortuary textual evidence from the Middle Kingdom can be used to expand our understanding of how the residence was perceived during the Middle Kingdom and informs the discussion of the relationship between the residence and Itj-tawy. There are five Middle Kingdom letters and four literary pieces that mention the residence.

Papyrus Brooklyn 35.1446 insert C (Wente 1990, 12), Papyrus Reisner II section D (Wente 1990, 42), and Kahun Letters UC 32128, 32200 and 32202 (Collier and Quirke 2002) show that the residence was perceived to be the focal point of reference for issues of justice. This judicial role of the residence in Itj-tawy is also attested to by a title relating to the Kenbet court of the residence (Doxey 1998, 312). There is an implication that the residence was a place of central control for the collection and distribution of goods.

The Tale of Sinuhe (Blackman 1972,1–41; Parkinson 1997, 27–53), the Prophecy of Neferti (Helck 1970; Parkinson 1997, 134–143), the Teaching of Amenemhat (Helck 1969; Parkinson 1997, 206–211) and the Dialogue of Ipuwer (Gardiner 1909; Parkinson 1997, 170–199) all contain references to the residence. It can be deduced that the residence is not simply a building but that the word is used to refer to an institution and a group of officials, in much the same way as 'Number Ten' (Downing Street) is used to refer to the Government offices, not simply the home of the British Prime Minister. These men are of great importance to the King, and to the stability (Maat) of Egypt.

Conclusions

The name of Itj-tawy ('Seizing of the Two Lands') is key to understanding much about the town. It was founded by Amenemhat I in order to symbolically re-unite the two lands, establish a northern base for his administration and to legitimise his own reign, and was strategically placed in a location that symbolically and practically upheld the idea of seizing the two lands. The fortified wall was inherent in the name ⌜☒⌝, and was critical to the message of domination that Amenemhat I seems to have been trying to convey.

Itj-tawy probably followed the tradition of other state towns and may well have been built to a similar plan; clear orthogonal layout with internal divisons for inhabitants of differing status, a harbour, temple and palace. Because Itj-tawy was seen as the capital, the 'residence' (the institution most responsible for law and order in the country) was also based there, and the two were synonymous.

The town was home to a body of elite officials, priests, craftsmen and the pharaoh and his family. The evidence for the palace in Itj-tawy has great implications; with the knowledge that there was a palace in the town it is possible to conclude that there was also a large population of general servant-class personnel residing in Itj-tawy, a population that is otherwise invisible. The presence of a temple in the town has similar implications; any temple would need a large number of priests to service it. Together these two establishments would require a considerable number of farmers and farm-land dedicated to producing supplies. The evidence for the workshops suggest that Itj-tawy became home to a state sponsored body of skilled craftsmen. It is possible that these individuals were heavily involved in the production of goods for the royal burials at Lisht but they were certainly involved in creating objects for national temples as well as privately owned stelae. Several of the inhabitants do seem to have been proud of having worked in Itj-tawy; in their offering stelae at Abydos their status at Itj-tawy was among the few achievements they mentioned.

However, by examining this information closely a number of questions are raised. Although there is clear evidence of the administrative and judicial activites in the town, the relative lack of evidence for the bureauocracy that must have been based there does lead to a question about the actual importance of the town. The quantity of evidence from Thebes could suggest that Itj-tawy, while being the new capital, did not actually house as many officials or bureaucratic activities as the southern city. Even taking into account the loss of evidence, the very small number of officials who claimed to have lived in Itj-tawy is surprising.

Itj-tawy was the capital in name and fulfilled the role in some ways (housing officials who were responsible for distribution of goods and judicial matters, royal craftsmen and a royal palace). But, in reality, much of the day-to-day running of Egypt probably continued to take place in Thebes. The symbolic role of Itj-tawy 'seizing the two lands' was the most important role the town played.

The absence of direct archaeological evidence for ancient settlements in Egypt should not prevent or restrain the study of their characters. By adopting a holistic framework and re-examining older hypotheses utilising new theoretical approaches, as well as evaluating all available relevant source material it should be possible to investigate other major towns in ancient Egypt. A fuller understanding of settlements and their roles in the bureaucracy of the country can only aid further research into the socio-economic history of ancient Egypt.

University of Liverpool

Acknowledgements

The paper is the result of an M.A. undertaken at Liverpool University. Thanks are due to all the staff of SACE, especially Dr. S. Snape, Dr. R. Enmarch and Dr. I. Shaw. Also to Janine Bourriau who spent time discussing this issue with me during the CRE VI conference, and all my collegues on the 2005 Chester Amphitheatre project.

References

Aldred, C. 1950, *Middle Kingdom Art in Ancient Egypt.* Alec Tiranti, London.

Arnold, D. 1988, *The South Cemeteries of Lisht Volume I: The Pyramid of Senwosret I.* Metropolitan Museum of Art, New York.

Arnold, D. 1991, Amenemhat I and the early Twelfth Dynasty at Thebes, *Metropolitan Museum Journal* 26, 5–48.

Arnold, F. 1996, Settlement Remains at Lisht-North, in M. Bietak (ed.), *Haus und Palast im Alten Ägypten,* 14–20. Österreichische Akademie der Wissenschaften, Vienna.

Bagh, T. 2002, Abu Ghâlib and Early Middle Kingdom Town in the Western Nile Delta, *Mitteilungen des Deutschen Archäologischen Instituts Abteilung Kairo* 58, 29–58.

Baines, J. 2003, Early definitions of the Egyptian world and its surroundings, in T. Potts, M. Roaf and D. Stein (eds.), *Culture through objects: Ancient Near Eastern studies in honour of P. R. S. Moorey,* 27–57. Griffith Institute, Oxford.

Berlin. 1913, *Ägyptische Inschriften aus den Königlichen Museen zu Berlin Volume 1.* Leipzig.

Bietak, M. 1979, Urban Archaeology and the 'Town problem' in Ancient Egypt, in K. Weeks (ed.), *Egyptology and the Social Sciences*, 97–144. American University in Cairo Press, Cairo.

Bietak, M. 1996, *Avaris, the Capital of the Hyksos.* British Museum Press, London.

Blackman, A. M. 1972, *Middle Egyptian Stories.* La Fondation Égyptologique Reine Élizabeth, Brussels.

Blackman, A. M. 1988, *The Story of King Kheops and the Magicians.* J. V. Books, Reading.

Borchardt, L. 1905, Ein Konigserlass aus Dashur, *Zeitschrift für Ägyptische Sprache und Altertumskunde* 42, 1–11.

Bourriau, J. 2003, The contribution of Lisht North Cemetery to Middle Kingdom Studies, in S. Quirke (ed.), *Discovering Egypt from the Neva. The Egyptological Legacy of Oleg D Berlev,* 51–59. Achet Verlag, Berlin.

Breasted, J. H. 1906, *Ancient Records of Egypt Volume I.* 2001 reprint. University of Illinois Press, Illinois.

British Museum 1913, *Hieroglyphic Texts from Egyptian Stelae etc in the British Museum Volume IV.* British Museum Press, London.

Bussmann, R. 2004, Siedlung im Kontext der Pyramiden des Alten Reiches, *Mitteilungen des Deutschen Archäologischen Instituts Abteilung Kairo* 60, 17–39.

Butzer, K. 1976, *Early Hydraulic Civilisation in Egypt: A study in cultural ecology.* University of Chicago Press, Chicago.

Butzer, K. 1982, *Archaeology as Human Ecology*. Cambridge University Press, Cambridge.

Callender, G. 2000, The Middle Kingdom Renaissance, in I. Shaw (ed.), *The Oxford History of Ancient Egypt*, 148–184. Oxford University Press, Oxford.

Caminos, R. A. 1956, *Literary Fragments in the Hieratic Script*. Griffith Institute, Oxford.

Collier, M. and Quirke, S. 2002, *The UCL Lahun Papyri: Letters*. British Archaeological Reports 1083. British Archaeological Reports, Oxford.

Czerny, E. 1999, *Tell el-Dab'a XI*. Verlag der Österreichischen Akademie der Wissenschaften, Vienna.

De Meulenaere, H. 1971, La Statue d'un contemporain de Sébekhotep IV, *Bulletin de l'Institut français d'archéologie orientale* 69, 61–64.

Doxey, D. M. 1998, *Egyptian non-royal epithets in the Middle Kingdom: A social and historical analysis*. Brill, Leiden.

el-Khouly, A. 1978, An offering table of Sesostris I from El-Lisht, *Journal of Egyptian Archaeology* 44, 44.

Erman, A. and Grapow, H. 1926, *Wörterbuch der aegyptische Sprache Volume 1*. J. C. Hinrichsische Buchandlung, Leipzig.

Erman, A. and Grapow, H. 1929, *Wörterbuch der aegyptische Sprache Volume 3*. J. C. Hinrichsische Buchandlung, Leipzig.

Eyre, C. J. 1999, The Village Economy in Pharaonic Egypt, in A. Bowman and E. Rogan (eds.) *Agriculture in Egypt. From Pharaonic to Modern times*, 33–60. Oxford University Press, Oxford.

Fakhry, A. 1940, Wadi el Natrun, *Annales du Services des Antiquités de l'Égypte* 40, 837–848.

Faulkner, R. O. 1952, The Stela of the Master-sculptor Shen, *Journal of Egyptian Archaeology* 38, 3–5.

Firth, C. and Gunn, B. 1926, *Excavations at Saqqara, The Teti Pyramid Cemeteries Volume I*. Imprimerie de l'Institut Français d'Archéologie Orientale, Cairo.

Franke, D. 1984, *Personendaten aus dem Mittleren Reich*. Otto Harrassowitz, Wiesbaden.

Gardiner, A. 1909, *The Admonitions of an Egyptian Sage*. J. C. Hinrichs, Leipzig.

Gardiner, A. 1935, Piankhi's instructions to his army, *Journal of Egyptian Archaeology* 21, 219–223.

Gardiner, A. 1959, *The Royal Canon of Turin*. Griffith Institute, Oxford.

Gauthier, H. 1925, *Dictionnaire des noms géographiques contenus dans les textes hiéroglyphiques, Volume I*. Imprimerie de l'Institut Français d'Archéologie Orientale, Cairo.

Gauthier, J. E. and Jéquier, G. 1902, *Mémoire sur les fouilles de Licht*. Imprimerie de l'Institut Français d'Archaéologie Orientale, Cairo.

Gomaà, F. 1986a, *Die Besiedlung Ägyptens während des Mittleren Reichs Volume One*. Tübinger Atlas des vorderen Orients, Reichert, Wiebaden.

Gomaà, F. 1986b, *Die Besiedlung Ägyptens während des Mittleren Reichs Volume Two*. Tubinger Atlas der vorderen orients, Reichert, Wiesbaden.

Griffith, F. L. 1898, *The Petrie Papyri; Hieratic Papyri from Kahun and Gurob, principally of the Middle Kingdom*. Bernard Quaritch, London.

Grimal, N. 1981, *La stèle Triomphale de Pi('ankh)y au musée du Caire: JE48862 et 47086–47089*. Institut français d'Archéologie Orientale, Cairo.

Hannig, R. 1995, *Die Sprache der Pharaonen. Grosses Handwörterbuch. Ägyptisch – Deutsch*. Phillip von Zabern, Mainz.

Hayes, W. C. 1947, Horemkha'uef of Nekhen and his trip to It̠-towe, *Journal of Egyptian Archaeology* 33, 3–11.

Hayes, W. C. 1953, Notes on the Government of Egypt in the late Middle Kingdom, *Journal of Near Eastern Studies* 12, 31–39.

Hayes, W. C. 1980, Itj-taui, in W. Helck and E. Otto (eds.), *Lexikon der Ägyptologie III*, col. 211. Harrasowitz, Wiesbaden.

Helck, W. 1958, *Zur Verwaltung des Mittleren und Neuen Reichs*. Brill, Leiden.

Helck, W. 1969, *Der text der 'lehre Amenemhats I für seinen Sohn'*. Otto Harrassowitz, Wiesbaden.

Helck, W. 1970, *Die prophezeiung des nfr.tj*. Harrasowitz, Wiesbaden.

Kempinski, A. 1992, *The Architecture of Ancient Israel*. Israel Exploration Society, Jerusalem.

Kuhrt, A. 1995, *The Ancient Near East*. Routledge, London.

Lange, H. O. and Schäfer, H. 1902, *Catalogue général des antiquités égyptiennes du Musée du Caire. Grab und Denksteine des Mittleren Reichs im Museum von Kairo Volume I*. Reichsdruckerei, Berlin.

Lansing, A. 1933, The Egyptian Expedition, *Bulletin of the Metropolian Museum of Art, New York* 28/2.

Larsen, H. 1936, Vorbericht über die Schwedischen Grabungen in Abu Ghalib 1932–1943, *Mitteilungen des Deutschen Archäologischen Instituts Abteilung Kairo* 6, 41–87.

Lehner, M. 2000, *The Giza Platau Mapping Project Annual Report*. http://oi.uchicago.edu/OI/PROJ/GIZ/ Giza.html. Accessed September 2003.

Lichtheim, M. 1975, *Ancient Egyptian Literature, Volume 1*. University of California Press, California.

Lichtheim, M. 1980, *Ancient Egyptian Literature, Volume 3*. University of California Press, California.

Malek, J. 1982, The Original Version of the Royal Canon of Turin, *Journal of Egyptian Archaeology* 68, 93–106.

Mariette, A. 1880, *Catalogue général des Monuments d'Abydos découverts pendant les fouilles de cette ville par Auguste Mariette*. Imprimerie Nationale, Paris.

Michałowski, K. 1968, The Labyrinth Enigma; Archaeological suggestions, *Journal of Egyptian Archaeology* 54, 219–222.

Moeller, N. 2004, Evidence for Urban Walling in the Third Millenium BC, *Cambridge Archaeological Journal* 14:2, 259–288.

O'Connor, D. 1987, The elite houses of Kahun in J. Phillips (ed.), *Ancient Egypt, the Aegean and the Near East: Studies in Honour of Martha Rhoads Bell*, 389–400. Van Sicklen, San Antonio.

Obsomer, C. 1995, *Sésostris 1er: Étude chronologique et historique du règne*. Connaissance de l'Egypte Ancienne, Brussels.

Parkinson, R. 1997, *The Tale of Sinuhe and other Ancient Egyptian Poems 1940–1640 BC*. Oxford University Press, Oxford.

Petrie, W. M. F. 1890, *Kahun, Gurob and Hawara*. Kegan Paul, Trench, Trubner and Co, London.

Petrie, W. M. F. 1891, *Illahun, Kahun and Gurob*. David Nutt, London.

Porter, B. and Moss, R. 1934, *Topographical Bibliography of Ancient Egyptian Hieroglyphic Texts, Reliefs and Paintings. Volume IV Lower and Middle Egypt*. Griffith Institute, Oxford.

Quirke, S. 1990, *The Administration of Egypt in the Late Middle Kingdom. The Hieratic Documents*. Sia Publishing, New Malden.

Quirke, S. 2004, *Titles and bureaux of Egypt 1850–1700 BC*. Golden House Publications, London.

Quirke, S. (ed.) 1998, *Lahun Studies*. SIA, Reigate.

Saleh, A. 1974, Excavations Around Mycerinus Pyramid Complex, *Mitteilungen des Deutschen Archäologischen Instituts Abteilung Kairo* 30, 131–154.

Saleh, A. 1996, Ancient Egyptian House and Palace at Giza and Heliopolis, in M. Bietak (ed.), *Haus und Palast im Alten Ägypten: Internationals Symposium 8. bis 11. April 1992 im Kairo*, 185–194. Österreichische Akademie der Wissenschaften, Vienna.

Simpson, W. K. 1963, Studies in the Twelfth Egyptian Dynasty: I–II, *Journal of the American Research Center in Egypt* 2, 53–59.

Śliwa, J. 1986, Die Siedlung des Mittleren Reichs bei Qasr el-Sagha, *Mitteilungen des Deutschen Archäologischen Instituts Abteilung Kairo* 42, 167–179.

Śliwa, J. 1992, Die Siedlung des Mittleren Reichs bei Qasr el-Sagha, *Mitteilungen des Deutschen Archäologischen Instituts Abteilung Kairo* 48, 177–187.

Stadelmann, R. 1996, Temple Palace and Residential Palace, in M. Bietak (ed.), *Haus und Palast im Alten Ägypten*, 225–231. Osterreichische Akademie der Wissenschaften, Vienna.

Strudwick, N. 1985, *The Administration of Egypt in the Old Kingdom.*. Keegan Paul International, London.

von-Beckerath, J. 1965, *Untersuchungen zur politischen Geschichte der zweiten Zwischenzeit in Ägypten. Ägyptologische Forschungen Heft 23*. Augustin, Glückstadt.

Ward, W. A. 1982, *Index of Egyptian Administrative and Religious Titles of the Middle Kingdom.* American University of Beirut, Beirut.

Wegner, J. 1998, Excavations at the Town of Enduring-are-the-places-of-Khakaure-Maa-Kheru-in-Abydos, *Journal of the American Research Center in Egypt* 35, 1–44.

Wegner, J. 2001, The Town of Wah-sut at South Abydos, *Mitteilungen des Deutschen Archäologischen Instituts Abteilung Kairo* 57, 281–308.

Wente, E. 1990, *Letters from Ancient Egypt.* Scholars Press, Atlanta.

A Study of Ramesside Royal Women's Tombs in the Valley of the Queens

Heather Lee McCarthy

I. Introduction

This paper derives from a wider, ongoing investigation into the tombs of Ramesside royal women to be presented in my forthcoming dissertation, *Queenship, Cosmography, and Regeneration: The Decorative Programs and Architecture of Ramesside Royal Women's Tombs*. A select group of tombs cut and decorated for 19th and 20th Dynasty royal women in the Valley of the Queens will be analyzed in order to reveal the nature of (and reasons for) Ramesside innovations in queens' burials, the most dramatic of which is the creation of a specifically 'queenly' netherworld landscape. Moreover, I will discuss the significance of these innovations as indicators of changes in the ideology of queenship and to the roles and status of royal women in the Ramesside period.

II. Context: The Valley of the Queens, Tombs of 18th Dynasty Royal Women, Ramesside Queens' Tombs

(a) The Valley of the Queens

At the beginning of the 19th Dynasty, a Y-shaped valley on the west bank of Thebes that contained the tombs of elite, 18th Dynasty male officials (Leblanc 1989b, 18–19, 69, n. 97–98) was adapted for use as a cemetery for 19th and 20th Dynasty royal women and, briefly, in the early 20th Dynasty, for the burials of five sons of Ramesses III. The necropolis is known from Ramesside documents as *T3 St Nfrw*—an appellation that has been translated variously as, 'The Place of Beauty', 'The Place of the Beautiful Ones' or, more recently, 'The Place of the Royal Children' (Leblanc 1989b, 14–19), but clearly encompasses the valley's primary purpose at this period as a cemetery for Ramesside royal women (Leblanc 1989b, 20).

The unprecedented creation of a queens' necropolis as a discrete spatial entity – geographically removed from and independent of the burial ground of contemporary pharaohs in the Valley of the Kings (Figure 1) – was just one of several significant changes made to the interment of New Kingdom royal women at the beginning of the Ramesside period. The other innovations included: consistently providing Ramesside royal women with their own tombs (ones that they did not have to share with co-queens or other royal relatives); endowing royal women with tombs that were larger and more architecturally complex than those attributed to the 18th Dynasty queens; and, most significantly, the decoration of each tomb with wall scenes and funerary texts. Moreover, each royal woman's independent ownership of her tomb is demonstrated by the content of these Ramesside decorative programs, which depict her direct interaction with the gods.

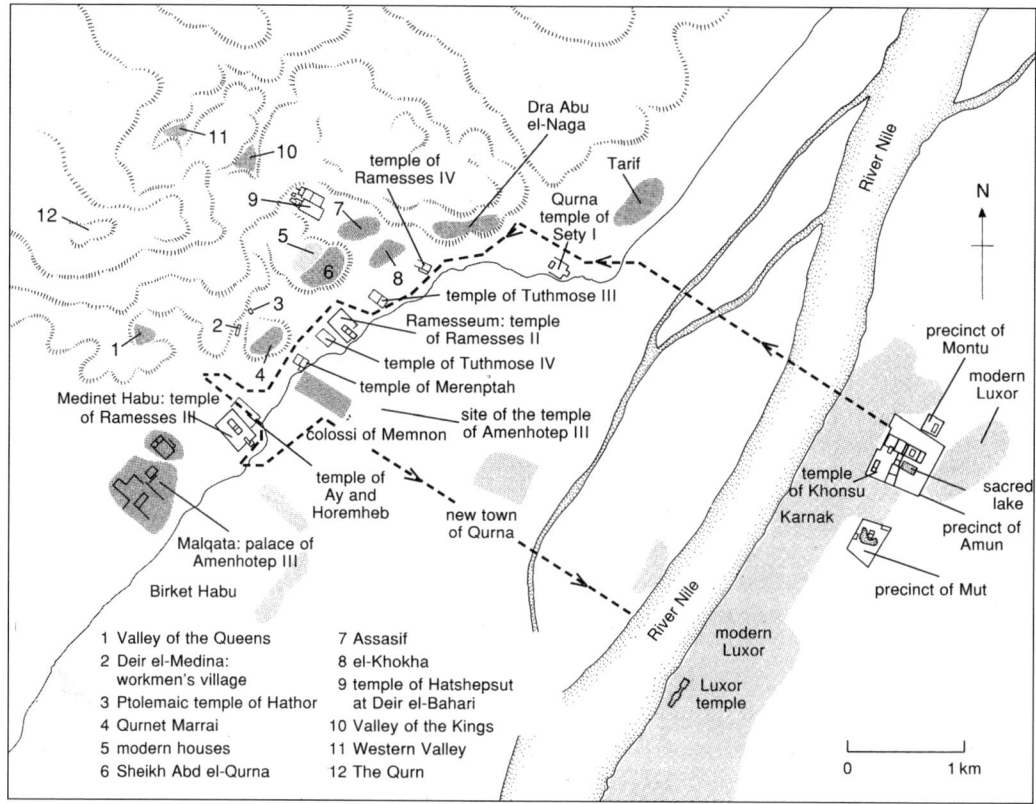

Figure 1. Map of Thebes (from Strudwick and Strudwick 1999, 11).

The dramatic transformation of the way royal women were buried at the start of the 19th Dynasty not only indicates the likelihood of a significant change in funerary beliefs pertaining to royal women in the Ramesside era, but also suggests corresponding changes, outside the funerary realm, to the ideological roles of 19th and 20th Dynasty queens, the mythic paradigms that underscored queenship, and the status (or outward expression of status) of queens.

(b) 18th Dynasty Royal Women's Burials

Before the advent of the Ramesside period, some 18th Dynasty queens were interred in undecorated chambers within the tombs of contemporary pharaohs in the Valley of the Kings and the West Valley – such as the planned burials of two queens (Tiye and possibly Satamun) within the tomb (WV 22) of Amenhotep III (Reeves 2003, 69–71, fig.1; 1990, 38–39, 54, n.77; Hayes 1990, 241). Alternatively, they could be buried (singly or in groups) in undecorated tombs in the Valley of the Kings and its neighboring wadi systems. Among these burials are the early 18th Dynasty tomb (DB 358) of Merytamun, the sister-wife of Amenhotep I at Deir el Bahri (Winlock 1932; Hayes 1990, 53–54; Romer 1976, 192, 194–197, figs. 2–4); the first, 'queenly', tomb (WA D) of Hatshepsut at Wadi Sikket Taqa el-Zeide (Carter 1916, 179–182;1917, 114–118; Thomas 1966, 195–196); the burial of Thutmose IV's mother, Tiaa in KV 32 (Giddy 2002, 29); and the group interment of three minor foreign wives (*hmt nswt*) of Thutmose III in a tomb in Wadi Qubbanat el Qurud (Winlock 1948; Lilyquist 2003).

(c) Ramesside Queens' Tombs

Eighteen tombs in the Valley of the Queens have been attributed to Ramesside royal women, but the focus of this study is the group of fifteen tombs (QV 31, 33, 36, 38, 40, 80, 60, 66, 68, 71, 73, 74, 75, 51, and 52) in which the titles and/or names of the royal female owners (or intended owners) are preserved (Figure 2). These tombs were cut and decorated over a period spanning approximately two centuries, from the beginning of the 19th Dynasty until the middle-to-late 20th Dynasty, and the tomb owners were among the highest ranking Ramesside royal women. The two most commonly held kinship titles were *ḥmt nswt wrt* (great royal wife) and *s3t nswt* (king's daughter). Thirteen of the fifteen royal women held the former title and eleven held the latter. There was, however, a high degree of overlap, as nine of the 'great royal wives' were also 'king's daughters'. This number includes the five known 'king's daughters', who each acted as a 'great royal wife' for her own father. The group of 'great royal wives' also included all five of the king's mothers (*mwt nswt, mwt nṯr*) buried in the valley. Of the two women who were not identified as 'great royal wife' in their tomb texts, both were king's daughters, and one, Ta-Nedjemy (QV 33), was, unusually, both a king's daughter and a king's secondary wife (*ḥmt nswt*) (Leblanc 1980, 45 and n. 17; Desroches-Noblecourt 1982, 228, 231). Therefore, only one of the tombs in the valley was intended for a 'princess' who was not also a king's wife. This strongly suggests that bearing the title *ḥmt nswt wrt* was an important criterion for being interred in the Valley of the Queens during the Ramesside period.

The tombs fall into three groups according to their topographical location in the valley -the south flank, the north flank, and the west flank. The tombs within each topographical cluster are not only linked by proximity, but also exhibit marked similarity to each other in plan (Leblanc 1989a, 240–245) and in decoration. Furthermore, the tombs within each cluster appear to be roughly contemporary, and the clusters developed sequentially – with the south cluster created first, the north group second, and the west tombs cut last.

The tombs on the south flank (QV 31, 33, 36, 38, 40), have been dated to the earliest part of the 19th Dynasty – the reigns of Ramesses I and Seti I (Leblanc 1984–1985, 52, n.1, fig. 1) – although one, QV 40, has a more complex plan and decorative program than the others and may belong to the reign of Ramesses II. All of the tombs on the northern flank of the valley (QV 60, 66, 68, 71, 73, 74, 75, 80) were cut and decorated during the long reign of Ramesses II. These tombs belonged to three generations of royal women related to Ramesses II by blood, marriage, or both – such as his mother, Tuy (QV 80); his most prominent great royal wife, Nefertari (QV 66); and his daughter-wives, including Merytamun (QV 68), Nebettawy (QV 60), and Bint-Anath (QV 71). QV 74, however, was later usurped by Duatentipet, the probable wife of Ramesses IV and mother of Ramesses V (Leblanc 1989a, 239, n. 26; Leblanc and Abdel-Rahman 1991, 164–169; Peden 1994, 6; Kitchen 1972, 189), and the identity of the tomb's first (or originally intended) owner is not known.

The last-built in the series of Ramesside royal women's tombs, which were cut and decorated for two 20th Dynasty queens, are located on the west flank of the valley. One tomb, QV 51, belongs to Isis, the wife of Ramesses III and mother of Ramesses VI (Soliman and Tosi 1996, 213–214, 224, n. 6; Peden 1994, 1–2, 4–5; Kitchen 1972, 189–190; Černy 1958, 31–37). The second, QV 52, was the burial place of Tyti, a queen who held the titles, 'great royal wife', 'king's daughter', 'king's mother', and 'king's sister' (*snt nswt*). Although she is sometimes identified as a wife (or daughter-wife) of Ramesses III (Grist 1985, 79–81), other scholars have placed Tyti in the late 20th Dynasty (Kitchen 1984, 131–132; Dodson 1987, 227–229).

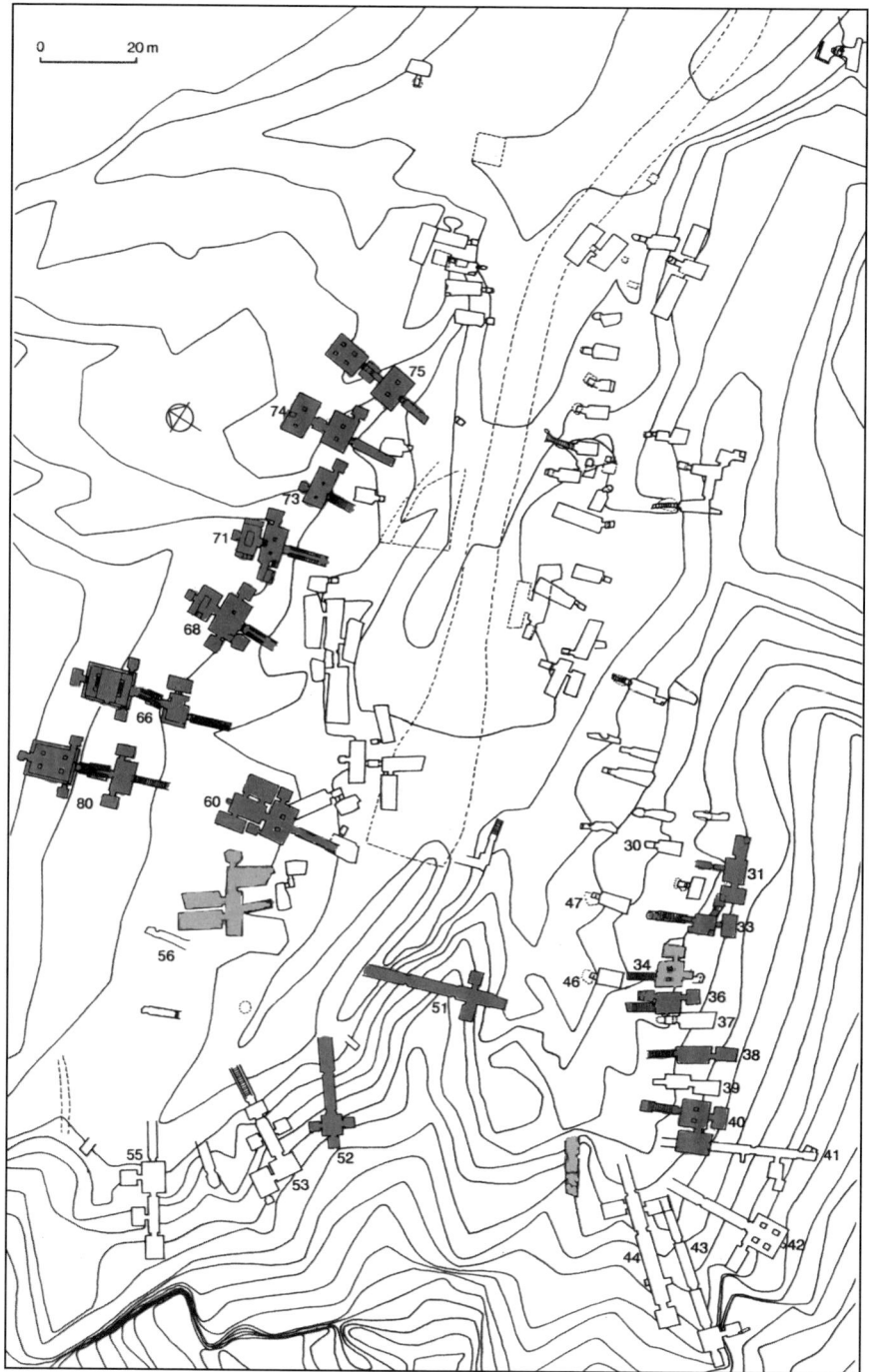

Figure 2. Map of the Valley of the Queens with all eighteen tombs attributed to Ramesside royal women shaded. The fifteen tombs discussed in this study are rendered dark grey (adapted from Willeitner 1994a, 88, Abb. 121).

III. Methodology

The basis of my current research was an examination, primarily, of the afore-mentioned fifteen Ramesside queens' tombs in the Valley of the Queens and, secondarily, of selected tombs of contemporary kings and princes in the Valley of the Kings and Valley of the Queens during two field research seasons in 2003 and 2004. A first-hand examination of these tombs was necessary due to a lack of published material. Most of the Ramesside royal women's tombs, with the exception of the tomb (QV 66) of Nefertari (Goedicke and Thausing 1971), have not been fully published according to modern scholarly standards. Moreover, even when tombs are published, certain aspects of their architecture and decoration are not adequately conveyed through photographs and verbal descriptions – such as the true color values of painted scenes and the relationship of the decorative schemes to the architecture – elements that help reconstruct the intended design of the tomb as a cosmographic representation of the deceased's 'netherworld landscape' and its full visual impact upon the viewer.

The secondary objective of my field research was the study of the decorative programs and architecture of selected tombs belonging to Ramesside royal males – kings and princes – and the late 19th Dynasty female pharaoh Tawosret (an 'honorary male') in order to establish a basis for comparison with the queens' tombs and to more fully define the relationship of status and gender to the architectural form and decoration of the tombs of Ramesside royal women.

IV. Tomb Cosmography, Rebirth and Regeneration, Queenship

The rationale for analyzing the decoration and architecture of the Ramesside royal women's tombs is to explore three interrelated issues, which are: (a) The function of the tomb as a document of the netherworld cosmography assigned to royal women and the impact of relative status and gender upon the content of the decorative programs, the architectural form, and layout of this 'document'; (b) the way royal women were believed to experience rebirth and regeneration in the afterlife; and (c) what these two issues may communicate about the ideological role and status of queenship and queens during the Ramesside Period.

(a) Netherworld Cosmography

The tomb functions as both a three-dimensional 'map' and embodiment of the netherworld landscape experienced by the deceased individual, in which different architectural components in the tomb evoke different areas or aspects of the netherworld. These associations are reinforced (with varying degrees of explicitness) by the decorative programs. The map provided by the tomb was tailored to the needs of the deceased so that it could perform its essential function as an aid to the tomb owner's regeneration. This netherworld cosmography varied from queen's tomb to queen's tomb – no two Ramesside royal women's tombs are identical in plan or decoration, but there are significant architectural similarities among these tombs. In addition, there are overarching themes expressed by texts and pictorial scenes that are consistent enough to allow us to identify what is characteristic of a queen's tomb and to distinguish a queen's tomb from that of another type of royal individual such as a king or a prince. Therefore, each type of royal individual – royal woman, king, and prince – possessed a distinctive type of tomb in terms of both architecture and decorative program content. Consequently, the vision of the netherworld for each type of royal individual was different and was tailored to that royal person's role, rank, and gender.

For example, kings are the only royal individuals whose tomb decoration depicts the perilous journey of the solar deity through the netherworld. The representations of this journey in the kings' tombs are taken directly from netherworld books such as the *Litany of Re*, the *Amduat* and the *Book of Gates*. The first text, which became the standard decoration for the first two corridors of king's tombs throughout most of the Ramesside Period (Hornung 1990b, 209–210; 1999, 136), associates the sun-god, Re, with Osiris (Hornung 1999, 138–144). It includes a passage in which the king identifies himself with the *ba*-souls of both Re and Osiris (Hornung 1990b, 87–88; 1999, 143–144) and lists the sun-god's numerous forms (Hornung 1999, 138–140). The *Amduat* and *Book of Gates* are each divided into twelve sections illustrating the events that occur during each hour of the sun's nocturnal, netherworld journey. These two texts decorate a substantial portion of the rest of the tomb (Hornung 1990b, 208–210).

This journey is given an appropriate presentation in the series of long corridors (Figure 3), architectural elements that function as passages and can be envisioned as concrete representations of dynamic, directed movement (Hornung 1991, 14; 1990b 75). The kings' tombs thus combine architectural elements that stress highly directed movement with scenes and texts that reinforce the sun-god's (and by association, the deceased king's) temporal and spatial progression through the netherworld (Hornung 1990b, 72).

The queens' tombs, by contrast, have more abbreviated plans (Leblanc 1989a, 239; Badawy 1968, 407) than do the vast, corridor-filled kings' tombs, and they evoke a more static and placid picture of the netherworld by means of architecture and decoration than the kings' tombs do. Not all queens' tombs possess internal corridors and those that do have only one that links the antechamber to the sarcophagus chamber (in the 19th Dynasty) or functions as an antechamber (in the 20th Dynasty). These corridors are, however, considerably shorter than those in kings'

Figure 3. *Tomb of Merenptah (KV 8). View into tomb from second internal corridor (photograph by H. L. McCarthy).*

tombs. Therefore, the architectural feature that embodies dynamic movement in kings' tombs is either absent from the tombs of royal women or truncated. The queens' tombs thus principally consist of square or rectangular chambers that represent specific regions or aspects of the netherworld – associations further reinforced in the decorative programs, which depict *Book of the Dead* vignettes and scenes of the queen interacting with deities.

Furthermore, the decorative programs in queens' tombs have no pictorial representations of the sun god's journey or any of its attendant perils, and there are no violent images of mutilated enemies undergoing a 'second death' in the netherworld (Figure 4), such as those found in the tombs of pharaohs (Hornung 1990b, 149–164). The inclusion of these supernatural hazards in kings' tombs and their omission from queens' tombs is a clear example of how decoration was tailored to the role of the deceased royal tomb owner. To wit, the presence or absence of these scenes parallels the fundamental difference between the highly active role of the pharaoh, whose responsibilities (ideal and actual) entailed the exercise of coercive, aggressive force in battling the various manifestations of chaos, and the more pacific, supportive functions of royal women. The queens'

Figure 4*. Naked, bound, decapitated male enemy. From the tomb of Ramesses IV (KV 2) (photograph by H. L. McCarthy).*

most important roles were as protectors (Troy 1986, 64) and supporters of the male aspect of kingship, performers of religious ritual, and agents for the sexual arousal and generative potential of the kings (Robins 1993, 41) and male deities (Troy 1986, 97–99; Robins 1995, 64). A concise pictorial demonstration of this gender-based royal role division is provided by a type of emblematic smiting scene sometimes found in Ramesside god's temples, wherein the king, his body shown in mid-stride, prepares to execute a foreign prisoner while the queen stands behind him and raises one hand in a protective gesture (Figure 5).

The tombs of queens and royal sons exhibit some affinities, in terms of decorative program content (Abitz 1986, 83, 89–92, 97–100, Abb. 27, 29) and architectural plan, but the differences between the tombs of royal women and princes are far more significant than the similarities. While the tombs of both types of royal individuals are decorated with scenes of the deceased among the gods and with *Book of the Dead* vignettes, the repertoire of *Book of the Dead* scenes in queens' tombs is greater than that employed in the tombs of the princes, many of which are decorated with *Book of the Dead* vignettes selected from chapter 145–146 alone (Hassanein and Nelson 1976, preface VII–VIII, 6, 10, 12–13, 15, pls. 1, 33–39; Hassanein *et al.* 1997, 85–87,

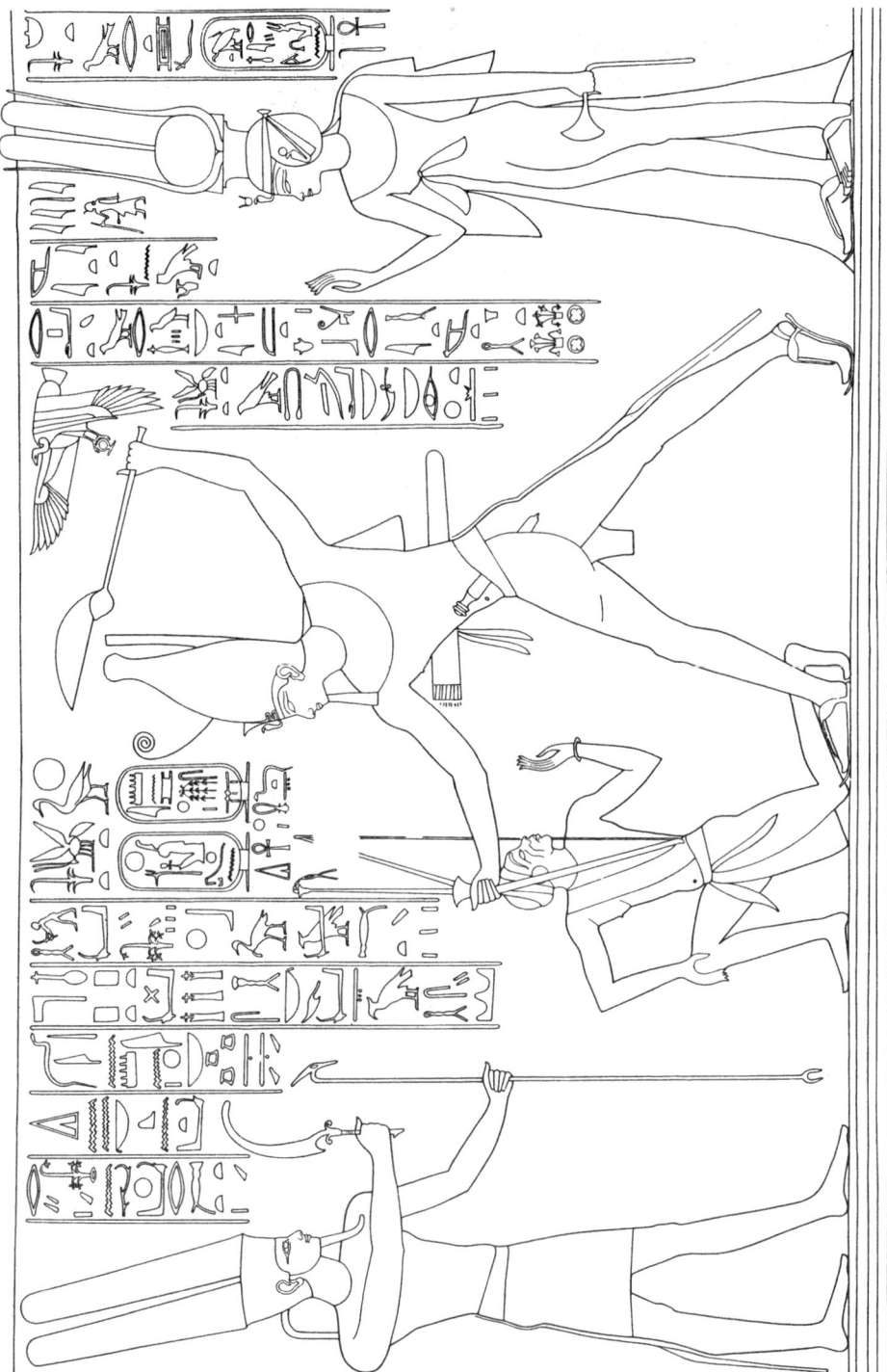

Figure 5. *Emblematic smiting scene from the Small Temple at Abu Simbel dedicated to Nefertari and Hathor of Ibshek (after Desroches-Noblecourt and Kuentz 1968, vol. 2, pl. 33).*

Figure 6. Nefertari and Anubis from the sarcophagus chamber of Nefertari's tomb (QV 66) (photograph © the J. Paul Getty Trust, [1990]. All rights reserved).

pls. 57–66; Abitz 1986, 12–13, 16–17, 19, 24–28, 77–80, Abb. 2–3, 5–6). Most importantly, royal women exhibit complete autonomy within the netherworld landscape of their tombs, where they always interact directly with the gods and the pharaoh is absent (Figure 6).

By contrast, the preserved decorative programs in tombs belonging to the sons of Ramesses II and Ramesses III convey the conceptual dependency of the deceased prince upon the king for his afterlife existence. Most of the princes' tomb scenes not only show the pharaoh acting as an intermediary between the royal sons and the gods of the netherworld (Brock 2000, figs. 45–49, 56, 60, 61a-c, 62, 69b; Abitz 1986, 13, 19, 23, 27, 31, 35, 42, 48, 65, Abb. 2–4, 6, 8–9, 11–12, 19; Hassanein and Nelson 1976, pls. 2, 11–12, 16–19, 22, 25, 33–37; Hassanein *et al.* 1997, pls. 23–24, 29, 31, 57–58, 62–65) (Figure 7), but in some cases depict a form of Osiris that fuses this god with the living king (Abitz 1986, 51–60, Abb. 14–15, 18; Hassanein *et al.* 1997, pls. 42, 75–76; Weeks 2000, 36–37, fig. 29c). The notion of the princes' dependency upon their fathers is further intensified by the depiction of the royal sons as children – despite evidence that some of these princes were middle-aged at death (Weeks 2000, 19–21).

In the late 20th Dynasty tomb (KV 19) of Prince Montuhirkhopshef in the Valley of the Kings, the notion of filial dependency is conveyed with more subtlety. Although the prince is

Figure 7. *Ramesses III (center), followed by his son, Sethhirkhopshef (left), greeting Anubis (right). From the first internal corridor of the tomb of Prince Sethhirkhopshef (QV 43) (photograph by H. L. McCarthy).*

(uniquely) depicted as an adult male who interacts with the gods directly, there is one scene in which the god Thoth wears a belt emblazoned with the prenomen of the prince's father, Ramesses IX (Ayrton 1908, 27, 29), thus suggesting that the deities in the tomb are identified with the living king as in the earlier princes' tombs.

The rules of decorum governing the location of Ramesside princes' tombs appear to have been less restrictive than were those determining the location of contemporary royal women's tombs. The reason for this may have been that wherever Ramesside royal sons were interred, whether in the Valley of the Kings or the Valley of the Queens, their conceptual proximity to the king (a concern not shared by Ramesside queens) was guaranteed by the ubiquity of images of the king in the decorative programs of the princes' tombs, if not by burial near their fathers' tombs in the kings' necropolis.

The plans of the archaeologically-known princes' tombs vary considerably. There is no 'standard plan' – even among those in the Valley of the Queens, which were all probably completed during the first decade of Ramesses III's reign (Kitchen 1982, 118–119). KV 5, cut for the sons of Ramesses II in the early 19th Dynasty, is not architecturally comparable to any other royal tomb. The plans of 20th Dynasty Ramesside princes' tombs (KV 3, KV 19, QV 42, QV 43, QV 44, QV 53, and QV 55), however, frequently strike a middle ground between kings' tombs and queens' tombs, sometimes combining features belonging to both. In general, princes' tombs are smaller, shorter, and less architecturally complex than kings' tombs, but sometimes have more and longer corridors than do queens' tombs.

(b) Afterlife Experience of Ramesside Royal Women
The afterlife experience of royal women, like that of kings, was structured by two highly complex, parallel, and interwoven mythic paradigms. The first paradigm was that of the solar deity who travelled through the sky during the day and entered and traversed the dangerous realm

of the netherworld at night – overcoming numerous supernatural obstacles in the process. The end result of his perilous nightly journey was his renewal and rebirth every morning at dawn (Hornung 1990a, 181). The cyclical journey that characterizes the solar mode of regeneration also had a parallel and interrelated sexual component wherein the sun god was reborn via intercourse with a goddess who had a tripartite, multigenerational aspect (Troy 1986, 25–30; Robins 1993, 17). This goddess was the solar deity's daughter, consort, and, ultimately, the mother of the sun god's renewed and regenerated aspect (Troy 1986, 27; Robins 1993, 17, 41; Hornung 1990b, 78, 89).

The second mythic paradigm was that of the god Osiris, who dwelt permanently in the depths of the netherworld and ruled over the realm of the dead and its inhabitants. Osiris awaited nightly rebirth and renewal achieved through a temporary union with the solar deity. In Egyptian funerary belief, Osiris and the sun god are united for a brief, but critical, moment in the midst of the netherworld (Hornung 1990a, 155–156; Hornung 1990b, 88, 121). They experience a transitory symbiotic relationship, in which each god absorbs the unique regenerative power of the other – effectively revitalizing both deities' capacity for rebirth and renewal. This unified form of the two gods is frequently depicted in art as the ram-headed and mummiform Re-Osiris (Figure 8).

Figure 8. Re-Osiris, from the upper east lateral chamber of Nefertari's tomb (QV 66) (photograph © the J. Paul Getty Trust, [1992]. All rights reserved).

The postmortem regeneration of the dead queen involved her identification with both Osiris and the solar deity – notions that are explicitly stated by texts on the walls of her tomb (*e.g.* Goedicke and Thausing 1971, pls. 35–36, 38, 41–42, 44, 46–48, 52–53, 59). The queen's identification with these two gods and her ability to partake of their respective modes of regeneration necessitated her assumption of a fluid postmortem sexual identity that included a temporary masculine aspect (Roth 2000, 199–200; McCarthy 2002, 190–195). In the decorative programs of the Ramesside royal women's tombs the queen's postmortem gender fluidity is conveyed both in writing and pictorially. In some of the tomb wall texts, such as *Book of the Dead* chapter 17 from the west half of the antechamber of Nefertari's tomb, masculine grammatical gender is used to refer to the queen (Goedicke and Thausing 1971, 39, n. 50).

Pictorially, this same notion is ex-

Figure 9. *Scene from the sarcophagus chamber of Nefertari (QV 66). Nefertari (far right) adoring the four sons of Horus (second from right) and three enthroned deities: Osiris (center), Hathor (second from left), and Anubis (far left). Nefertari, Anubis, and two sons of Horus have "masculine" red-brown skin, while the goddess Hathor is depicted with "feminine" yellow flesh. Osiris and two sons of Horus are shown with the green skin color characteristic of chthonic deities (photograph © the J. Paul Getty Trust, [1992]. All rights reserved).*

pressed by painting the otherwise feminine-looking images of Ramesside royal women with skin tones usually reserved for male figures – red-brown and orange-brown flesh tones – in contrast to the canonical 'feminine' yellow skin tones that are consistently employed in images of goddesses throughout these same queens' tombs (McCarthy 2002, 191–193) (Figure 9).

The deliberate omission of kings' images from all of the royal women's tombs (Hornung 1990b, 187; McCarthy 2002, 175) and, with the exception of Isis's tomb (where Ramesses VI's cartouches appear on the jambs of the sarcophagus chamber doorway) (Soliman and Tosi 1996, 222), the omission of kings' names, appears to be a rule of decorum (Roth 1999, 45–53) that was developed to protect each queen's postmortem gender fluidity, her identification with Osiris and the solar deity, and her assumption of the two gods' regenerative modes (McCarthy 2002, 176, 193–195). The king's presence in a royal woman's tomb would have hindered that queen's capacity for regeneration and renewal because the pharaoh, by virtue of his male sex and his position as the highest-ranking royal individual, was more appropriately identified with Osiris and Re than was the queen, who as the feminine (and subordinate) aspect of kingship was identified with the goddess Hathor (Troy 1986, 3, 53–72). Moreover, the dyadic relationship of the king and queen, when they are shown together on monuments, necessitates the placement of the royal woman in a secondary, subordinate position *vis-à-vis* the king (Robins 1994, 33,

36–37; 1995, 13, 19; McCarthy 2002, 188–190) and locks her in to an unambiguously female role. Thus, if the king were present in the queen's tomb, this would force the royal woman into the specific subordinate position that reinforces her ideological role (in life) as the king's complementary (and female) opposite – a role that impedes her ability to assume the gender fluidity she needed to identify with Osiris and Re and to regenerate.

The rule of decorum necessitating the absence of the king in Ramesside queens' tombs stands in sharp contrast to that governing the role of the king in the decorative programs of contemporary princes' tombs. While queens are necessarily drawn in complementary opposition to the king by virtue of their sex and roles, the princes, who were male and served as potential heirs of the reigning king, can be envisioned as the younger half of the generational duality of the masculine aspect of kingship. Thus the divine paradigm of the father-son generational continuum (Troy 1986, 27–28) exemplified by Osiris and Horus, Ptah and Nefertum, Amun and Khonsu, or Atum and Re-Horakhty underscores masculine kingship. Furthermore, this paradigm not only structures the relationship between the king and his heir in life, but also determines the relationship between the king and any of his deceased sons (who serve as 'notional' rather than 'actual' heirs to the throne) in the netherworld landscape of the princes' tombs (Abitz 1986, 63–67). Furthermore, while deceased Ramesside queens need conceptual distance from their king in order to undergo the process of regeneration, nearly all of the Ramesside princes need to be identified with the person of the king in order to embark upon his successful afterlife journey.

(c) Changes in Role, Mythic Paradigms and Status

The creation of elaborately decorated, individual royal women's tombs and their situation in a discrete necropolis are mortuary developments that coincide with certain substantial changes in Ramesside royal women's roles and titles outside the funerary sphere. Examples of these changes include the reinstatement of the title 'god's wife' for royal women at the beginning of the 19th Dynasty after a lapse of almost a century (Robins 1983, 68, fig. 5.1, n.2, 71, 76) and the Ramesside application of the title *wrt ḫnr*, which designated the leader of a special musical group that performed during cult activities, to royal women – demonstrating a complete convergence of the roles of queen and priestess (Troy 1986, 76, 86, 180, 186–187).

Furthermore, Troy demonstrates that Ramesside texts such as the ancient Egyptian Onomastica provide evidence of a mythologization of the role of queenship and a consequent elevation of its properties (Troy 1986, 68, 70–71). Troy suggests that the role of divine queenship materializes during the later 18th and early 19th Dynasties "as a[n] independent expression of the [divine] feminine prototype" (Troy 1986, 68). Thus, the notion of deified queenship emerges as an entity unto itself – taking its place alongside goddesses such as Hathor or Isis. The notion of a mythologized conception of Ramesside queenship is also made manifest in the frequent employment of the queens' title *mwt-nṯr*, which was first used in the late 18th Dynasty and emphasized the royal woman's role as mother of the divine child (Troy 1986, 75) (and, not coincidentally, was an epithet commonly used for the goddess Isis in the New Kingdom).

In two and three-dimensional art, the divinization of queenship is expressed by the way Ramesside royal women and goddesses share iconographic attributes that had been principally associated either with one or the other. For example, queens adopt the iconography of Hathor (Troy 1986, 70), and the goddess Isis, by the reign of Seti I, is sometimes shown wearing the uraei, double-plumes, and vulture headdress of queenship (Troy 1986, 70; Calverley and Gardiner 1933, pls. 17–20, 22–23). In one scene from the tomb (QV 60) of Nebettawy, the goddess Selket is depicted with the flat-topped 'platform' crown regularly worn by Ramesside queens

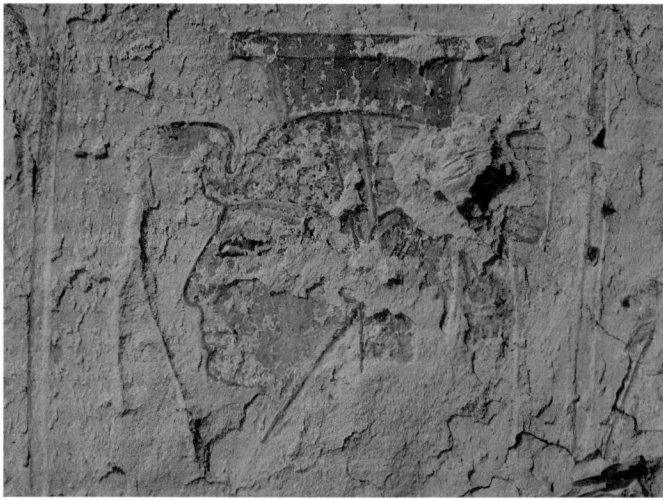

Figure 10. *The goddess Selket wearing the queenly platform crown from the tomb (QV 60) of Nebettawy, a daughter-wife of Ramesses II (photograph by H. L. McCarthy).*

instead of her usual scorpion emblem (Figure 10). Furthermore, as elements of queenly regalia changed during the Ramesside period, contemporary representations of goddesses reflect these changes. This is demonstrated by a depiction of Meretseger from the tomb (QV 43) of Prince Sethhirkhopshef, which shows the goddess wearing a 'platform' crown surmounted by divine figures (Figure 11), a headdress worn by late-19th Dynasty and 20th Dynasty queens.

Although Troy does not offer an explanation for the mythologization of queenship and its effects, it seems entirely plausible that a shift in the estimation of the role of queenship was part of a larger re-organization, re-evaluation, and re-establishment of traditional Egyptian religion and notions of kingship produced in response to the revolutionary theological and ideological changes wrought by Akhenaten during the Amarna period. The Amarna period, although brief, created a cultural and ideological rift of sufficient power to trigger a Ramesside 'classicism' – exemplified by Seti I's presentation of his rule as a 'renaissance' – a notion imbued with an implicit, self-conscious awareness of a breach in tradition that needed to be closed (Assmann 2002, 272–274).

The Amarna period transformation of the roles of king and queen (and the mythic paradigms that underscored these roles) appears to have been among the ideas that motivated a Ramesside counter-reaction. During the reign of Akhenaten, the divine dyad of Shu and Tefnut was given special

Figure 11. *The goddess Meretseger depicted with a type of headdress worn by late-19th and 20th Dynasty queens (a "platform" crown surmounted by a vulture protecting a rearing cobra). From the sarcophagus chamber of Prince Sethhirkhopshef (QV 43) (photograph by H. L. McCarthy).*

prominence as a mythic paradigm underpinning kingship (Fecht 1960, 105ff; Troy 1986, 21, 136–137); accordingly, the previously well-defined distinction between the 'masculine' and 'feminine' halves of kingship embodied in the royal couple was de-emphasized in order to highlight the equivalency of the roles of Akhenaten and Nefertiti (Troy 1986, 137). The limestone relief in the Museum of Fine Arts, Boston (64.521, 63.260) showing Nefertiti on a royal barge smiting a female enemy illustrates this notion, because the queen is performing an act that was previously the sole prerogative of the pharaoh – thus illustrating a greater permeability between the gendered halves of kingship. The Ramesside response to the Amarna revision of these roles appears to have been to return to an even more acute gender role division between king and queen outside the funerary realm.

It is not entirely clear whether the ideological enhancements to Ramesside royal women's roles translated into a real increase in status, authority, and wealth for the individual women who held these titles. It has been argued, for example, that 18th Dynasty queens, especially those who were also 'god's wives', possessed a high degree of power and wealth (independent of the king) that is not attested for queens of the Ramesside period and that the divinization of queenship, though resulting in the elevation of the role, also led to a higher degree of depersonalization and interchangeability among the royal women as they became absorbed into their divine identities (Troy, personal communication).

The mortuary evidence, however, strongly suggests that there was a greater expenditure of effort for the burials of Ramesside royal women than for those of earlier New Kingdom queens, since the Ramesside queens' tombs were conceived as complex fusions of architecture and pictorial art that created an individual netherworld landscape for each woman. The creation of these tombs entailed the design of a new corpus of tomb scenes, the selection of texts, and their programmatic layout on the tombs wall – all of which were specific to the Ramesside royal women's tombs. Furthermore, the notion that the Ramessides chose to express the divine feminine element through the image of individual, named, royal women does not appear to lead inexorably to de-personalization. While there is a depiction of an unnamed, 'generic' *ḥmt nswt wrt* in the mortuary temple of Ramesses III at Medinet Habu (Epigraphic Survey 1940, pls. 205, 207; Troy 1986, 95), there are also examples of Ramesside monuments where the identities and roles of individual women appear to be of great significance, and particular women were chosen for special commemoration and cult at places such as the Small Temple of Nefertari at Abu Simbel (Desroches-Noblecourt and Kuentz 1968) and the temple dedicated to Tuy and Nefertari on the north side of the Ramesseum (Desroches-Noblecourt 1982, 239–243; Willeitner 1994b, 80–83).

V. Conclusion

The sudden introduction of large, decorated tombs for individual, high ranking royal women in a discrete necropolis at the beginning of the 19th Dynasty is a complex phenomenon that indicates significant changes in funerary beliefs vis-à-vis Ramesside queens. To wit, each royal woman's tomb, for the first time, served as a unique document of her identity, the process of her postmortem regeneration, and her netherworld landscape by: (i) reflecting her identity as an individual and as executor of the queenly role through the writing of her name and titles, the employment of a distinctive iconography of queenship in her pictorial images, and the depiction of her sacerdotal role through scenes of offering to the gods and/or being in their presence and partaking of offerings; (ii) identifying the deceased queen with Osiris and Re, the paradigmatic male deities of linear and cyclical modes of time and regeneration, a process that required the queen's assumption of a postmortem gender fluidity; and (iii) serving as a pictorial representation and embodiment of a netherworld landscape specific to queens that depicts different regions of the netherworld and the inward and outward movement of the deceased while excluding representations of activities that belong to the realm of the male kingly role.

These changes coincide with conspicuous enhancements to the ideological role of queens (outside the funerary sphere) manifested in new queenly titles and iconography. All of these changes appear to have been underscored by a Ramesside shift in mythic paradigms that produced a heightened polarization of the gendered halves of kingship, an intensified interest in portraying the royal women as a multigenerational feminine collective (a principle that may have informed the selection of women buried in the Valley of the Queens), and a new emphasis on the father-son dynamic of the masculine half of kingship.

The increase in the complexity of mortuary arrangements and the elevation of the queenly role through divinization can be interpreted in diverse ways – either as evidence that status and power held by Ramesside royal women was greater or lesser than that possessed by 18th Dynasty queens. The picture, however, was probably more complex, with selected women in the 18th Dynasty and the Ramesside period holding significant power, but with changes in the expression of status.

Institute of Fine Arts at New York University

References

Abitz, F. 1986, *Ramses III. In Den Gräbern Seiner Söhne*. Orbis Biblicus et Orientalis 72. Universitätsverlag Freiburg Schweiz and Vandenhoeck & Ruprecht, Freiburg and Göttingen.

Assmann, J. 2002, *The Mind of Egypt: History and Meaning in the Time of the Pharaohs* (trans. A. Jenkins). Metropolitan Books, New York.

Ayrton, E. R. 1908, The Tomb of Mentuherkhepshef. (No. 19), in T. M. Davis, G. Maspero, E. Ayrton, G. Daressy and E. H. Jones, *The Tomb of Siptah: The Monkey Tomb and the Gold Tomb*, 20–29. Archibald Constable and Co., Ltd., London.

Badawy, A. 1968, *A History of Egyptian Architecture: The Empire (The New Kingdom) From the Eighteenth Dynasty to the End of the Twentieth Dynasty 1580–1085 B.C. Volume 3*. University of California Press, Berkeley and Los Angeles.

Brock, E. C. 2000, Wall Decoration, in K. R. Weeks (ed.), *KV 5: A Preliminary Report on the Excavation of the Tomb of the Sons of Ramesses II in the Valley of the Kings*, 55–94. The American University in Cairo Press, Cairo and New York.

Calverley, A. and Gardiner, A. H. 1933, *The Temple of Sethos I at Abydos. Volume I: The Chapels of Osiris, Isis and Horus*. Egypt Exploration Society and University of Chicago Press, London and Chicago.

Carter, H. 1916, A Tomb Prepared for Queen Hatshepsuit Discovered by the Earl of Carnarvon (October 1916), *Annales du Service des Antiquités de l'Égypte* 16, 179–182.

Carter, H. 1917, A Tomb Prepared for Queen Hatshepsuit and Other Recent Discoveries at Thebes, *Journal of Egyptian Archaeology* 4, 107–118.

Černy, J. 1958, Queen Ese of the Twentieth Dynasty and Her Mother, *Journal of Egyptian Archaeology* 44, 31–37.

Desroches-Noblecourt, C. 1982, Touy, Mère De Ramsès II, La Reine Tanedjmy et Les Reliques de L'Expérience Amarnienne in *Colloques Internationaux du C.N.R.S.*

No. 595—L'Égyptologie En 1979. Axes prioritaires de recherches. Volume II, 227–243. Editions Centre National de la Recherché Scientifique, Paris.

Desroches-Noblecourt, C. and Kuentz, C. 1968, *Le Petit Temple d'Abou Simbel*. Volumes 1.2. Centre de Documentation et d' Etude sur l'ancienne Egypte, Cairo.

Dodson, A. 1987, The Takhats and Some Other Royal Ladies of the Ramesside Period, *Journal of Egyptian Archaeology* 73, 224–229.

Epigraphic Survey. 1940, *Festival Scenes of Ramesses III. Medinet Habu. Volume IV*. Oriental Institute Publication, Volume 51. University of Chicago Press, Chicago.

Fecht, G. 1960, Amarna-Probleme (1–2), *Zeitschrift für ägyptische Sprache und Altertumskunde* 85, 83–118.

Giddy, L. 2002, Digging Diary 2001–2002, *Egyptian Archaeology* 21, 27–32.

Goedicke, H. and von Thausing, G. 1971, *Nofretari: Eine Dokumentation der Wandgemälde ihres Grabes*. Akademische Druck-u Verlagsanstalt, Graz.

Grist, J. 1985, The Identity of the Ramesside Queen Tyti, *Journal of Egyptian Archaeology* 71, 71–81.

Hassanein, F. and Nelson, M. 1976, *La Tombe du Prince Amon-(Her)-Khepchef*. Centre de Documentation et d'Étude sur l'ancienne Égypte, Cairo.

Hassanein, F., Nelson, M. and Lecuyot, G. 1997, *La Tombe du Prince Khaemouaset [VdR n° 44]*. Centre de Documentation et d'Étude sur l'ancienne Égypte, Cairo.

Hayes, W. C. 1990, *The Scepter of Egypt II. The Hyksos Period and the New Kingdom (1675–1080 B.C.)*. Fourth Edition (revised). Metropolitan Museum of Art, New York.

Hornung, E. 1990a, *Conceptions of God in Ancient Egypt: The One and the Many*, (trans. J. Baines). Cornell University Press, Ithaca.

Hornung, E. 1990b, *Valley of the Kings: Horizon of Eternity* (trans. D. Warburton). Timken Publishers, New York.

Hornung, E. 1991, *The Tomb of Pharaoh Seti I/Das Grab Sethos I*. Artemis Verlag, Zurich and Munich.

Hornung, E. 1999, *The Ancient Egyptian Books of the Afterlife* (trans. D. Lorton). Cornell University Press, Ithaca and London.

Kitchen, K. 1972, Ramesses VII and the Twentieth Dynasty, *Journal of Egyptian Archaeology* 58, 182–194.

Kitchen, K. 1982, The Twentieth Dynasty Revisited, *Journal of Egyptian Archaeology* 68, 116–125.

Kitchen, K. 1984, Family Relationships of Ramesses IX and the Late Twentieth Dynasty, *Studien zur altägyptischen Kultur* 11, 127–132.

Leblanc, C. 1980, Le dégagement de la Tombe de Ta-nedjemy: Une Contribution à l'histoire de la Vallée des Reines, *Bulletin de la Société française d'égyptologie* 89, 32–49.

Leblanc, C. 1984–1985, Les Tombes No 58 [Anonyme] et No 60 [Nebet-Taouy] de la Vallée des Reines: Achèvement des Dégagements et Conclusions, *Annales du Service des Antiquités de l'Égypte* 70, 51–68.

Leblanc, C. 1989a, Architecture et Évolution Chronologique des Tombes de la Vallée des Reines, *Bulletin de l'Institut française d'archéologie orientale* 89, 227–247.

Leblanc, C. 1989b, *Ta Set Neferou: Une Nécropole de Thebes-Ouest et Son Histoire*. Vol. 1. Nubar Printing House, Cairo.

Leblanc, C. and Abdel-Rahman, I. 1991, Remarques Relatives à La Tombe de la Reine Douatentipet, *Revue d'Égyptologie* 42, 147–169.

Lilyquist, C. 2003, *The Tomb of Three Foreign Wives of Tuthmosis III*. Yale University Press, New Haven and London.

McCarthy, H. L. 2002, The Osiris Nefertari: A Case Study of Decorum, Gender, and Regeneration, *Journal of the American Research Center in Egypt* 39, 173–195.

Peden, A. J. 1994, *The Reign of Ramesses IV*. Aris and Phillips Ltd., Warminster.

Reeves, C. N. 1990, *Valley of the Kings: The Decline of a Royal Necropolis*. Kegan Paul International, London and New York.

Reeves, C. N. 2003, On some queens' tombs of the Eighteenth Dynasty, in N. Strudwick and J. H. Taylor (eds.), *The Theban Necropolis: Past, Present and Future*, 69–73. British Museum Press, London.

Robins, G. 1983, The God's Wife of Amun in the Eighteenth Dynasty in Egypt, in A. Cameron and A. Kuhrt (eds.), *Images of Women in Antiquity*, 65–68. Billings and Sons, Worcester.

Robins, G. 1993, *Women in Ancient Egypt*. Harvard University Press, Cambridge, Massachusetts.

Robins, G. 1994, Some Principles of Compositional Dominance and Gender Hierarchy in Egyptian Art, *Journal of the American Research Center in Egypt* 31, 33–40.

Robins, G. 1995, *Reflections of Women in the New Kingdom: Ancient Egyptian Art from the British Museum*. Van Siclen Books, San Antonio.

Romer, J. 1976, Royal Tombs of the Early Eighteenth Dynasty, *Mitteilungen des Deutschen Archäologischen Instituts Abteilung Kairo* 32, 191–206.

Roth, A. M. 1999, The Absent Spouse: Patterns and Taboos in Egyptian Tomb Decoration, *Journal of the American Research Center in Egypt* 36, 37–53.

Roth, A. M. 2000, Father Earth, Mother Sky: Ancient Egyptian Beliefs about Conception and Fertility, in A. E. Rautman (ed.), *Reading the Body: Representations and Remains in the Archaeological Record*. 187–201. University of Pennsylvania Press, Philadelphia.

Soliman, I. M. and Tosi, M. 1996, La Tombe de la Reine Isis [VdR 51], Grande Épouse de Ramsès III *Memnonia* 7, 213–225.

Strudwick, N. and Strudwick, H. 1999, *Thebes in Egypt: A Guide to the Tombs and Temples of Ancient Luxor*. Cornell University Press, Ithaca.

Thomas, E. 1966, *The Royal Necropoleis of Thebes*. N.p., Princeton.

Troy, L. 1986, *Patterns of Queenship in Ancient Egyptian Myth and History*. BOREAS 14. University of Uppsala, Uppsala.

Weeks, K. R. 2000, Archaeological and Architectural Description, in K. R. Weeks (ed.), *KV 5: A Preliminary Report on the Excavation of the Tomb of the Sons of Ramesses II in the Valley of the Kings*, 7–54. American University in Cairo Press, Cairo and New York.

Willeitner, J. 1994a, Das Grab der Nefertari im Tal der Königinnen und seine Wiederentdeckung in H. C. Schmidt and J. Willeitner (eds.), *Nefertari: Gemahlin Rameses' II*, 88–103. Verlag Philipp von Zabern, Mainz.

Willeitner, J. 1994b, Ein weiterer Kultbau für Nefertari? Zur Diskussion um ihren Totentempel in H. C. Schmidt and J. Willeitner (eds.), *Nefertari: Gemahlin Rameses' II*, 80–83. Verlag Philipp von Zabern, Mainz.

Winlock, H. E. 1932, *The Tomb of Queen Meryet-Amun at Thebes*. Metropolitan Museum of Art Egyptian Expedition Publication, Volume 6. Metropolitan Museum of Art, New York.

Winlock, H. E. 1948, *The Treasure of Three Egyptian Princesses*. Metropolitan Museum of Art. Publications of the Department of Egyptian Art, Volume 10. Metropolitan Museum of Art, New York.

Designing Materials for Language Self-Instruction: A Case Study of Middle Egyptian

Anne Morrison

Introduction

Compared to other ancient writing systems, the Egyptian hieroglyphic script generates a substantial level of interest amongst members of the general public. While linguists have paid surprisingly little attention to written Egyptian, Egyptologists have responded to public interest by publishing an array of books about Egyptian writing, language and literature, aimed at both the casual reader and the serious amateur. However, for members of the public who wish to take their interest further, opportunities to learn the reconstructed language of Middle Egyptian, and the associated hieroglyphic script, are limited. Unless learners are eligible for, and interested in, tertiary education, self-instruction may be the only available option.

Although empirical research is limited, all available evidence suggests that self-instruction is a demanding way to learn *any* language. Jones notes that, "Even with the best course package in the world, solo language learning would still operate under certain severe constraints" (1994, 43). It is therefore all the more important to ensure that independent learning materials are pedagogically sound and effective, in order to maximise the chances of learner success.

Using Middle Egyptian as a case study, the current project focuses on the design of self-instructional language learning materials. In this action research project, self-instructed volunteers contribute towards the development of course materials by providing feedback to the researcher during the writing process. This paper investigates existing pedagogical approaches to self-instruction in Middle Egyptian, and suggests an alternative. The action research project, in which the alternative approach is tested on a cohort of 27 adults, is described. Several of the instructional strategies employed in the alternative materials are discussed, and finally, the preliminary outcomes of the project are presented.

Byrd comments that "the work of the [language] materials writer is an interdisciplinary mix" (1995, 6). The project draws on insights from applied linguistics, linguistics and educational psychology, and the new learning materials incorporate strategies that are derived from these fields. In particular, the International Phonetic Alphabet is introduced as a transliteration system, and interlinear translation is exploited as a pedagogical tool.

One of the limitations of action research is that findings cannot always be generalised to other contexts (Wallace 1998, 17). Given the small size of the research cohort, it is not claimed that this group is representative of all learners who may attempt to teach themselves Egyptian or another language. By virtue of their independence from institutions, self-instructed learners of *any* language are difficult to identify, recruit and monitor for research purposes (*cf.* Jones 1998, 382). Nevertheless, although the project focuses on Middle Egyptian as a case study, it is anticipated that some of the research findings may apply to other low-demand languages, for which appropriate learning materials are often scarce (Janus 2000, 28; Walker 1991, 444). Jones argues that, while each limited study of language self-instruction can provide only one small piece in a mosaic, cumulatively, "a larger picture will gradually appear" (1994, 444).

Self-Instructional Pedagogies

The challenge of language self-instruction

Jones defines language self-instruction as "a deliberate long-term learning project instigated, planned, and carried out by the learner alone, without teacher intervention" (1998, 378). Despite their perennial market presence, self-instructional language learning materials have only recently attracted significant applied linguistic scrutiny. Published studies that focus on self-study materials for various target languages, or on the learners using them, include those of Dickinson (1987), Fernández-Toro and Jones (1996), Jones (1993; 1994; 1998), Heafford (1995), Roberts (1995) and Rowsell and Libben (1994).

From these studies, it is possible to glimpse the challenges faced by fully self-instructed language learners. Unless they are able to find suitable study partners, independent learners have no teachers or fellow students to turn to for support, clarification, correction, debate, practice, inspiration and motivation. Typically, learners "flounder around in frustration, making little or no progress" (Rowsell and Libben 1994, 668). At beginners level, language self-instruction is fraught with low success and high attrition (Fernández-Toro and Jones 1996). In his survey of cassette-based learning packages, Roberts (1995) found that materials were often methodologically dated, dull in content, and instead of addressing the needs of solo language learners, tended to mimic classroom instruction minus the classroom. Overall, these studies support Rowsell and Libben's anecdotal observation that:

> "Most people (with the possible exception of those who market teach-yourself learning materials) know that learning in isolation is a poor way to learn a language" (1994, 668).

Jones argues that if "teach-yourself learners have the learning odds stacked against them, good materials are vital to help shorten these odds" (1998, 403).

Conventional approaches to Middle Egyptian self-instruction

In recent years, several new coursebooks for the self-instructed learner of Middle Egyptian have become available. Focusing on those written for English-speakers, the publications fall into two categories: books explicitly designed for self-instruction (*e.g.* Collier and Manley 1998) and those catering simultaneously for classroom and self-instructed learners (Allen 2000; Hoch 1996). Irrespective of their target audiences, these coursebooks are underpinned by a similar methodology, which applied linguists variously refer to as 'the academic style', 'the classical method' or 'grammar-translation'.

Grammar-translation involves the sequential presentation of explicit grammatical rules and vocabulary, which learners then apply to translation exercises. Deriving from the pedagogy of classical Greek and Latin, grammar-translation has been one of the primary strategies for foreign language instruction for over 200 years, and only in recent decades has the approach been challenged. Referring to the pedagogy of modern foreign languages, Klapper observes that:

"Grammar-translation was dealt a serious blow by the findings of second language acquisition [research] which showed that grammatical structures are not acquired in a regular, linear, once-and-for-all fashion, i.e. in the way the traditional grammar textbook presents and seeks to teach them, but in a fairly lengthy and complicated process which bears little resemblance to a steady learning curve" (1997, 24).

The applicability of these findings to the pedagogy of non-contemporary languages, such as classical Greek and Latin, remains the subject of debate (for example, see discussions in LaFleur 1998).

Undeniably, grammar-translation is very successful for some learners. Most applied linguists agree that grammar-translation matches the learning style of two student sub-groups: those who are highly analytical and those who respond to rote learning. However, these groups represent only a small proportion of language learners (Cook 1996, 178). Whereas educators may have sound reasons for targeting particular learner sub-groups in the context of tertiary education, self-instructed learners are likely to have diverse learning orientations, motives, and goals. According to Sadler-Smith (1997), learner uniformity is largely over-estimated in the self-instructional environment, and an approach that caters for a range of learning styles is likely to benefit a wider target audience.

Accommodating alternative learning styles

'Learning style' refers to a person's habitual manner of undertaking learning tasks, and is closely linked to 'cognitive style' (Sadler-Smith 1997, 186). Although specific models vary, cognitive style is often seen as a composite of two independent dimensions: the verbal-imagery dimension, and the holist-analytic dimension. Following the model of Riding and Sadler-Smith (1992), the verbal-imagery dimension relates to the *representation* of information during thinking. Verbalisers generally learn best from verbal (written or oral) presentation, while imagers tend to learn best from pictorial representations (Riding 2001). The holist–analytic dimension relates to information *processing*. Holists approach a learning task in a generalised manner, but with less attention to detail. Analysts tend to proceed one step at a time with less consideration of the overall perspective (Banner and Rayner 2000, 40). Although cognitive style is not related to intelligence (Riding and Pearson 1994), the extremes of these dimensions are associated with both learning strengths and weaknesses.

Riding and Sadler-Smith (1992) have confirmed that a mismatch between instructional materials and cognitive style has significant effects on learning outcome. However, unless consideration is given to learning preferences and cognitive styles, instructional materials tend to reflect the disposition of the designer, and are likely to result in a program lacking in balance, breadth and differentiation (Banner and Rayner 2000, 40).

Unlike adaptive computer-based learning systems in which students can select their preferred learning path, printed self-instructional materials are inherently non-adaptive. Under these circumstances, Sadler-Smith argues that materials should include "a range of activities only some of which [are] congruent with the style or preferences of the individual" (1997, 189). It is expected that individual learners will:

"(a) focus on those elements of the learning materials which most suit their particular style; (b) be encouraged or required to undertake activities which are not congruent with their preferences but which, nevertheless, will lead to a more complete learning experience" (Sadler-Smith, 1997, 191).

In the context of language learning, conventional grammar-translation materials that present language through the sequential introduction of detailed rules are primarily verbal and analytic. Self-instructional courses based solely on this approach are likely benefit the verbal-analysts, to the exclusion of other learner profiles. Consequently, in the project described here, materials are intentionally designed to accommodate a wider range of learning styles than is possible by grammar-translation alone.

The Action Research Project

Project Design

The current project is based on an action research framework that involves collaboration between the researcher and those who will hopefully benefit from the research: independent learners of ancient Egyptian. In an educational environment, action research is orientated towards practical problem solving, and aims to improve or change educational practice through cycles of understanding, evaluation and change (Costello 2003, 5). The process is usually conceptualised as a series of steps:

1. identification or refinement of the research problem
2. data collection, research and reflection
3. change to educational practice
4. monitoring and evaluation of the changes

Action research is frequently, but not always, cyclical in nature, since the process can be repeated as often as necessary in order to adequately address the research problem.

The current study is in progress in an Australian city where there are no opportunities for formal Middle Egyptian instruction, either through tertiary institutions or community-based Further Education organisations. In order to make contact with potential recruits, a leaflet briefly describing the project was distributed via adult education courses that focus on ancient Egyptian culture and history. Adults interested in piloting self-instructional materials for introductory Middle Egyptian were invited to contact the researcher for further information. Recruitment took place over a period of several months. A total of 27 adults volunteered to participate in the project. Participants were able to withdraw from the project at any time.

Upon recruitment, participants completed a questionnaire, designed to yield basic demographic data and other relevant information, such as motives for learning Middle Egyptian and previous language learning experience. Draft chapters of a self-instructional textbook and accompanying workbook were mailed to each participant in instalments. Working independently at their own pace, learners returned completed exercises and a standardised 'feedback' questionnaire at the end of each chapter. At this point, participants could opt to receive further materials, or formally withdraw from the project. The cyclical nature of this process enabled the researcher to: (1) identify problems with the materials; (2) modify the materials where necessary; and (3) test the modifications with learners.

For several reasons, this project does not replicate true self-instruction, even though the materials are studied independently. With full self-instruction, learner progress is not monitored by another individual. Under normal circumstances, self-instructed learners are free to work 'backwards' from the supplied answers to exercises, often a valuable strategy. In the current study, answers are not provided until after the participants have submitted the completed exercises, enabling the researcher to check the appropriateness of the tasks. Furthermore, while fully self-instructed language learners have no teacher to ask for guidance, these participants are invited to, and often do, seek additional assistance from the researcher via the feedback questionnaires. Individual requests for assistance provide further opportunities to identify inadequacies in the materials, enabling the evolving draft to be adjusted and re-tested with learners until problems are overcome as far as possible.

Despite the potential for interaction with the researcher, these participants nevertheless consider themselves to be self-instructed. They work at their own pace, fitting their study around other commitments, and exchanging coursework as time permits. This pattern is entirely consistent with the self-instructional environment, where learners are not restricted by externally determined goals, expectations and time-lines.

The target audiences

Regardless of the target language, the materials writer must consider the characteristics of the intended audience. The new materials are aimed at two different groups: members of the general public and interested linguists. The cohort of 27 research participants, comprising of twenty females and seven males, represents the public audience. Three participants are aged 18–25, nine are aged 26–40, eleven are aged 41–60 and the remaining four are over 60. In terms of occupational status, the cohort includes nurses, retired teachers, scientists, students, sales assistants, a mechanic, a training officer and a property developer.

Fourteen of the 27 participants report that they have had no previous experience in learning a foreign language. Most of the remaining participants were taught a language at school, although the majority consider that their fluency in that language is limited. Note that this profile contrasts significantly with the tertiary student of Egyptian, for whom fluency in at least one foreign language is often an admission requirement. While the project recruitment criteria precluded those who have previously learnt Middle Egyptian in an institutional setting (in any case, an unlikely scenario in this region of Australia), five participants report that they have previously attempted to teach themselves from books.

It comes as no surprise that most participants are interested in learning Middle Egyptian because of a personal interest in ancient Egypt in particular, or in ancient cultures generally. A few individuals express other motives, such as a broad interest in languages, the challenge of a new hobby, or spiritual beliefs. Prompted to consider their short and long-term goals, most learners have quite modest expectations. For example, some participants have planned holidays to Egypt, and would like to be able to identify some hieroglyphs, and maybe read a few words and phrases during their travels. Others participants would like to be able to read connected text on monuments or tomb walls. Only a few learners hope to eventually become fluent in Middle Egyptian, probably a good thing given the inherent limitations of language self-instruction, and the lack of formal learning opportunities in this region of Australia.

The materials are also designed with members of the linguistic community in mind. As mentioned previously, linguists have shown only limited interest in ancient Egyptian, which is surprising given the very long documented history of the language, and its consequent potential for testing theories of language change. Speculating on this situation, Loprieno suggests that:

> "... over the last decades, we [in the Egypological community] have preferred to engage in a dialog among ourselves, rather than with the broader audience of comparative and general linguists, and we have developed conceptual and terminological conventions that often appear opaque, if not downright incomprehensible to the non-initiated" (1995, xii).

In his exhaustive and detailed treatment of the ancient Egyptian language continuum, Loprieno addresses this problem by introducing linguists to the conventions of the Egyptological community. While the materials currently under development are, of necessity, only a very superficial introduction to Middle Egyptian, a reverse approach is experimentally adopted, and linguistic practices are substituted for Egyptological conventions. The materials are checked for linguistic and pedagogical soundness by the project supervisors, who are professional linguists and educators.

The materials integrate linguistic methodologies with applied linguistic theory and practice, in order to meet the needs and expectations of two very different target audiences: members of the general public and linguists. At first glance, these two audiences may seem quite incompatible. However, referring to Middle Egyptian, Ritter argues that:

> "a more linguistically oriented presentation of the language can make things easier for the beginner, as it is not only descriptively and explanatorily more adequate, but also more intuitive" (1999, 201).

The view that foreign language pedagogy and linguistics can be usefully integrated is echoed by Paul, who argues that "the development of ... linguistic awareness is a major factor in the successful acquisition of another language" (1993, 4).

New materials for self-instruction in Middle Egyptian

According to Stern, "the development of linguistics and applied linguistics over the past quarter of a century has brought about a better understanding of how we proceed in developing pedagogic grammars" (1992, 130). Stern refers here to the development of teaching grammars for contemporary languages in a classroom situation. However, these insights are equally relevant to the development of materials for non-contemporary languages (such as Middle Egyptian) and for the self-instructional environment.

The project materials are divided into two major components: a textbook (including the dictionary and sign lists), and a workbook. Compared to conventional materials for Middle Egyptian, each textbook chapter is relatively short, providing learners with frequent opportunities to test their understanding of the text before tackling new concepts. The workbook is designed for practical use, with spaces provided for exercise responses.

Throughout the course learners are introduced to some of the main features of Middle Egyptian and the hieroglyphic script. Topics are selected on the principle that "they can be justified in relation to the length and purpose of the course and the characteristics of the student population" (Stern 1992, 137). No attempt is made to treat each concept exhaustively. For example, the verbal system is introduced at a superficial level only, but learners are explicitly advised to investigate the various Egyptological approaches if they wish to gain a sophisticated understanding of verbal behaviour.

While traditional pedagogical grammars for any language tend to introduce items in a linear lock-step fashion, the project materials are structured on a 'spiral syllabus' in which grammatical topics are introduced in a gradual, cyclical manner:

> "No item in the syllabus that has once been introduced should ever be lost sight of. Each item is periodically reintroduced, and not simply in its original form; instead it is place in ever new contexts, or associated with additional information" (Stern 1992, 139).

According to Stern, "[I]t may be necessary for a grammatical item to be encountered several times in different situations before the learners become aware of its relevance" (1992, 144). This is consistent with the researcher's own experiences in attempting to learn Egyptian, and other languages, by self-instruction. In addition, three revision chapters are included at appropriate intervals throughout the materials, providing further opportunities for consolidation of grammatical concepts.

In terms of instructional tools, the materials exploit some well-established practices from linguistics. For example, the transliteration system is based on the International Phonetic Alphabet (IPA). The IPA assigns a unique symbol to every documented human speech sound, enabling linguists around the world to transcribe language as unambiguously as possible. This system has also used by historical linguists to represent the hypothetical speech sounds of reconstructed languages (*e.g.* Crowley 1992).

In the context of Egyptian, the use of the IPA was suggested two decades ago by Gregersen (1985), and is occasionally found in academic discussions (*e.g.* Reintges 1998b). However, to the knowledge of the researcher, Egyptologists have not used this system for instructional purposes. The sound values that are adopted in the new materials generally correspond to those proposed by Loprieno (1995), although the learner is warned that some of these sounds are hypothetical (*c.f.* Peust 1999). All IPA symbols used throughout the materials are placed in *italics* to indicate the uncertain status of the sound system.

IPA:	*b*	*c*	*ç*	*d*	*f*	*g*	*h*	*ħ*	*j*	*jj*	*ɟ*	*k*
Standard:	*b*	*ṯ*	*ḫ*	*d*	*f*	*g*	*h*	*ḥ*	*j* or *i*	*y*	*ḏ*	*k*

IPA:	*m*	*n*	*p*	*q*	*r*	*R*	*s*	*ʃ*	*t*	*w*	*χ*	*ʕ*
Standard:	*m*	*n*	*p*	*ḳ* or *q*	*r*	*ꜣ*	*s*	*š*	*t*	*w*	*ḫ*	*ꜥ*

Figure 1. *IPA sympols used in the materials.*

In many cases, the IPA symbols match the standard Egyptological symbols. Where there are differences, the IPA is already familiar to linguists, who form part of the intended target audience. In addition, some learners from the general public may also be aware of the IPA system through pronunciation guides in English and foreign language dictionaries. In the cohort under investigation, seven of the twenty-seven participants reported that they had encountered the system when using dictionaries, or in other contexts.

Given that the materials are designed for English-speakers, entries in the dictionary component are sequenced in accordance with the Roman alphabet. According to Peust, the conventional Egyptological sequence is neither indigenous to ancient Egyptian practice, nor based on any other alphabet, but is the outcome of various "accidental decisions" (1999, 65).

Another tool borrowed from linguistics is the use of interlinear translation. In conventional learning materials for Egyptian, novices are required to identify word boundaries, transliterate and translate each word, then rearrange the components into fluent English, in one smooth process. On cognitive processing grounds alone, it is suggested here that this is not a realistic expectation for self-instructed beginners.

Harrington describes the complex process by which a foreign language learner decodes a single sentence:

"A range of cues are used to identify and assign words to parts of speech, define the constituent boundaries, and then to integrate the constituents into the developing structure... These cues include lexical category information (e.g., whether a word is a noun, verb or adjective); thematic role information (e.g., the role a word plays in an event, as agent, source, goal, etc.); information concerning phrase structure (noun phrase..., verb phrase..., prepositional phrase ..., as well as lexico-semantic information concerning who can normally do what to whom...); and frequency information concerning how likely a particular form yields a specific interpretation" (2001, 95).

Harrington refers here to the processing of *spoken* foreign language, however, in the case of Egyptian, we can substitute the complexity of decoding the hieroglyphic script. Red (1999) discusses the specific difficulties that adults experience when learning to read a foreign language in a new script. Studies indicate that reading in a different writing system poses significant problems, even where learners already have advanced oral skills in the foreign language (Red 1999, 7). It would therefore seem reasonable to offer considerable support to novice self-instructed learners of the hieroglyphic script.

In order to address this issue, the new materials promote a four-step translation process. First, the text in presented in its original format. Secondly, the individual words, and their morphological components are identified and transliterated. Thirdly, a translation is made in Egyptian word order. Finally the wording is adjusted into fluent English (in the following example, PART = particle, FEM = feminine and INF = infinitive):

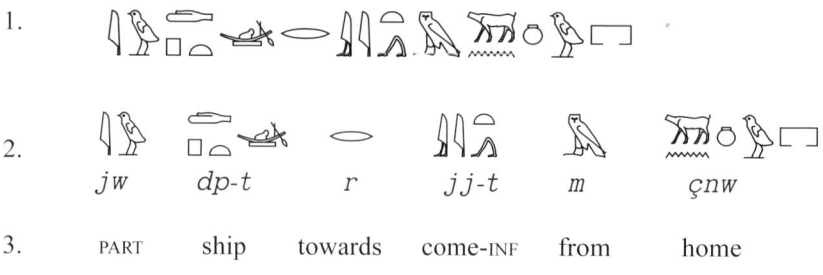

1.						
2.	*jw*	*dp-t*	*r*	*jj-t*	*m*	*çnw*
3.	PART	ship	towards	come-INF	from	home

4.   'A ship will come from home'

This process breaks the translation task into manageable steps, enabling the learner to identify all linguistic elements, and to determine or demonstrate how the English interpretation is derived and justified. Although interlinear translation is not always valued positively in Egyptian language classrooms (see, for example, comments by Junge 1991, 400), it is regarded as an indispensable tool in the linguistic disciplines, and has been used in scholarly works by some Egyptologists (*e.g.* Callender 1975; Reintges 1998a). Of course, interlinear translation is ideally a temporary tool designed to assist the learning process until the student develops an independent grasp of the grammar and script, and an adequate working vocabulary. Based on the findings of Red (1999), this may take some considerable time, particularly in the demanding self-instructional environment.

In order to avoid an excessive dependence on grammar-translation, the materials cater for a range of learning styles. For the visual learners, activities based on diagrams and illustrations are ideal, and have been used to excellent effect in the self-instructional materials of Collier and Manley (1998). The current materials offer a range of exercises that are based on pictures, maps and diagrams. For example, the task opposite is designed specifically for visual learners, and has been well-received:

While grammar-translation is primarily a deductive learning process, the project materials incorporate several inductive learning activities. Whereas deductive exercises supply the rules to the learner, inductive exercises encourage learners to work out the linguistic rules for themselves. Fortune (1992, 161) has found that many language learners view inductive grammatical exercises favourably, and recommends that they should be incorporated into self-study materials. Ellis offers four arguments in support of an inductive approach:

Identify the regions on the map

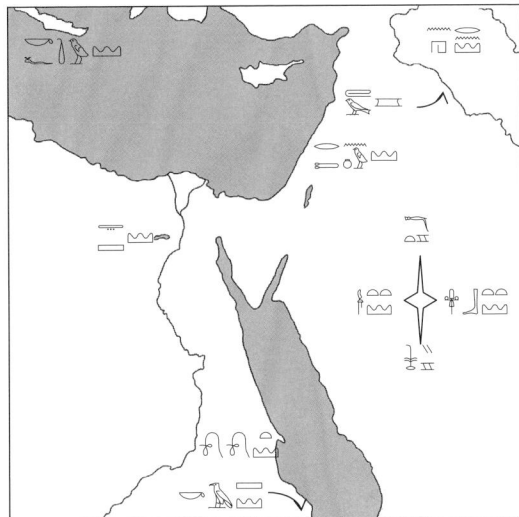

Figure 2. An exercise for inductive learners

"First, it is potentially more motivating than simply being told a grammatical rule and, for this reason, students may be more likely to remember what they learn. Second, it can encourage students to form and test hypotheses about the grammar [of the foreign language]. Third it can lead to powerful insights about the grammar of a language that cannot be found in any published descriptions …… Fourth, and perhaps most important, discovery grammar tasks have a learner -training function. They help to develop the skills learners need to investigate language autonomously – to become field linguists" (2002, 164–165).

Perhaps even more so than in a classroom environment, self-instructed learners need to develop independent investigative skills, especially if they wish to continue their language learning once they exhaust the information available in their current coursebook.

The following exercise is an example of an inductive activity:

From the feedback offered by the research participants, it has been possible to establish the kinds of tasks that learners particularly enjoy. For example, early in the study, one participant suggested that he liked to learn from puzzles. As well as engaging and maintaining learner interest, a crucial factor in a non-compulsory learning environment such as self-instruction,

Here is some reconstructed data from Middle Egyptian (remember that the vowels, in particular, are hypothetical). Identify the root consonants of each word. How does the suffix -w change the meaning of the word?

ʕanaχ	'oath'	raaʀaw	'mouths'
taʀʃaaw	'provinces'	nacar	'god'
raʀ	'mouth'	radwaw	'plants'
nacuuraw	'gods'	taʀaʃ	'province'
raaduw	'plant'	ʕanaχw	'oaths'

Figure 3. An exercise for inductive learners.

puzzles may actually stimulate more effective and efficient language learning (Danesi 2003, 111–115). Consequently, puzzles such as word finds and crosswords have been included in the project materials, and have received positive learner feedback.

Even the more analytically orientated puzzles can offer some variation to the usual grammar-translation sequence:

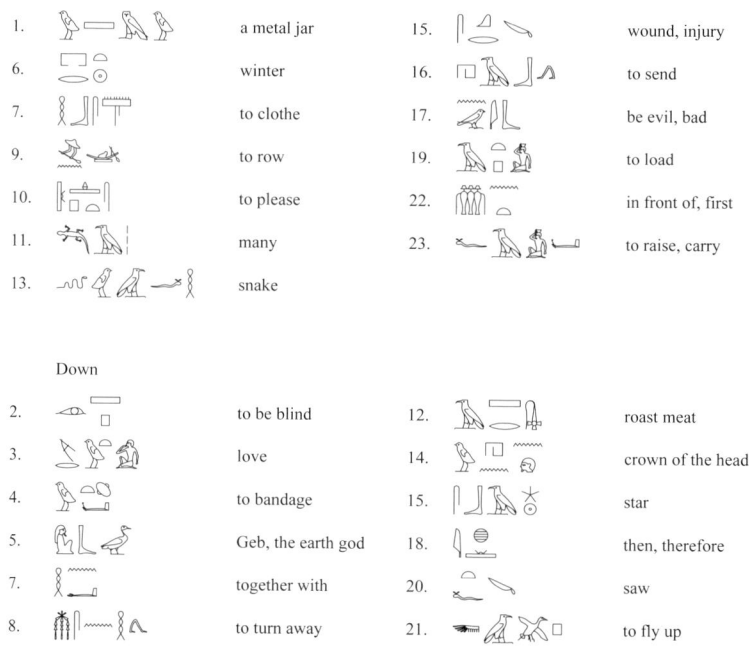

Figure 4. A Middle Egyptian crossword.

Of course, the new materials also include purely analytical exercises that have much in common with conventional materials.

Preliminary Outcomes

Match the sentence on the left with one of the three options on the right

(a)  [hieroglyphs]

1. He makes the seasons in a month.

2. He makes the seasons with the months.

3. He makes a season in a month.

(b) He sends a message to the residence.

1.  [hieroglyphs]

2.  [hieroglyphs]

3.  [hieroglyphs]

(c) He arrives at his house.

1.  [hieroglyphs]

2.  [hieroglyphs]

3.  [hieroglyphs]

Figure 5. *A grammatical exercise.*

At present, the introductory course in Middle Egyptian consists of twenty chapters. A specialist in Egyptian language has checked the language content and made a number of helpful recommendations. The research participants offer invaluable feedback as they work through the materials. As well as identifying which activities they like and dislike, the participants frequently offer suggestions about the pace of the materials, sequencing, quantity and quality of exercises, and level of difficulty. They also identify typographical errors (in the English, hieroglyphs and transliteration), mistakes and inconsistencies in the exercises or answers, and omissions from the dictionary and sign lists. It is the responsibility of the materials writer to address these issues and make adjustments as necessary.

To date, two learners have completed the entire course, and several remain active participants. Although only one participant has formally withdrawn from the project, some learners have not corresponded with the researcher for several months. Given that learners are explicitly advised to work at their own rate, participation is unpredictable, and some learners have re-entered the project after lengthy intervals. On the other hand, high attrition is to be predicted in the self-instructional environment, and there are no parallel studies of self-instruction in Middle Egyptian against which retention rates can be assessed. Bearing in mind that self-instructed learners differ in their personal goals, attrition should ideally be measured against the learner's own targets.

The participants appear to cope well with interlinear translation and the International Phonetic

Alphabet. One of the advantages of the IPA is the relatively high level of discrimination between symbols, compared with conventional transliteration systems for Middle Egyptian. For example, where traditional systems have four similar symbols distinguished by the presence or absence diacritics (*h ḥ ḫ ẖ*), the equivalent IPA symbols are easier to disambiguate (*h ħ χ ç*). Once learners are familiar with the IPA, transliteration mistakes are uncommon, with the exception of occasional confusion between ʀ and ɾ. Of course, learners who ultimately swap to other Middle Egyptian coursebooks will encounter alternative transliteration systems, and for this reason a comparative table is provided in the materials. Given that a fully standardised transliteration system has yet to be finalised (see, for example, recent treatments in Schenkel 2005; Schneider 2003), this problem is not exclusive to the current materials. It is, however, acknowledged that the IPA departs from conventional systems more so than other approaches.

In terms of catering for learner diversity, participants frequently offer positive feedback regarding the nature and scope of the tasks and activities presented in the new materials. For example, some learners report that they find the inductive exercises challenging but rewarding. Others particularly like activities based on diagrams and maps. Word puzzles seem to be popular with almost all of the participants, especially during the early stages of mastering the hieroglyphic script. For these learners, the materials appear to offer a satisfying learning route.

Naturally, one may ask how much Middle Egyptian the participants are actually learning. Referring to the piloting of language materials destined for the compulsory education market, Donovan warns that, "learning is a particularly slippery parameter to measure, and this is one of the most difficult to assess in piloting" (1998, 169). Given that there are no empirical 'benchmarks' against which self-instructed language learning can be measured, it is not possible to comment about the success of the new materials in terms of learning achievement.

Furthermore, it is suggested here that in the self-instructional environment, the success of learning materials should not be measured only in terms of language outcomes. Successful self-instructional language materials are, in addition, those that encourage the learner to feel confident and positive about independent study in general, or language learning in particular. Learners who are left believing that they must be 'bad learners' or 'bad at languages' have not had a positive learning experience. The extent to which the materials themselves may contribute towards a successful or unsuccessful outcome is a vital issue.

Conclusion

Self-instruction is not an easy way to learn any foreign language, yet for those who wish to learn a low-demand language, such as Middle Egyptian, independent learning may be the *only* available option. Unlike the tertiary student of Egyptian, who qualifies for enrolment according to external criteria and is expected to meet academic goals, self-instructed learners are more likely to come from diverse backgrounds and have individualised and relatively modest goals. It has been argued here that materials intended for self-instruction should consequently be designed to cater for learner diversity, rather than uniformity.

In the case of Middle Egyptian, where grammar-translation appears to be the norm, conventional materials may suit only a proportion of language learners. In the self-instructional environment, there would seem to be no justification for excluding the majority of learners for whom grammar-translation is problematic. In this paper, examples of exercises that are designed to accommodate alternative learning routes have been presented. In the demanding self-instructional environment, any tools that may support learning should be exploited as far as possible. For this purpose, the International Phonetic Alphabet and interlinear translation have been tested on a small cohort of adult learners, with promising feedback.

Of course, compared to contemporary languages, it is not really possible to learn Middle Egyptian "following the normal principles of studying a foreign language" (Eyre 1987, 22). Middle Egyptian can only be approached as a reconstructed written language, and its correspondence to the vernacular of the time is uncertain. In particular, the details of the verbal system remain contentious, and learners who change coursebooks will inevitably encounter differences in this regard, even if the underlying theories are not explicitly discussed.

In the project materials, the verbal system has been tackled by providing the self-instructed learner with a superficial overview, without ascribing to one theory or another. This is justified on the basis that, if independent learners have modest goals, as suggested by the research sample, a superficial treatment of verbs may be adequate for beginners.

However, learners who wish to move beyond an introductory level must inevitably confront the competing verbal theories. While academic learners of Middle Egyptian can engage with the literature in order to make informed decisions, self-instructed learners must either attempt to reconcile, or arbitrarily choose between, the various verbal paradigms that are presented in currently available materials. Until the issue of the verbal system is satisfactorily resolved within the Egyptological community, advanced self-instruction in Middle Egyptian is likely to remain all the more problematic.

Acknowledgements

Many thanks to Rachel Mairs, Dr. Carsten Peust, Dr. Mia Stephens, Alice Stevenson and Professor Claire Woods.

School of Communication, Information and New Media, University of South Australia

References

Allen, J. P. 2000, *Middle Egyptian: An Introduction to the Language and Culture of Hieroglyphs*. Cambridge University Press, Cambridge.

Banner, G. and Rayner, S. 2000, Learning language and learning style: Principles, process and practice, *Language Learning Journal* 21, 37–44.

Byrd, P. 1995, *Materials Writer's Guide*. Heinle and Heinle, Boston.

Callender, J. B. 1975, *Middle Egyptian*. Undena Publications, Malibu.

Collier, M. and Manley, B. 1998, *How to Read Egyptian Hieroglyphs: A Step-by-Step Guide to Teach Yourself*. British Museum Press, London.

Cook, V. 1996, *Second Language Learning and Language Teaching*, (2nd edition). Arnold, London.

Costello, P. 2003, *Action Research*. Continuum, London.

Crowley, T. 1992, *An Introduction to Historical Linguistics*, (2nd edition). Oxford University Press, Oxford.

Danesi, M. 2003, *Second Language Teaching: A View from the Right Side of the Brain*. Kluwer Academic Publishers, Dordrecht.

Dickinson, L. 1987, *Self-Instruction in Language Learning*. Cambridge University Press, Cambridge.

Donovan, P. 1998, Piloting – a publisher's view, in B. Tomlinson (ed.), *Materials Development in Language Teaching*, 149–189. Cambridge University Press, Cambridge.

Ellis, R. 2002, Methodological options in grammar teaching materials, in E. Hinkel and S. Fotos (eds.),

New Perspectives on Grammar Teaching in Second Language Classrooms, 155–179. Lawrence Erlbaum Associates Inc., New Jersey.

Eyre, C. J. 1987, Speculations on the structure of Middle Egyptian: Considerations on the lines of syntactical and morphological research towards a new teaching grammar, in J. D. Ray (ed.), *Lingua Sapientissima: A Seminar in Honour of H. J. Polotsky*, 22–46. Fitzwilliam Museum and the Faculty of Oriental Studies, Cambridge.

Fernández-Toro, M. and Jones, F. R. 1996, Going solo: Learners' experiences of self-instruction and self-instruction training, in E. Broady and M.-M. Kenning (eds.), *Promoting Learner Autonomy in University Language Teaching*, 185–214. CILT, London.

Fortune, A. 1992, Self-study grammar practice: learners' views and preferences, *English Language Teaching Journal* 46(2), 160–171.

Gregersen, E. A. 1985, On the transliteration of Ancient Egyptian, *Göttinger Miszellen* 86, 13–20.

Harrington, M. 2001, Sentence processing, in P. Robinson (ed.), *Cognition and Second Language Instruction*, 91–124. Cambridge University Press, Cambridge.

Heafford, M. 1995, Getting going in Greek – better some than all, *Language Learning Journal* 12, 66–70.

Hoch, J. E. 1996, *Middle Egyptian Grammar*. Society for the Study of Egyptian Antiquities Publications (15). Benben Publications, Mississauga.

Janus, L. E. 2000, An overview of less commonly taught languages in the United States, *National Association of Secondary School Principals Bulletin* 84, January, 25–29.

Jones, F. R. 1993, Beyond the fringe: A framework for assessing teach-yourself materials for ab initio English-speaking learners, *System* 21(4), 453–469.

Jones, F. R. 1994, The lone language learner: A diary study, *System* 22(4), 441–454.

Jones, F. R. 1998, Self-instruction and success: A learner-profile study, *Applied Linguistics* 19(3), 378–406.

Junge, F. 1991, How to study Egyptian grammar and to what purpose. A summary of sorts, *Lingua Aegyptia* 1, 389–426.

Klapper, J. 1997, Language learning at school and university: The great grammar debate continues (1), *Language Learning Journal* 16, 22–27.

LaFleur, R. A. (ed.) 1998, *Latin for the 21st Century: From Concept to Classroom*. Addison-Wesley Educational Publishers Inc., Glenview, Illinois.

Loprieno, A. 1995, *Ancient Egyptian: A Linguistic Introduction*. Cambridge University Press, Cambridge.

Paul, P. 1993, *Linguistics for Language Learning*. Macmillan Education Australia, Melbourne.

Peust, C. 1999, *Egyptian Phonology: An Introduction to the Phonology of a Dead Language*. Peust and Gutschmidt, Göttingen.

Red, D. L. 1999, Adults learning to read in a second script: What we've learned, *Georgetown University Round Table on Languages and Linguistics*, 2–18.

Reintges, C. H. 1998a, Ancient Egyptian in 3D: Synchrony, diachrony and typology of a dead language, *Orientalia (Nova Series)* 67(4), 447–476.

Reintges, C. H. 1998b, Mapping information structure to syntactic structure: one syntax for *jn*, *Revue d'Égyptologie* 49, 195–220.

Riding, R. 2001, The nature and effects of cognitive style, in R. Reigeluth and L. Zhange (eds.), *Perspectives on thinking, learning and cognitive styles*. LEA, Mahwah, New Jersey.

Riding, R. and Sadler-Smith, E. 1992, Type of instructional material, cognitive style and learning performance, *Educational Studies* 18(3), 323 - 338.

Riding, R. J. and Pearson, F. 1994, The relationship between cognitive style and intelligence, *Educational Psychology* 14, 413–425.

Ritter, T. 1999, Review of E. Graefe *Mittelägyptische Grammatik für Anfänger*, *Lingua Aegyptia* 6, 185–202.

Roberts, J. T. 1995, An anatomy of home-study foreign language courses, *System* 23(4), 513–530.

Rowsell, L. V. and Libben, G. 1994, The sound of one hand clapping: How to succeed in independent language learning, *The Canadian Modern Language Review* 50(4), 668–687.

Sadler-Smith, E. 1997, 'Learning styles' and instructional design, *Innovations in Education and Training International* 33(4), 185–193.

Schenkel, W. 2005, *Tübinger Einführung in die klassisch-ägyptische Sprache und Schrift.* Tübingen.

Schneider, T. 2003, Etymologische Methode, die Historizität der Phoneme und das ägyptologische Transkriptionsalphabet, *Lingua Aegyptia* 11, 187–199.

Stern, H. H. 1992, *Issues and Options in Language Teaching.* Oxford University Press, Oxford.

Walker, G. 1991, Gaining place: the less commonly taught languages in American schools, *Foreign Language Annals* 24(2), 131–150.

Wallace, M. J. 1998, *Action Research for Language Teachers.* Cambridge University Press, Cambridge.

New Considerations on Campbell's Tomb

Mike Stammers

Introduction

When Campbell's Tomb was described by the excavators, they raised two questions, neither of which, in my opinion, has been satisfactorily answered. The first was the purpose of the trench, present in this and other similar tombs, for which several uses have been mooted, while the second was the question of why the main shaft was not placed centrally within the tomb. This paper addresses these questions and suggests an answer to them.

Discussion

Campbell's tomb in Giza, to the north of Khafre's causeway and to the west of the Sphinx, is of the type of tomb called the 'Saite-Persian Shaft Tomb' – a phenomenon of the 26th and 27th Dynasties primarily to be found in the Memphite necropoleis of Saqqara and Abusir. This tomb was designated LG 84 by Lepsius (1897, 100) and excavated in April 1837 by Vyse and Perring, who named it 'Campbell's tomb' in honour of the then British Consul to Egypt, Colonel Campbell (Vyse 1840, 136). It was the burial place of Pakap (Ranke 1935, 120, no. 5).

Typically, the 'Saite-Persian Shaft Tomb' consisted of a huge shaft containing a burial chamber within which was a sarcophagus of white limestone. Within the white limestone sarcophagus there was sometimes an inner anthropoid sarcophagus of black stone, and a wooden coffin inside this contained the mummy of the deceased, although on occasion only a wooden coffin or even just the mummified body was placed directly into the limestone sarcophagus. The body was laid with the head towards the west, the north or even the east. The burial chamber itself was shaped like a traditional Old Kingdom coffin, vaulted and with posts at the four corners, which was inscribed with religious formulae taken from the Pyramid Texts, the Coffin Texts and the Book of the Dead. A secondary shaft, much smaller than the first, was cut, usually to the east of the main shaft, with which it communicated by means of a short passage. The passage typically entered the burial chamber at the foot of the sarcophagus. In Campbell's tomb, however, it entered at the head. The main shaft was filled with fine, sifted sand, and after burial the secondary shaft and burial chamber were also filled with sand and the passage between the shafts was blocked, usually with stone, making intrusion by tomb robbers extremely difficult. However, in spite of the difficulties of digging through sixteen metres of fine sand, Pakap's tomb and coffins had been entered and the bodies removed before Vyse and Perring excavated them. The main shaft was sometimes surrounded by a trench, and a 'pit' descended into the bedrock, either as a continuation of the secondary shaft or from the connecting passage or burial chamber. A superstructure was built over the tomb, which may have been shaped as a mastaba or as a truncated pyramid (Bareš 1999, 48). Campbell's tomb conforms generally to this model of a 'Saite-Persian Shaft Tomb'.

Vyse and Perring were primarily interested in the enormous main shaft of the tomb, some 53 feet 6 inches (16m) deep, and in the burial chamber of *Pakap,* Overseer of the Scribes of the King's Repast (Porter and Moss 1974, 290), that was within it. They were, after all, looking for museum exhibits, and archaeology was of secondary importance to them. Indeed, some fine objects from this tomb are now in the British and Ashmolean Museums. The inner sarcophagus of Pakap, the granite sarcophagus of Neskedet, son of Ahmosi, and part of the basalt sarcophagus of Neskedet, son of Pasherinhet, are in the British Museum, while the inner basalt sarcophagus of *Ptahhotep,* also from Campbell's Tomb, is in the Ashmolean Museum (Porter and Moss 1974, 290). The provenance of relief fragments BM 537–46, thought to have come from Campbell's Tomb, is disputed (Leahy 1989, 239–243). The drawing by Vyse and Perring (Figure 1) gives some indication of the scale of this vast tomb.

In Campbell's tomb the four sides of the trench (marked CCCC on Figure 2) are some distance from the main shaft of the tomb itself, from which they are not equidistant. The trench is about 1.5 metres wide internally and lies approximately 3 metres from the north and east, 5 metres from the west and 6.5 metres from the south of the main shaft. The bottom of the trench is about 22 metres below ground level and is some six metres lower than the bottom of the main shaft. The walls of the trench have been stabilised by leaving pieces of rock (numbered 1–7 on Figure 2) at intervals to support the sides. In this tomb there is a third shaft, to the south of the main shaft, leading to burials 'w', 'y' and 'z'. A pit lies at the foot of the sarcophagus. The present article aims to investigate the purpose of the trench and of the pit, and why the main shaft was not placed centrally within the trench.

Vyse reported that the bottom of the trench was under 15 feet 6¾ inches (about 4.75 metres) of water during the Nile flood in 1838 and concluded that "it seems... to have been made for the purpose of insulating the tomb" (1840, 131). The average Nile flood level was 1.5 metres (Butzer 1976, 17) leaving the bottom of the trench, by Vyse's measurements, still some 3.25 metres below the 1838 water level when the Nile was not in flood. The bed of the river Nile has risen by about 1m every 1,000 years (Bunbury 2005), so that

Figure 1. *The excavators' drawing of the main shaft of Campbell's Tomb (Vyse 1840, 216).*

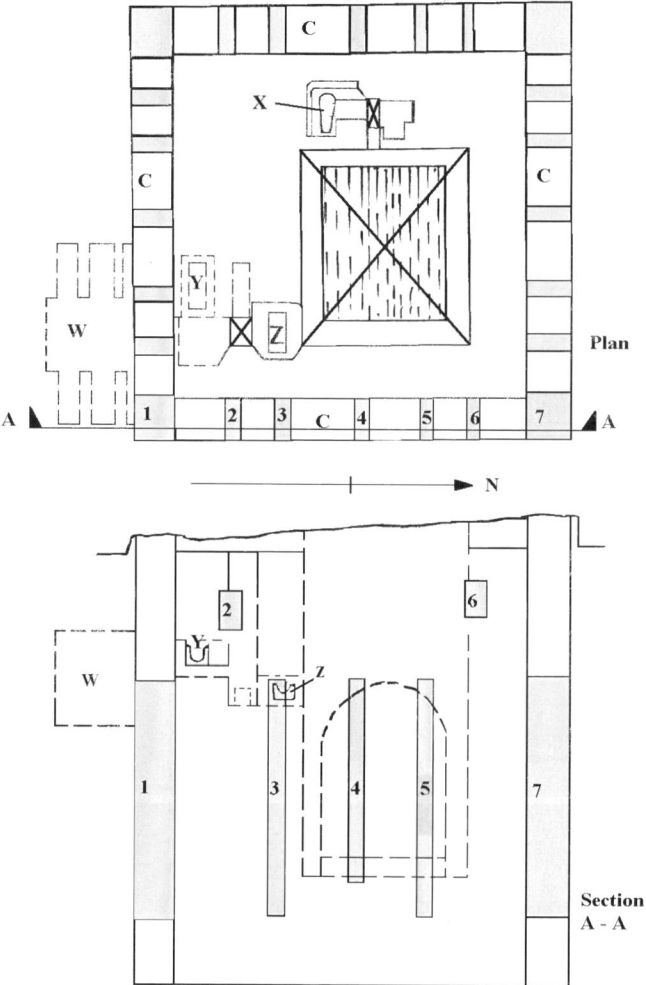

Figure 2. *Plan and Section of Campbell's Tomb, after Vyse (1840, Figure 1).*

at the time of the construction of Campbell's Tomb the water level was some 2.5 metres lower than in 1838; there would still, however, have been about 0.75 metres of water in the trench at normal river levels, rising to 2.25 metres during the inundation. Although he was unspecific, it is to be assumed that by "insulating the tomb" Vyse meant that the trench would protect the tomb from rain and river flood water by draining it safely away. Vyse's figures indicate that the bottom of the burial chamber was about 6 metres above the bottom of the trench, and therefore some 3.75 metres above the ancient flood level, so that flood water would not have entered it. Giza has a climate in which cloudbursts are not uncommon and it may have been considered necessary to divert rainwater from the burial chamber.

The burial chamber rests on a bed of sand about 0.75 metres thick, above the bedrock. This sand was left when the massive burial chamber complex was lowered into the tomb shaft by 'sand hydraulics' at the time of construction. Eigner (1984, 164) pointed out that, during the annual ritual of the burial of the Osirian relic, the coffin was laid on a mound of sand representing the primeval mound. It was from this mound that Osiris was resurrected (Bonnet 1971, 567). Pakap's entire burial chamber rests on a layer of sand, while there was sand below the burial chamber in the tombs of Djanehibu (Bresciani *et al*. 1977, Tav. II), Neferibra-sa-neit (Drioton and Lauer 1951, 477) and Udjahorresnet (Bareš 1992, 111): such sand layers may well also represent the primeval mound. Eigner (1984, 178) also suggested that the sand hill of Sokar is to be equated with the primeval mound of Osiris. Brock (2002, 23) described the Osireion in Abydos as having a deep water-filled moat leaving an island in the centre where the sarcophagus would be placed.

The tomb of Udjahorresnet in Abusir has the only known 'trench' similar to that of Pakap and there is an additional trench inside the eastern side of the main one. The series of passages within other tombs, passing below the burial chamber, may represent an early attempt at the trench or may be a later degeneration of the feature, possibly because of the cost of cutting the external trench, or because there was no likelihood of reaching water. These passages can be seen below the burial chamber in the tombs of Amentafnakht (Saad 1947, 383), Hor (Lauer 1954, planches I and II) and the double tomb of Neferibra-sa-neit and Wahibramen (Drioton and Lauer 1951, planche 1). It is difficult to tell from the excavators' reports whether or not these features existed in other tombs, although it is clear that no trench existed in the tomb of Amentafnakht (author's visit to the tomb, April 2005), and there was no room for a trench around the connected tombs of Padineit (Barsanti 1901), Psamtek and Setariban (Barsanti 1900a) and Djanehibu (Barsanti 1900c).

The purpose of Udjahorresnet's 'trench', which was more than eleven metres deep (Bareš 1988, 158), has been considered by Bareš, who stated that they "resemble the situation of the cenotaph of Sethi I at Abydos imitating the tomb of Osiris" (1999, 63, n. 314). Lauer (1954, 133) thought these passages were for defence, arguing that they would save the burial from attack from below (Drioton and Lauer 1951, 477). However, the task of attacking the burial chamber from below would only have threatened an attacker with a deluge of fine sand: a religious reason for these features must be more compelling. We know from research into the 25th and 26th Dynasty tombs at Assassif in Western Thebes that the cult of Osiris proved a potent and important motivation in tomb design (Eigner 1984, Chapter 7).

Rather than taking water away from Campbell's tomb, the trench could equally have been designed to bring water into the tomb. Bonnet (1971, 567) has stated that a feature of the Osireion in Abydos was a platform surrounded by a trench which filled with water during the Nile inundation. During the inundation, Pakap's burial chamber would also have been an island above the water that surrounded it in the trench. The only parallel to the 'trench' at Saqqara lies in the corridor round the tomb of Bakenrenef (Eigner 1984, 178), and the phenomenon is represented in the tomb of Harwa in Thebes (Porter and Moss 1960, 64, 68–69). In both these instances the corridor was thought by Eigner (1984, 178) to represent the cavern of Sokar, which, according to the Book of the Amduat, is traversed during the fifth hour of the night (Hornung 1999, 37). Bonnet (1971, 576) suggested that the concentric arrangement of passages round a central burial chamber was based on an island surrounded by water, such as the primeval mound. Campbell's tomb was also concentrically organized.

According to Frankfort (1961, 114), the dead had to cross water to reach the Field of Rushes. This water is Nun, from which the sun rises at dawn, and in which the old and worn have to be immersed if they are to be regenerated (Hornung 1996, 161). Nun was vital to the deceased and was a central part of the cult of Osiris, which was just as important in Memphis as it was in Thebes. Herodotus described the "Vaults of Cheops ... built on a sort of island, surrounded by water introduced from the Nile by canal" (Book II, 124 – Rawlinson's translation), which Kerisel (1991, 79) thought ran from the bottom of the escarpment to a structure like the Osireion that must have been in the vicinity of the causeway and therefore also of Campbell's tomb. The island at the end of the canal represents the mound of creation (Wilkinson 1994, 395). The importance of Osiris is clearly shown by inscriptions in many contemporary tombs. Unfortunately, in Campbell's tomb there is very little inscriptional evidence: apart from the inscriptions on the sarcophagus, there is only a single, damaged line of text in a plastered groove running around the walls of the burial chamber. However, the text, translated by Birch (Vyse 1840), includes the phrases: "I am your sister Isis: rejoice" (Vyse 1840, 133) and "Your mother Nut has spread herself over you" (Vyse 1840, 134) – the latter from Pyramid Text Utterances 356 (§580), 368 (§638) and 588 (§1607) (Faulkner 1998, 114, 121 and 241). Both of these phrases refer to the family of Osiris, and on his coffin the deceased is, as usual, frequently referred to as Osiris. The text also includes part of the resurrection text of Chapter 178 of the Book of the Dead – the Spell for Setting Upright the Corpse, Opening the Eyes, Strengthening the Ears and Making Fast the Head Put in its Place (Allen 1974, 186). Osiris is the very epitome of resurrection, and this resurrection is demonstrated by the eternal rhythms of the earth: the annual changes in the level of the Nile, rising to inundation and subsiding back to normal levels, are seen to be an important aspect, not only of these natural cycles but also of resurrection: not only did the Nile flood recur on a regular and predictable basis, but it also brought fertility to the land, enabling the growth of new crops. The annual, cyclical ebb and flow of the Nile followed the monthly cycle of the moon and the daily cycle of the sun in representing death and resurrection to the ancient Egyptians. Surely, then, it is likely that the trench, which allowed this annual ebb and flow of the Nile flood waters to be part of the tomb, was a deliberate Osirian feature. If this interpretation is correct, it also adds meaning to the masonry-lined pit (Figure 3) descending 2.75 metres deep into the bed rock at the foot of the sarcophagus, which Vyse (1840, 217) thought might lead to another burial chamber below the first. No such second burial chamber existed.

Secondary shafts exist in all the 'Saite-Persian Shaft Tombs' and are a characteristic feature of them. It has always been assumed that their main purpose was two-fold: it was primarily to allow the mummy of the deceased to enter the burial chamber after death (Bareš 1999, 25) but, in addition, it enabled the evacuation of those who caused the entry of sand into the tomb after the funeral. However, the downward extension of the secondary shaft, or the pit below the passage adjacent to it or the burial chamber, would not have been needed for either purpose. Eigner (1999, 438) saw the pit as playing some part in the evacuation of sand from the main shaft during the sinking of the burial chamber from ground level to its place of permanence. Lauer (Drioton and Lauer 1951, 472) argued that these pits were for security against a possible overflow of sand when the main shaft was filled after burial; Verner (2002, 181) suggested they were for protection and Bareš (1999, 62–63), considering the shaft that lies below the corridor connecting the secondary shaft to the burial chamber in Udjahorresnet's tomb, also thought that the pit was probably for protection, although he surmised that it could have been part of the structure abandoned at an early stage of construction, or that it could have had a religious meaning. A pit exists in all the 'Saite-Persian Shaft Tombs' for which detailed evidence is available: in those of Udjahorresnet (Bareš 1992, 108), Djanehibu (Barsanti and Maspero 1900, 162), Amentafnakht (Saad 1947, 383), Hor (Lauer 1954, planches I and II), Padenisis (Barsanti 1900b, 230) and the joint tomb of Neferibra-sa-neit and Wahibramen (Drioton and Lauer 1951,

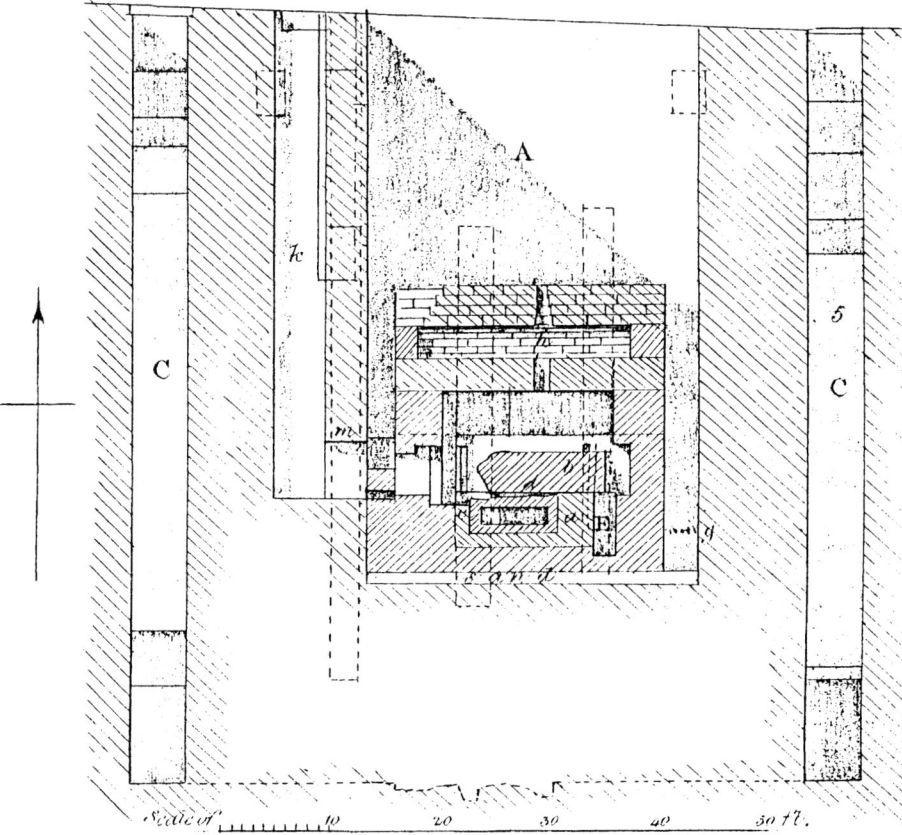

Figure 3. *Section through Campbell's Tomb, after Vyse (1840, Figure 5).*

planche I). Because of its isolation from the main shaft, the secondary shafts in Sharuna tomb S-14 (Brinka 1986, 78) must be considered only as a pit. The pit would have allowed the deceased easy access to join the solar barque at the end of the fifth hour of the night, when the souls of Osiris and Re become united (Hornung 1999, 37). Bareš (1999, 63) follows Brock in thinking that it was a symbolic burial for Sokar, and Gestermann in agreeing that it was religious. If the pit was designed to remove water or for the handling of sand, it seems unlikely that it would have been lined with masonry, as in Campbell's tomb and that of Djanehibu (Bresciani *et al.* 1977, Tav. II), but an important religious function would make this necessary. It is possible that the trench and pit were designed to drain water from the tomb – an insulation in Vyse's terms – although, as there were natural fissures that enabled water to flow into and out of the tomb area when the Nile flooded, it seems that the construction of this massive trench would have been unnecessary for the purpose. They seem rather to have had a deeply religious significance, and not to have been for purely practical purposes.

Eigner (1984, 164), in discussing the tomb of Osiris at Abydos, identified several other details of the Osiris Tomb that had been carried into the design of Late Period tombs in the Assassif in Thebes. Amelineau (1899, 150) had commented that there were some sixteen Osiris graves in Egypt, placed as reliquaries for parts of Osiris' body, and that the tomb for Osiris' head was the tomb of Djed in Abydos. Bonnet (1971, 576) thought the Osiris tomb had originated on an island in Busiris. The tomb was divided into the 'Upper Duat' and the 'Lower Duat', and as a representation of the 'Lower Duat' the burial chamber had a proportion of 4:3 with seven 'gates', including that of entry into the tomb. The proportion 4:3 equates to the sides of the 'Sacred Triangle', mentioned by Plutarch (Lauer 1977, 55), of which the angle enclosed by those two sides is exactly 90°. The cenotaph tomb of Seti I in Abydos has these features (Eigner 1984, 166). In Campbell's tomb the burial chamber of Pakap also has a proportion of 4:3 and the seven 'gates' are represented by the entrance from the passage, a recess on each of the northern and southern sides of the burial chamber and one at each of the four corners (Vyse 1840, 132). The eleven other 'Saite-Persian Shaft Tombs' of which measurement is possible vary in proportion from 3.5:3 to 5:3 – although it must be said that accurate measurement is not possible in most cases. The exact proportion of 4:3 occurs in over a third of the tombs, and it is also the mean figure.

The design of the tomb, with the trench giving access to Nun, the pit giving access to the solar barque, the burial chamber placed on a mound of sand, and its sacred proportions, must have a basis in Osirian ritual.

There seems little doubt that the structure of Campbell's tomb, and of other 'Saite-Persian Shaft Tombs', was designed to follow Osirian tradition: these are 'Osiris Tombs'. Although they were not designed to guard against the incursion of water or tomb robbers, they have proved ideally suited for this.

The second difficulty with Campbell's tomb lies in Vyse's contention, obvious from the plan of the tomb (Figure 2), that the main shaft was not placed centrally within the trench. The Egyptians loved symmetry and in the tomb of Udjahorresnet – the only other case where a trench has been described by the excavators – the shaft is equidistant from it, so why was this tomb asymmetrical? Vyse (1840, 131) suggested that this was because of the existence of the "sepulchral grotto proceeding from the shafts on the southern side". El-Sadeek (1984, 128), writing nearly one hundred and fifty years later, argued that it was this southern shaft for tombs 'w', 'y' and 'z' (Figure 2) which stopped the main shaft from being built where Pakap wanted it to be. In order to establish whether this might have been correct we need to examine the chronology of the complex and to consider whether the other burials were earlier or later than that in the main tomb.

The main burial chamber, which contained Pakap's sarcophagus, now in the British Museum with Number 1384, (Buhl 1959, 25, A.6) is generally accepted as dating to the 26th Dynasty. The only cartouche within the tomb is given as part of Pakap's title 'Overseer of scribes to Wahibra' (Vyse 1840, text facing 134), found as part of the inscription on the North side of the burial chamber. Pakap's '*rn nfr*' – his 'good name' – given on the lid of his sarcophagus, is Wahibra-em-akhet (Ranke 1935, 73, no. 3), dated by de Meulenaere (1966, 30) to the time of Psamtek II, who reigned from 595 B.C. to 589 B.C. and by Zivie-Coche (1991, 285) to the later reign of Apries. This is a clear indication that Pakap must have lived under the reign of one of these kings and that the tomb cannot be earlier than that date.

Chamber 'x' leads directly from the secondary shaft of Pakap's tomb and is not in contention: it has to be of a similar but probably slightly later date than the main structure, for it could not have been placed there without the shaft. This secondary tomb held the basalt sarcophagus of Ptahhotep (Ranke 1935, 141, no. 5), of which the lid is now in the Ashmolean Museum with Number 1947.295 (Buhl 1959, 140, K.1). The son of Horenpatesnakht, Porter and Moss dated

Ptahhotep's burial to the time of Darius I (Porter and Moss 1974, 290); el-Sadeek (1984, 132) dated it to the 26th Dynasty on epigraphic grounds but Josephson (1997, 11) is of the opinion that a statue of Ptahhotep in the Brooklyn Museum (Brooklyn Museum 37.353) can be securely dated to the 27th Dynasty. A stele of Ptahhotep, dated to Year 34 of Darius I was found in the Serapeum (Zivie-Coche 1991, 285).

Chambers 'w', 'y' and 'z' all lead from the third shaft, to the south of the main shaft of the tomb. Chamber 'y' contained the sarcophagi of two people, both confusingly called Neskedet (Ranke 1935, 179, no. 10). Both were $w^c b$ priests of the Temples of Memphis; one was the son of *Ahmosi* and *Tasaenankh*, while the other was the son of *Pasherinhet* and *Wasetemhat*. A fragment of the coffin of the former is in the British Museum, BM 3, while the basalt sarcophagus of the latter is also in the British Museum, BM 525. The similarity of the names and professions of the occupants of chamber 'y' suggests that they may well have been related. A white granite sarcophagus, found in chamber 'z', was left *in situ* by the excavators and the contents of chamber 'w' were not reported.

Vyse (1840, 136), on the basis of comparison with other sarcophagi in the Ashmolean and the Louvre, dated the two people named Neskedet to the 26th Dynasty. Buhl (1959, 147) decided, on the basis of its shape and style, that one was of a Greek and de Meulenaere, early in the 1970s, suggested that they were from the 30th Dynasty (Zivie-Coche 1991, 287). Later, however, Porter and Moss (1974, 290) dated them both to the 30th Dynasty. El-Sadeek (1984, 132) agreed, dating them to perhaps the 27th Dynasty and stated that they were both certainly later than the 26th Dynasty. The white granite sarcophagus was not described, so it offers us no help.

The evidence, then, suggests that the burials of Pakap and Ptahhotep date from the 27th Dynasty. Those in 'y' were contemporary with or later than the main burial of Pakap: they cannot be earlier and probably also date from the 27th Dynasty. The burial chamber at 'z', which contained the white granite sarcophagus, would appear to have been constructed between the main and the southern shafts and is probably contemporary with them, or maybe slightly later. It is certainly not earlier. The position of tomb 'w', cut as it is through the wall of the trench, suggests that it is much later. What is certain, however, is that these burials are not earlier than the main burial. Pakap would therefore not have needed to design his tomb to avoid these other shafts and burial chambers. Certainly, it is most unlikely that a rich and powerful man like Pakap, who could afford the immense cost of building this tomb, would have bothered — he would probably either have demolished any unwanted structures or built elsewhere. Similarly, it is inconceivable that Pakap would have left space within his design for possible later tombs.

It is clear that the main shaft and the secondary shaft at the west, leading to the main burial chamber and to chamber 'x' are part of the same structure. If we now assume that the southern shaft is also contemporary, we obtain an entirely different view of the tomb complex. The northern side of the main shaft is the same distance from the trench as is the southern side of the southern shaft, which leads to 'w', 'y' and 'z'. The eastern sides of both the main and southern shafts are, again, the same distance from the trench, as is the western side of the secondary shaft, leading to Pakap's burial chamber and to burial chamber 'x'. Therefore, although the main shaft itself is not equidistant from the four sides of the trench, the totality of all the shafts, encompassing the main shaft, the secondary shaft and the southern shaft, is now equidistant from the trench. The tomb would thus seem to have been designed as a whole, and the southern shaft must have been considered as part of the design, probably intended to be used for a family burial.

El-Sadeek stated that "it is now clear that (the tomb) had no superstructure" (1984, 126). Vyse (1840, 148) thought that there had been a superstructure that had been destroyed or robbed out.

Perring had found stones remaining that suggested an arched roof, giving him cause to conjecture "that the whole monument (including the trench) may have been covered by a pyramid" (Vyse 1840, 133). If that is so, it reinforces the opinion that the entire structure of trench, shafts, burial chambers and superstructure, was designed and built as a single entity. Lauer (Drioton and Lauer 1951, 470–471) conjectured the existence of a colonnaded chapel above the main shaft of the 'Saite-Persian Shaft Tombs' in Saqqara; Verner (Bareš 1999, 48) thought it was a pyramid; Eigner (1999, 437) suggested a mastaba and Bareš (1999, 23) has stated that, with the present state of our knowledge it is not possible to confirm which shape the superstructure may have taken. In the tomb of Udjahorresnet in Abusir (Bareš 1999, 48) it seems likely that a battered, truncated pyramid with a flat roof covered the main shaft and that the whole tomb was surrounded by an enclosure wall, the area between being paved with limestone blocks.

It would now seem entirely credible that the entire complex of 'Campbell's Tomb', including all the shafts and the trench, is to be seen as a single family tomb, designed to represent the tomb of Osiris.

University of Wales, Swansea

References

Allen, T. G. 1974, *The Book of the Dead or Going Forth By Day*. The University of Chicago Press, Chicago.

Amelineau, E. 1899, *Les Nouvelles Fouilles d'Abydos, 1898–1898*. E. Leroux, Paris.

Bareš, L. 1988, Late Period Shaft Tombs, in *Akten des Vierten Internationalen Ägyptologenkongresses, München 1985*, 155–160. Buske, Hamburg.

Bareš, L. 1992, Excavations at Abusir. Season 1990/91. Preliminary Report. The Shaft Tomb of Udjahorresnet, *Zeitschrift für Ägyptische Sprache und Altertumskunde* 119, 108–116.

Bareš, L. 1999, *The Shaft Tomb of Udjahorresnet at Abusir*. The Karolinium Press, Praha.

Barsanti, M. A. 1900a, Fouilles autour de la Pyramide d'Ounas – Les Tombeaux de Psammétique et de Setariban, *Annales du Service des Antiquités de l'Égypt* 1, 161–188.

Barsanti, M. A. 1900b, Fouilles autour de la Pyramide d'Ounas – Le Tombeau de Péténisis, *Annales du Service des Antiquités del'Égypt* 1, 230–261.

Barsanti, M. A. 1900c, Fouilles autour de la Pyramide d'Ounas – Le Tombeau de Zanehibou, *Annales du Service des Antiquités del'Égypt* 1, 262–271.

Barsanti, M. A. 1901, Fouilles autour de la Pyramide d'Ounas – Le Tombeau de Péténéit, *Annales du Service des Antiquités de l'Égypt* 2, 97–111.

Barsanti, M. A. and Maspero, G. 1900, *Fouilles Autour de la Pyramide d'Ounas*. Institut Français d'Archéologie Orientale, Le Caire.

Bonnet, H. 1971, *Reelexicon der Ägyptischen Religiongeschichte*. Walter de Gruyter, Berlin.

Bresciani, E., Pernigotti, S. and Giangeri Silvis, M. P. 1977, *La Tomba di Ciennehebu, Capo della Flotta del Ra*. Biblioteca degli Studi Classici e Orientali 7. Giardini, Pisa.

Brinka, J., Gestermann, L., Gomaà, F., Israel, A., Jürgena, P. and Schenkel, W. 1986, al-Kôm al-Ahmar/ Šhārūna 1986, *Göttinger Miszellen* 93, 65–80.

Brock, E. 2002, *The Temples of Abydos*. The Palm Press, Cairo.

Buhl, M-L. 1959, *The Late Egyptian Anthropoid Stone Sarcophagi*. Nationalmuseet, København.

Bunbury, J. 2005, *Impact of an active Nile on archaeological sites*. Abstract of a paper given to the British Egyptological Congress, Cambridge, 24–25 September 2005. Online from www.fitzmuseum.cam.uk/projects/ae/Congress/Abstracts

Butzer, K. 1976, *Early Hydraulic Civilization in Egypt.* University of Chicago Press, Chicago.

Drioton, E. and Lauer, J-P. 1951, Fouilles à Saqqara. Les Tombes Jumellées de Neferibré-Sa-Neith et Ouahibré-Men, *Annales du Service des Antiquités de l'Égypt* 51, 469–490.

Eigner, D. 1984, *Die Monumentalen Grabbauten der Spätzeit in der thebanischen Nekropole.* Verlag der Österreichischen Akademie der Wissenschaften, Wien.

Eigner, D. 1999, Late Period Private Tombs, in K. A. Bard (ed.), *Encyclopaedia of the Archaeology of Ancient Egypt,* 432–438. Routledge, London.

El-Sadeek, W. 1984, *Twenty-sixth Dynasty Necropolis at Gizeh. An Analysis of the Tomb of Thery and its Place in the Development of Saite Funerary Art and Architecture.* Afro-Pub, Wien.

Faulkner, R. O. 1998, *The Ancient Egyptian Pyramid Texts.* Oxford University Press, Oxford.

Frankfort, H. 1961, *Ancient Egyptian Religion.* Harper and Row, London.

Herodotus, 1910, *Histories,* translated by G. Rawlinson. J. M. Dent and Sons Ltd., London.

Hornung, E. 1996, *Conceptions of God in Ancient Egypt.* Cornell Paperbacks, Ithaca, New York.

Hornung, E. 1999, *The Ancient Egyptian Books of the Afterlife.* Cornell University Press, Ithaca, New York.

Josephson, J. A. 1997, Egyptian Sculpture of the Late Period Revisited. *Journal of the American Research Center in Egypt* 34, 1–20.

Kerisel, J. 1991, *La Pyramide à Travers les Âges.* Presses de l'École Nationale des Ponts et Chausses, Paris.

Lauer, J-P. 1954, La Structure de la Tombe de Hor à Saqqara (XXVIe Dynastie), *Annales du Service des Antiquités de l'Égypt* 52, 133–136.

Lauer, J-P. 1977. Le Triangle Sacré dans les Plans des Monuments de l'Ancien Empire, *Bulletin de l'Institut Français d'Archéologie Orienta:* 77, 55–78.

Lepsius, C. R., 1897, *Denkmäler aus Ägypten und Äthiopien. Text.* 3 volumes. Reprinted 1975. Éditions des Belles Lettres, Genève.

Meulenaere, H de. 1966. *Le Surnom Égyptien à la Basse Époque.* Nederlands Historisch-Archaeologisch Instituut in het Nabije Oosten, Istanbul.

Leahy, L.M. 1989, Wahibreemakhet at Giza, *Journal of Egyptian Archaeology* 75, 239–243.

Porter, B. and Moss, R. L. B., 1960, *Topographical Bibliography of Ancient Egyptian Hieroglyphic Texts, Reliefs and Paintings. Volume I, The Theban Necropolis, Part 1.* (Reprinted 1994.) Griffith Institute, Oxford.

Porter, B. and Moss, R. L. B., 1974, *Topographical Bibliography of Ancient Egyptian Hieroglyphic Texts, Reliefs and Paintings. Volume III, Memphis, Part 1.* (Reprinted 1994.) Griffith Institute, Oxford.

Ranke, H. 1935, *Die Ägyptischen Personennamen. Vol. I.* Verlag von J J Augustin, Glückstadt.

Saad, Z. 1947, Preliminary Report on the Excavations at Saqqara and Helwan 1941–42, *Annales du Service des Antiquités de l'Égypt* 41, 381–393.

Verner, M. 2002, *Abusir – Realm of Osiris.* American University in Cairo Press, Cairo and New York.

Vyse, Col, H. 1840, *Operations Carried Out at the Pyramids of Gizeh. Vol. 1.* James Fraser, London.

Wilkinson, A. 1994, Landscapes for Funeral Rituals in Dynastic Times, in Eyre, C., Leahy, A. and L. M. Leahy (eds.), *The Unbroken Reed – Studies in the Culture and Heritage of Ancient Egypt in Honour of A. F. Shore.* Egypt Exploration Society, London.

Zivie-Coche, C-M. 1991, *Giza au Premier Millenaire.* Museum of Fine Arts, Boston.

The Material Significance of Predynastic and Early Dynastic Palettes

Alice Stevenson

Introduction

The discussion presented here derives from a broader theoretical appraisal of the significance of a class of artefact known as the palette, an esoteric object of the Predynastic and Early Dynastic periods of Egypt (*c.* 4100 B.C. – *c.* 3000 B.C.). The most widely recognised examples are the relief-carved 'ceremonial' palettes (Petrie 1953), such as the iconic Narmer Palette. Yet this piece is in fact the culmination of over a millennium of engagement with this type of object; it is these plainer, more frequently encountered palettes which form the focus of this paper. The wider investigation into these articles was driven by three main questions: (i) how and why these objects were promoted by an emerging elite in the Late Predynastic and Early Dynastic periods; (ii) what their relationship to the relief-carved palettes was; and (iii) why these palettes, as a distinctive class of artefact, disappeared in the mid-1st Dynasty, never to be incorporated into the stylistically familiar Dynastic cultural tradition. The common thread running through all three of these lines of investigation is the question of how these artefacts were valued, and what social dynamics were integral to the ongoing negotiation of such value. Part of this interpretive process involves challenging some of the assumptions that we make in attributing meanings to things.

Previous interpretations of palettes have either been descriptive, focusing on typology, chronology and basic 'function' (*e.g.* Cialowicz 1991; 2001; Regner 1996; Kroeper 1996), or speculative, centring upon the symbolic 'meanings' of the different palette forms and designs (*e.g.* Westendorf 1982; Largacha 1986; Sherkova 1998). Although it is necessary to move beyond a typological and chronological emphasis, it is not the intention here to linger upon the potential meanings of the symbolic forms. Rather, the approach adopted stems from the premise that we can consider how objects may be used as symbols without attempting to ascertain their 'meaning' (*cf.* Renfrew 1994, 6). In order to do this, and to understand how objects become imbued with value, we have to go beyond defining a date and a function, both of which fix an object too rigidly in temporal and social space.

Following the ideas first advocated by Appadurai (1986) and Kopytoff (1986) it has become recognised that meanings and functions can become recategorised through the phases of production, distribution and consumption, phases which may be repeated over the course of an object's existence: things, in the manner of humans, can therefore be considered to have 'lives' (Shanks 1998; Gosden and Marshall 1999). A life-history approach is not just a constructive metaphor, but is also a useful framework for analysis, as it encourages us to evaluate the wider network of significance into which the meaning of the artefact was articulated.

The following discussion will be limited to a consideration of some aspects of how palettes may have been valued in terms of their material, as well as in terms of their consumption, and how this value was transformed over time. After reviewing these aspects, the question of why this changed will be approached. It is proposed here that palettes were symbols that were traditionally valued within the community, and which were appropriated by an emerging elite as a source of social power.

What Were Palettes?

Palettes derive from a wider cultural practice of using grinding-stones that originated at least as early as early Neolithic times, as the rough unworked examples from the Fayum region (Caton-Thompson and Gardner 1934) and El-Omari (Debono and Mortensen 1990) attest. It is only in the Predynastic, however, that such objects took on a new dimension, through being fashioned into a variety of geometric and zoomorphic shapes (Petrie 1921). The earliest such examples were the elongated Badarian specimens with notches carved at each end. The dominant forms in Naqada I were simple rhomboid-shaped stones (Figure 1), but by mid-Naqada II this had given way to variety of designs, from roughly worked stones to more finely carved pieces. The fish was a particularly popular form (Figure 2), as were birds, and, to a lesser extent, turtles. Hippopotami and gazelles occur less frequently. Shield-shaped (scutiform) palettes were also introduced in this phase, and it is these types which were the direct stylistic predecessors of the later ceremonial palettes. In the terminal Predynastic and Early Dynastic period this spectrum of design gradually became limited to the production of rectangular (Figure 3) or circular pieces.

The wear marks and traces of pigment, particularly green malachite and occasionally red ochre or black galena, upon the surfaces of the palettes proclaim that at least part of their function was the preparation of mineral matter. As such, they have often been referred to as 'cosmetic' palettes, although this is perhaps a rather pejorative term, since from a modern Western perspective cosmetics may be assumed to be used merely to 'beautify'.

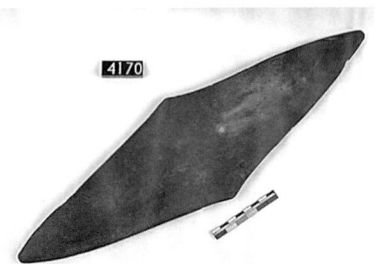

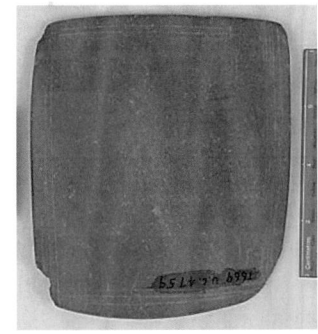

Figure 1 (top). Mudstone rhomboidal palette from Naqada tomb 1409. UC4170. (Courtesy of the Petrie Museum of Egyptian Archaeology, UCL).

Figure 2 (middle). Mudstone palette in the shape of a fish from Naqada tomb 177. UC 4374. (Courtesy of the Petrie Museum of Egyptian Archaeology, UCL.)

Figure 3 (bottom). Mudstone rectangular palette with a border of three incised parallel lines from Naqada tomb 1669. UC4759. (Courtesy of the Petrie Museum of Egyptian Archaeology).

The term 'cosmetic' also bears connotations of 'superficiality'. This perspective is seen in the recent interpretation of the palettes from Nekhen (Hierakonpolis) as evidence of 'vanity' (Friedman 2001, 12). We must, however, be cautious in our imposition of modern Western notions of 'cosmetics' on the past. Indeed, historical evidence from the Old Kingdom informs us that cosmetics had, in certain contexts, a greater significance than our terminology may impart. For instance, the Pyramid Texts refer to the role of cosmetics in the affective restoration of the eye of Horus (Faulkner 1969, 19; Troy 1993) whilst the 5th Dynasty reliefs from Sahure's mortuary temple depict a priestess applying eye-paint to a sacrificial ox (Borchardt 1910, pl. 47). Cosmetics could thus form an important tool for the enactment of cult ritual (Manniche 1999; Hassan and Smith 2002, 62). There is the potential, then, to posit a greater contextual significance for palettes, as an active component of Predynastic culture and ritual, than has sometimes been credited to them.

More often than not these enigmatic objects have been cited only in passing within discussions of the artistically revered ceremonial palettes, such as the 1st Dynasty Narmer Palette. Thus, while much has been written about ceremonial palettes from an art historical perspective (*e.g.* Davis 1989; 1992), little scholarly attention has been paid to the fact that they are made from the same material as the 'ordinary' palettes that were used for over a millennium prior to the advent of the more elaborately decorated versions. The significance of the connection between these forms has been commented on previously (*e.g.* Köhler 2002, 505), although the focus of discussion here has again been on the symbolic forms that the artefacts take, rather than any engagement with palettes as material culture in their own right.

Material Significance

There has been a considerable amount of confusion regarding the correct material identification of the stone used for palettes. This material has often been termed 'slate' and this geological identification has become almost synonymous with that of palettes. The term, however, has been incorrectly applied, as has the term 'schist' (Klemm and Klemm 1993, 369; Aston 1994, 61). Other geological names often encountered in the literature include greywacke and siltstone. The confusion over the precise terminology which should be followed is therefore understandable. To a great extent, this is a result of geological semantics: even geologists are inclined to ambivalence over the classification of rocks, the term 'greywacke' being a case in point. It is not my intention here to encumber this paper with in-depth terminological discussions, as these have been well covered previously (Klemm and Klemm 1993, 369; Aston *et al.* 2000, 57–58; Harrell 2002, 239). To summarise briefly, whilst 'slate' and 'schist' are incorrect labels for the material, the terms greywacke, siltstone and mudstone are geologically more accurate descriptions. All three of these sedimentary rocks are related on a scale, known as the Wentworth scale, of decreasing grain size, with greywacke having larger grains than siltstone, and mudstone possessing finer grains still. The prefix 'meta-' is sometimes added, and refers to the apparent incipient metamorphism that the greywacke series in the Eastern Desert has undergone, as is evident from the chlorite and epidote minerals in the stone from which the distinctive green quality of the rock originates.

In order to resolve some of this confusion, a number of palettes held in the University of Cambridge's Museum of Archaeology and Anthropology were analysed, to identify their mineral composition and possible provenance. The samples were compared to specimens collected from the Wadi Hammamat in the Eastern Desert. All the samples were identified as chlorite rich meta-mudstone which bore close visual resemblance to the samples taken from the Wadi Hammamat. The close visual correlation between the palettes analysed and the Wadi Hammamat samples accords with the present consensus that it was the sole location for collection of the type of stone favoured for palettes.

This assertion is not unwarranted and it is the most likely source from which a large proportion of the material for palettes must have been harvested. First, the Wadi Hammamat is the shortest course across the Eastern Desert between the core of the Naqada culture on western approaches to the Wadi and the Red Sea (Harrell 2002, 298). Secondly, the abundance of Predynastic rock art within the Wadi Hammamat, particularly in the mudstone quarry vicinity, is testimony to considerable Predynastic activity in this area (Morrow and Morrow 2002). Thirdly, the Wadi Hammamat was a source of, and a route to, other important materials including galena (Hassan and Hassan 1981) and malachite which were ground on the palettes themselves. Finally, Debono (1951) recorded the presence of 'archaic' villages and a number of tombs in the Wadi. Debono (1951, 77) further mentioned a large quantity of malachite that was also found on the site, although the precise details of the find are not clear. Hence we cannot doubt the extensive use of the Wadi Hammamat by early peoples.

This specific source was perhaps selected because, from a technical point of view, the chlorite rich mudstones were particularly amenable to the manufacture of palettes, on account of the pronounced rock cleavage which facilitates the production of flat plates. We should, however, bear in mind that the source of mudstone in the Wadi Hammamat is approximately 90 km from the Nile itself (Klemm and Klemm 1993, 355). Throughout the Eastern Desert there are in fact a wide variety of sedimentary stones readily available (Stevenson 2004), including red, brown and purple varieties of mudstone, as well as purple types of siltstone, situated within the Wadi Hammamat itself, which were not utilised. If palettes were the basic, technically functional artefacts that some proclaim them to be, why is it that other types of stones, which were to be found closer to the Predynastic Nile settlements, were not used for the 'everyday' purpose of grinding pigment?

Different rocks were occasionally used for palettes in other contexts. For example, in addition to the imported Egyptian mudstone palettes, a large proportion of Nubian specimens were also regularly manufactured in other locally available stones including granite, diorite, sandstone and quartzite (Firth 1912; 1915). In Lower Egypt limestone palettes were excavated at Maadi (Rizkana and Seeher 1989, 47–48), whilst at Heliopolis roughly worked calcite and flint pieces stained with pigment were recovered (Debono and Mortenson 1988, 35). The materials from which some of the earliest Predynastic palettes were made were also more varied than in succeeding phases. For instance, in Badarian contexts at Mostagedda alabaster and limestone were utilised in addition to mudstone (Brunton 1937, 25, 30), while at Badari a pair of black and white porphyry palettes were discovered (Brunton and Caton-Thompson 1928, 6). These examples suggest that 'functionally' many other stones were perfectly amenable to categorisation and utilisation as palettes. Indeed, when we consider the wide repertoire of materials which was exploited for the manufacture of Predynastic and Early Dynastic stone vessels (Aston 1994), it is apparent that early Egyptian peoples were perfectly capable of skilfully carving a large variety of stones and would not have been precluded from producing palettes in other materials.

The exclusivity of this rock for the production of palettes in the Predynastic can be gauged by considering different artefacts that were made in the same material. Although stone vessel manufacture became more commonplace during Naqada II, studies of stone vessels have shown that mudstone vessels were not common until the 1st Dynasty (Aston 1994, 32). El-Khouli's

(1974) compilation of all published stone vessels, together with many previously unpublished vessels from the Predynastic to the 3rd Dynasty, forms a valuable resource for stone vessel analysis. A cursory quantification of the vessels documented by el-Khouli indicates that only 0.9% (4 typological forms, 4 singular occurrences) of 'slate' and 'schist' vessels were Predynastic. In comparison, over 84.6% of the 'slate' and 'schist' forms (367 forms, over 857 occurrences) recorded were from the 1st Dynasty, which may be of significance in explaining the demise of palettes, an issue which will be considered further below. Similarly, beads, although the next most common artefact in burials after pottery, were rarely made of mudstone. A wide variety of both common and rare stones were used for beads "…particularly carnelian, garnet, lapis lazuli, steatite, serpentine and limestone; calcite, quartz, chalcedony, fluorspar, obsidian, haematite, diorite and turquoise …are not nearly so common" (Payne 1993, 204). Notably absent from this list are any references to 'slate' or 'schist'. It is only with the 1st Dynasty that these rocks again began to be exploited for jewellery, particularly bangles (Andrews 1981, 37). Thus, at the height of the popularity of palettes, the material used was seemingly quite particular to palettes and appears to have been recognised almost exclusively for this purpose.

It can be proposed, then, that the preferential selection for one type of stone may be evidence of the investment of social value. Certainly we cannot ignore the physical characteristics of the Wadi Hammamat stone, with its pronounced rock cleavage, which would have lent itself to the production of palettes in the stone's raw and unworked state. It would be short-sighted, however, to assume that technical function is the sum of an artefact's meaning. The implication is that the significance and value of the palette may have resided as much in its originating area, or visually perceptible qualities, as in its functional capabilities (see also Chapman 2002, 57 on place-based biographies and the importance of colour symbolism). Indeed, the qualitative significance of stone has been acknowledged for later Pharonic history (Baines 2000; Aufrère 2001), where ideological concerns were often privileged over technical ones.

An in-depth consideration of what form such an investment of meaning would have taken is beyond the scope of the present study. However, some qualitative observations can be presented. We know that much later in Egyptian history the rock of the Wadi Hammamat was specifically distinguished by the name *Bekhen* (Lucas and Rowe 1938; Shiah 1942; Aston *et al.* 2000, 58; Harrell and Brown 1992), and its importance is apparent from royally-sponsored expeditions, such as that undertaken by Ramesses IV, to quarry this favoured stone (Harrell and Brown 1992). Its appeal may have derived from the grey-green quality of the stone, green having positive connotations of fertility and growth (Brewer and Friedman 1989, 9; Harrell 2002, 239). In this regard, it has been commented that the green qualities of both the malachite – the most frequently ground mineral on the palettes in funerary contexts (see below) – and the palettes themselves could be viewed as a transformative act promoting health and vitality (Hassan and Smith 2002, 60). The proposal might therefore tentatively be advanced that the mudstone was perceived to impart or enhance the life-giving properties of the pigment which was ground upon its surface.

Mortuary Consumption

For the most part, the provenanced examples of palettes derive from burial contexts (Figure 4). Before engaging with this evidence, however, an important caveat must be stated. As Parker Pearson (1993) has discussed, comparative information from settlement data and other cultural deposits is necessary for a cross-contextual analysis which can more accurately assess the symbolic value of different artefact types and expose the selection processes for grave goods. Unfortunately, such well-excavated and published Predynastic settlement contexts are, at present, rare and our understanding of the period is therefore biased.

Another area of potential significance for which we are unfortunately lacking detailed information is that of early temple sites, which have revealed some limited evidence for palettes. At Abydos, plain and incised palettes were found in the Osiris/Khenti-amentiu temple/town area, but the stratigraphic contexts are unclear (Petrie 1902). Similarly, the rectangular palettes from the Hierakonpolis temple area have no clear stratigraphic context (Adams 1974). A fragment of a rectangular palette was also found in a 5th Dynasty temple deposit at Elephantine (Dreyer 1986). Without any further information it is difficult to gauge the significance of palettes in these contexts, and it is hoped that future research will be able to redress such vagaries in the data. In the meantime, however, it is necessary to maintain an optimistic outlook, predicated upon using what sources we do have in the most productive way possible, whilst sustaining caution in our interpretations. For the remainder of this section it is therefore the burial contexts, on which we are best informed, which will be considered.

Figure 4. *Tarkhan burial No. 634. Shield-shaped palette lying on body.*

In these contexts, it is notable that vivid green malachite stains are often visible upon the surface of many of the excavated specimens, and it is likely that palettes were employed in the funerary ritual. This scenario would be in keeping with the possible ideological connection between palettes, regeneration and rebirth proposed above, the primary ideological motivator of much of Ancient Egyptian mortuary cult elaboration.

Many hundreds of palettes have been excavated from cemetery sites, but if a cursory examination of the actual frequencies of finds is tabulated it becomes apparent that, despite the fact that palettes are one of the more numerous categories of grave goods, the actual number of palettes is still relatively small (Podzorski 1996, 288; Stevenson 2004) with, on average, only 15% of graves in a cemetery containing a palette. This indicates that these objects were certainly not 'standard' mortuary equipment. By the beginning of the 1st Dynasty there had been a significant decrease in numbers and only about 1–2 % of graves per cemetery in this phase contained a palette, and by the end of this Dynasty mudstone palettes, as a distinctive artefact class, had disappeared from the archaeological record. It seems as if there was some factor, or combination of factors, that limited their distribution, factors which may perhaps have become accentuated during the creation and consolidation of the early state.

Social discrimination of access to resources on the basis of age or gender is one such area that may be considered to impact on grave good selection, and a statistical methodology was adopted in order to assess this (see Fletcher and Lock 1994 and Shennan 1997 for further information on statistical approaches in archaeology). The chi-square statistic (χ^2), which is used for determining the presence of an association between two qualitative variables, was calculated for the cross-tabulation of palettes with age and with gender from eleven Predynastic cemeteries. The resulting statistic allows for the evaluation of the probability of the observed result by comparison with standard statistical tables. A significance level (α) of 0.05 for two-by-two contingency tables was chosen and in statistical tables this corresponds to a value of 3.84. A significant association is indicated by figures larger than this number. For contingency tables where there was a low frequency of a variable, usually below five, it was necessary to use Fischer's Exact Test where a figure below 0.05 is considered to be significant. Chi-square, however, only establishes the existence of a statistical association, not the strength of that association. Cramer's V was chosen to gauge this, as it standardizes the strength of association as a measure from 0 to 1, where a value of 1 signifies absolute association between variables.

From the cross-tabulation of the presence of palettes with age it was apparent that palettes were deemed appropriate accompaniments in the tomb for all age gradations from the smallest infant to the most elderly in society. Gender has been propounded as one of the prime limiting factors and it is commonly reiterated that palettes were "essentially feminine property" (Randall-MacIver and Mace 1902, 47) which were primarily associated with women (Brunton 1948, 28; Petrie 1953, 1; Fattovich 1979, 215; Ellis 1992; 1996; Kroeper 1996). Testing this assumption is problematic, given that few sex determinations were noted in early excavation reports and, where determinations were provided, their accuracy is questionable (Mann 1989). Any interpretation of statistical patterns must therefore be tentative, but the approach was deemed to be a valid attempt to at least quantify early sweeping statements. The occurrence of palettes by sex was tabulated for the mortuary data from the sites of Armant, Naqada, el-Amrah, Mahasna, Naga-ed-Dêr, Badari, Hemamia, Matmar, Mostagedda, Tarkhan and Minshat Abu Omar (Tables 1–3). Out of

Table 1. *Association of sex and palettes in Upper Egypt.*

	Armant	Naqada	el-Amrah	Mahasna	Naga-ed-Dêr
χ^2	0.49*	0.825	5.25	7.552*	0.735
Cramer's V	0.05	0.055	0.235	0.46	0.040
Fisher's Exact	1.000	0.385	0.024	0.010	0.463
Graves represented in sample # (%)	59 (30.1)	213 (20.6)	95 (66.4)	32 (22)	462 (52)
Palettes represented in sample # (%)	6 (35.3)	38 (17.1)	29 (70.1)	7 (33)	17 (57.1)
Graves sexed # (%)	59 (51.8)	242 (23.4)	108 (75.5)	36 (25)	462 (52)
# published graves at site	169	1032	143	145	889

* contingency table contains cells that have expected counts less than 5

α = 0.05 with 1d.f.; *p*= 3.8

Table 2. *Association of sex and palettes in Middle Egypt.*

	Badari	**Hemamia**	**Matmar**	**Mostagedda**
X^2	0.135*	1.25*	0.540	2.209
Cramer'sV	0.046	0.289	0.062	0.194
Fischer's Exact	1.000	0.329	0.591	0.187
Graves represented in sample# (%)	64 (20.9)	15 (19.2)	142 (46)	59 (27.2)
Palettes represented in sample# (%)	10 (22.7)	6 (40)	16 (43.2)	11 (39.2)
Graves sexed # (%)	76 (25)	15 (19.2)	185 (59.9)	93 (42.9)
# published graves at site	305	78	309	217

* contingency table contains cells that have expected counts less than 5

$\alpha = 0.05$ with 1d.f.; $p= 3.84$

Table 3. *Association of sex and palettes in Lower Egypt.*

	Tarkhan Valley	**Tarkhan Hill**	**Minshat Abu Omar**
X^2	45.2	2.79*	16.03
Cramer'sV	0.28	0.177	0.276
Fischer's Exact	–	0.122	–
Graves represented in sample	578	89	210
palettes represented in sample #(%)	165 (56.1)	7 (18.4)	21 (56.8)
Graves sexed #(%)	578 (54.8)	89 (29.2)	296[1]
# published graves at site	1054	305	420

* contingency table contains cells that have expected counts less than 5

[1] (Kroeper, personal communication)

$\alpha = 0.05$ with 1d.f.; $p= 3.84$

these, only el-Amrah, Mahasna, Tarkhan Valley and Minshat Abu Omar indicated a statistically valid association between sex and palette ownership, with females more likely to possess these articles. The low value of Cramer's V tempered this, however, and suggested a weak relationship, although this does not necessarily mean that the correlation is any less real. What this indicates is that these are not mutually exclusive relationships, in that palettes are not avoided by one sex in particular. Whilst palettes were probably not female objects *per se* they may nonetheless have been associated with feminine qualities, as suggested by the factor analysis undertaken by Hassan and Smith (2002, 49).

Another very broad and generalised variable that can be considered is that of the wealth of the funerary interments, as calculated by the sizes of tombs and the number of pots. The validity of such a calculation has been extensively reviewed in the literature (*e.g.* Griswold, 1992; Wason 1994; Bard 1994) but its applicability to the current study was seen as justified, since it may be used as a preliminary springboard for the identification of possible patterns and future, more in-depth, analysis. The cross-tabulation of tomb sizes and numbers of pots with the presence of palettes (Stevenson 2004) suggested that there were a wide variety of wealth categories represented from the poorest graves to notably rich, well-endowed tombs. In particular, it appeared that middle-sized graves were more likely to be provided with palettes, although as always we must recognise that since many of the wealthier tombs were the focus of intensive plundering our data may be somewhat distorted. Yet, despite some instances of exceptionally well-crafted and large palettes deriving from prominent graves, the pattern of association seemed to indicate that palettes were not wealth items *per se*. A case in point may be the exceptional 'Hathor palette' from Gerzeh, which although deemed to be ancestral to the later elaborate relief carved palettes, was in fact discovered in a very modest tomb of a standard size and with a limited repertoire of other material goods, as can be seen from the original tomb card (held in the Petrie Museum of Egyptian Archaeology, London). Having thus considered correlates of hierarchy it is apparent that although sizeable, well-crafted palettes may occasionally have been used as a materialised form of wealth – perhaps representing a certain social role writ large – they were on the whole not restricted by this criterion alone. How are we then to explain the phenomenon whereby palettes were not always 'wealth' items economically but nevertheless achieved enough social value to be worthy of elite mortuary consumption and display in the Late Predynastic/1st Dynasty?

One avenue of investigation is to consider alternative facets of value other than that of 'wealth' or 'rank', since value is not always conceived of in economic terms. Other aspects of social complexity that may be taken into account include concepts such as heterarchy, a recent focus of archaeological enquiry that considers more horizontal differences in addition to hierarchical patterns (Crumley 1995). Palettes in this framework could perhaps be considered to be sumptuary items, where 'sumptuary' refers to social rules that limit access to specialized artifacts to certain groups within society. Consequently, the significance of palettes may not have resided in their use to mediate the single meaning of prestige, but in their ability to convey multiple meanings including social role.

The Disappearance of Palettes

The cross-tabulations mentioned above also presented a pattern chronologically. Although the concentration of palettes in middle-ranking burials was a general trend throughout the Predynastic, in the final stages of the Predynastic and the early 1st Dynasty a significant shift in consumption context was noted (Stevenson 2004). As commented above, the frequency of palettes in mortuary arenas decreased towards, and especially during, the 1st Dynasty. The few graves that were furnished with palettes at these later sites seem to have been the richest in terms of their material wealth, the quality of their goods and effort expended upon the construction of the tomb. At Tarkhan (Petrie 1914, 15), for instance, in the last phase the cemetery's use the only palette discovered derived from one of the site's three early 1st Dynasty mastabas.

Similarly, at elite 1st Dynasty cemetery M at Abu Rawash only one palette was recovered, and this was from the largest of the seven mastabas excavated (Klasens 1961). The temporal span of ceremonial palettes, not coincidentally, traverses this period, although only one recently recovered ceremonial palette to date has a seemingly securely datable context in the form of a 1st Dynasty elite mastaba at Minshat Ezzat (el-Baghdadi 1999). It is tempting to suggest, therefore, that the social restrictions surrounding access to these items constricted during the intensification of state formation at the Predynastic/ Early Dynastic intersection.

The reasons for this contextual shift are only beginning to be theorised in more complex terms. The upshot of the explanatory model put forward here is that certain elements of tradition, whether consciously understood as such or not, were "politicised" (Pauketat 2000): that is, actively appropriated as a source of social power by an emerging and highly competitive elite. As sumptuary items valued traditionally within communities or households for small-scale social reproduction, palettes were symbols that were ripe for materialising the emergent ideology of kingship, where ritual focused on, and was propagated by, the king and the initiated elite on the notional behalf of communities (*cf.* Yoffee 2005, 37). Change is often more successful when built upon processes that begin with the familiar, especially in instances where domestic rituals recognizable to all members of society were the basis of larger scale ceremonies (Walker and Lucero 2000). Ceremonial palettes were thus intimately bound into a historical trajectory, from traditional symbols understood by communities, to a new state 'community' writ large (*cf.* Lehner 2000, 280). Baines (1989) has touched upon this connection between the earlier palettes and the ceremonial palettes. In this view the phenomenon was considered to be a by-product of the emergence of high culture, with the concomitant impoverishment of the majority, although the possible strategies by which this may have been achieved have not been fully explored.

By appealing to the concept of 'materialisation' (DeMarrais *et al.*1996), we may postulate some strategies. This term refers to the process by which ideas and myths are transformed into a material reality, permitting them to be manipulated. The significance of an ideology rooted in a tangible medium means that it can be controlled in much the same way as utilitarian goods. Hence, while the message of ideology is important, it is emphasised that the connections to other systems of control also require consideration, such as over the raw material used to make palettes, over the craftsman that made them, or control of the trade and social networks within which palettes were exchanged. Therefore, whilst a focus on palettes has been needed, they cannot be studied in a vacuum and these wider issues will need to be considered in greater depth.

Given the evidence for the specificity of the stone procured for palettes it is easy to see how, in order to increase the value and exclusive associations of these objects, an elite may have sought to limit access to the raw materials used in their manufacture. Records of royal activity in the Wadi Hammamat certainly attest to the interest of the court in this area. For instance, the *serekh* of Narmer is inscribed in a tributary of the Wadi Hammamat and in the mudstone quarry region an inscription dated to the Early Dynastic period mentions an overseer of craftsmen (Wilkinson 1999, 169). By the Old Kingdom titles such as 'master of the roads' within the wadi testify to the influence of the Egyptian administration in this area (Aston *et al.* 2000,18).

This elite interest in the Hammamat mudstone resource is further reflected in the material record. As discussed above, stone vessels were rarely made out of mudstone before the 1st Dynasty, but thereafter there was a dramatic increase in production in this material. This pattern has been noted recently at a number of sites in the Delta, such as Minshat Abu Omar. The earliest phases were not characterised by mudstone vessels, yet by the latest phases at the site they comprise the majority of forms (Rowland 2004, 202). Aston (1994, 32) notes, for instance, that the great majority of mudstone vessels were made in the Early Dynastic Period, with almost 20% of the stone vessels excavated from the Abydos Royal tombs being of mudstone. A further example of this exponential increase in craft output in this medium derives from tomb 3506 at Saqqara which contained 217 identical 'schist' vessels (Emery 1958, 59). The sheer scale and standardisation of production, together with the evidence for conspicuous consumption within an elite context, is surely indicative of craft specialisation, which was state-sponsored and controlled. This is particularly meaningful in the context of the present argument, given that the craftsmen involved in the production of stone vessels may also have been responsible for the relief sculpturing of the ceremonial palettes (see Davis 1989, 154), as is perhaps indicated by the examples of relief work rendered on a number of Late Predynastic and Early Dynastic pieces (*cf.* Hendrickx and Depraetere 2004).

A second class of artefact reveals a similar pattern. Whereas the inclusion of beads or pendants of mudstone had been sporadic during much of the Predynastic, the Early Dynastic jewellery repertoire came to include mudstone bangles, which appeared in significant numbers at this time (Andrews 1981). At least one specialised workshop for the production of these artefacts has been located in the Wadi Hammamat itself (Debono 1951, 77).

As argued above, the significance of this stone may have resided as much in ideological as in technical domains. Accordingly, elite regulation of the material resource, in addition to those craft specialists who carved them, was equivalent to control of the means to materialise ideology. If the stone medium preferred for palettes was integral to their use, contributing to the efficacy of pigment production, restriction of this material constrained its traditional use and meanings as ordinary people became excluded from crucial social arenas, such as exchange networks, which permitted access to, and everyday experience of, this resource. By appropriating traditional community roles and their symbolic expression through the limitation of their material manifestation in this way, an elite stratum could be both created and consolidated. Mudstone as a symbolic medium, however, was perhaps rendered redundant through its increasing use for artefacts other than palettes in contexts of conspicuous consumption from the Early Dynastic period.

The phenomenon of ceremonial palettes was in fact relatively short-lived, with the early 1st Dynasty Minshat Ezzat palette being the latest chronologically confirmed ceremonial palette. Both the mudstone palettes and the ceremonial palettes had thus exited the archaeological record by the mid-1st Dynasty. Perhaps in their briefly elevated context, dislocated from broader arenas of social action, they lost their wider relevance to people, becoming a short-lived experiment in the elevation and transformation of 'folk culture' (Kemp 1989, 64) that did not fully accord with other elements of the expression of the emergent ideology of kingship. The alteration of relations and forms of early symbols by an aspiring elite acting in the short-term could thus have had unintended consequences in the long-term.

It is evident that cosmetics retained a potent symbolic role throughout Pharaonic history, as the inclusion of malachite and galena, or kohl, in tomb offering lists demonstrates (Troy 1993). There are also infrequent examples of grinding mortars recovered from later tombs, such as the Middle Kingdom tombs at Beni Hassan (Garstang 1907, 114), but no standard material was used in their production and their forms were not elaborate. The distinctive and prominent role that the mudstone palettes initially had in early Egyptian culture never emerged again.

Conclusion

Ideology is not simply about ideas, but also about the means to communicate and control them (DeMarrais *et al.* 1996). Ceremonial palettes thus materialise not just certain concepts central to kingship but also some of the means by which kingship was created and consolidated – the economic, political and ideological control, direct and indirect, of traditionally valued resources such as palettes (maceheads and flint knives may be further examples of this). Without the material so valued for palettes, without the craftsmen to produce those palettes, and perhaps even without the specialists initiated in the correct use of these sumptuary items, communities were slowly deprived of their old symbols. We are just beginning to understand these processes, and the case introduced here is only an aspect of the complex biographies of palettes. There are certainly many more facets which may be explored in this account, but it is hoped that at the very least some foundations for further theoretical engagement with this material has been laid.

Acknowledgements

I am grateful to Professor James Harrell of the University of Toledo for providing me with geological samples to examine and for all his helpful advice on geological matters. I am further indebted to my supervisor, Professor Barry Kemp, for his assistance throughout the course of my MPhil study on this subject. Finally, I would like to express my gratitude to the anonymous referees whose comments on this paper were extremely insightful and constructive. Any remaining errors are my own.

Gonville and Caius College, University of Cambridge

References

Adams, B. 1974, *Ancient Hierakonpolis Supplement*. Aris and Phillips, Warmister.

Andrews, C. 1981, *Jewellery I. From the Earliest Times to the Seventeenth Dynasty*. Catalogue of Egyptian Antiquities in the British Museum 6, London.

Appadurai, A. 1986, Introduction, in A. Appadurai (ed.) *The Social Life of Things: Commodities in cultural perspective,* 3–63. Cambridge University Press, Cambridge.

Aston, B. 1994, *Ancient Egyptian Stone Vessels: Materials and forms*, Studien zur Archaologie und Geschichte Ältagyptens 5. Heidelberg Orientverlag, Heidelberg.

Aston, B., Harrell, J. and Shaw, I. 2000, Stone, in P. Nicholson and I. Shaw (eds.) *Ancient Egyptian Materials and Technology*, 5–77. Cambridge University Press, Cambridge.

Aufrère, S. H. 2001, The Egyptian temple, substitute for the mineral universe, in W. V. Davies (ed.), *Colour and Painting in Ancient Egypt,* 158–161. British Museum Press, London.

Baines, J. 1989, Communication and display: the integration of early Egyptian art and writing, *Antiquity* 63, 471–482.

Baines, J. 2000, Stone and other materials in Ancient Egypt: usages and values, in C. Karlhausen and T. De Putter (eds.), *Pierres Égyptiennes, chefs d'oeuvre pour l'eternité,* 29–41. Faculté Polytechnique de Mons, Mons.

Baines, J. and Yoffee, N. 1998, Order, legitimacy and wealth, in G. M. Feinman, and J. Marcus (eds.), *Archaic States,* 199–260. School of American Research, Mexico.

Bard, K. 1994, *From Farmers to Pharaohs*. Sheffield Academic Press, Sheffield.

Borchardt, L. 1910, *Das Grabdenkmal des Königs Sa hu – Re*. Hinnidis, Leipzig.

Brewer, D. and Friedman, R. F. 1989, *Fish and Fishing in Ancient Egypt*. Aris and Phillips, Warminster.

Brunton,G. 1937, *Mostagedda and the Tasian Culture*. London.

Brunton, G. 1948, *Matmar*. London.

Bruton, G. and Caton-Thompson, G. 1928, *The Badarian Civilisation*. British School of Archaeology in Egypt, London.

Caton-Thompson, G. and Gardner, E. W. 1934, *The Desert Fayum*. Royal Anthropological Institute, London.

Chapman, J. 2002, Colourful prehistories: the problem with the Berlin and Kay colour paradigm, in A. Jones and G. MacGregor (eds.), *Colouring the Past: The Significance of Colour in Archaeological Research*, 45–72. Oxford, Berg.

Cialowicz, K. 1991, *Les Palettes égyptiennes aux motifs zoomorphes et sans décoration: etudes de l'art prédynastique*. Instytut Archaeologii Uniwersytetu Jagiellonskiego, Kraków.

Cialowicz, K. 2001, Palettes, in D. Redford (ed.), *The Oxford Encyclopaedia of Ancient Egypt*, 17–20. Oxford University Press, Oxford.

Crumley, C. 1995, Introduction, in R. Ehrenreich, C. Crumley, and J. Levy (eds.), *Heterarchy and the Analysis of Complex Societies*, 1–6. American Anthropological Association, Arlington.

Davis, W. M. 1989, *The Canonical Tradition in Ancient Egyptian Art*. Cambridge University Press, Cambridge.

Davis, W. M. 1992, *Masking the Blow. The Scene of Representation in Late Prehistoric Egyptian Art*. University of California Press, Berkeley.

Debono, F. 1951, Expedition archéologique royale au desert oriental (Keft-Kosseir): rapport préliminaire sur la campagne 1949, *Annales du Service des Antiquités de l'Égypte* 51, 59–110.

Debono, F. and Mortensen, B. 1988, *The Predynastic Cemetery at Heliopolis: Season March – September 1950*. Archäologische Veroffentlichungen 63. Philipp von Zabern, Mainz am Rhein

Debono, F. and Mortensen, B. 1990, *El Omari, A Neolithic Settlement and Other Sites in the Vicinity of Wadi Hof, Helwan*. Archäologische Veröffentlichungen 82. Philipp von Zabern, Mainz am Rhein.

DeMarrais, E., Castillo, L. J., and Earle, T. 1996, Ideology, materialization, and power strategies, *Current Anthropology* 37 (1), 15–31.

Dreyer, G. 1986, *Elephantine VIII. Der Tempel der Satet. Die Funde der Frühzeit und des Alten Reiche*. Archäologische Veröffentlichungen 39. Philipp von Zabern, Mainz am Rhein.

el-Baghdadi, G. S. 1999, Le Palette décorée de Minshat Ezzat, *Archéo-Nil* 9, 9–11.

el- Khouli, A. 1974, *Egyptian Stone Vessels. Predynastic Period to Dynasty III. Typology and Analysis*. Unpublished Ph.D. thesis, University College London.

Ellis, C. 1992, A statistical analysis of the Protodynastic "valley" cemetery of Kafr Tarkhan, in C. M. van den Brink (ed.), *The Nile Delta in Transition: 4th – 3rd Millennium B.C.*, 241–258. R. Pinkhaus, Israel.

Ellis, C. 1996, Expression of social status: a statistical approach to the Late Predynastic/Early Dynastic cemeteries of Kafr Tarkhan, in L. Kryzaniak, K. Kroeper, and M. Kobusiewicz (eds.), *Interregional Contacts in the Later Prehistory of North Eastern Africa*, 151–164, Pozna'n.

Emery, W. 1958, *Great Tombs of the First Dynasty* III. Egypt Exploration Society, London.

Fattovich, R. 1979, Trends in the study of Predynastic social structures, in W. F. Reineke (ed.), *First International Congress of Egyptology. Acts*, 215–220. Akademie-Verlag, Berlin.

Faulkner, R. O. 1969, *The Ancient Egyptian Pyramid Texts*. Oxford University Press, Oxford.

Firth, C. M. 1912, *The Archaeological Survey of Nubia, Report for 1908–1909*. Government Press, Cairo.

Firth, C. M. 1915, *The Archaeological Survey of Nubia, Report for 1909–1910*. Government Press, Cairo.

Fletcher, M. and Lock, G. 1991, *Digging Numbers: Elementary Statistics for Archaeologists*. Oxford University Committee for Archaeology, Oxford.

Friedman, R. F. 2001, The archaeology of vanity, *Nekhen News* 13, 12.

Garstang, J. 1907, *The Burial Customs of Ancient Egypt; as illustrated by tombs of the Middle Kingdom, being a report of excavations made in the necropolis of Beni Hassan during 1902–4*. London.

Gosden, C. and Marshall, Y. 1999, The cultural biography of objects, *World Archaeology* 31(2), 169–178.

Griswold, W. A. 1992, Measuring inequality at Armant, in R. F. Friedman and B. Adams (eds.), *The Followers of Horus. Studies Dedicated to Michael Allan Hoffman 1944–1990*, 193–198. Oxbow Publications, Oxford.

Harrell, J. 2002, Pharonic stone quarries in the Egyptian desert, in R. Friedman (ed.), *Egypt and Nubia; Gifts of the desert*, 232–243. British Museum Press, London.

Harrell, J. and Brown, M. 1992, The oldest surviving topographical map from Ancient Egypt, *Journal of the American Research Center In Egypt*, 24, 81–105.

Hassan, A. A. and Hassan, F. A. 1981, Source of galena in Predynastic Egypt at Nagada, *Archaeometry* 23 (1), 77–82.

Hassan, F. and Smith, S. 2002 Soul birds and heavenly cows, in S. Nelson and M. Rosen-Ayalon (eds.), *In Pursuit of Gender*, 43–65. Altamira Press, Oxford.

Hendrickx, S. and Depraetere, D. 2004, A theriomorphic Predynastic stone jar, in S. Hendrickx, R. F. Friedman, K. M. Cialowicz, and M. Chlodnicki (eds.), *Egypt at its Origins; Studies in memory of Barbara Adams*, 801–822. Leuven, Peeters Publishers.

Kemp, B. 1989, *Ancient Egypt; Anatomy of a Civilisation*. Routledge, London.

Klasens, A. 1961, The excavations of the Leiden Museum of Antiquities at Abu-Roash. Report of the third season: 1957. Part II. Cemetery M, *Oudheidkundige Mededelingen uit het Rijksmuseum van Oudheden te Leiden* 42, 108–128.

Klemm, R. and Klemm. D. D. 1993, *Steine und Steinbrüche im Alten Ägypten*. Springer-Verlag, Berlin.

Köhler, C. 2002, History or Ideology? New Reflections on the Narmer Palette, in van den E. Brink and T. Levy (eds.), *Egypt and Levant: Interrelations from the 4th Through the Early 3rd Millennium BCE*, 499–513. Leicester University Press, London.

Kopytoff, I. 1986, The cultural biography of things: commoditization as process, in A. Appadurai (ed.), *The Social Life of Things. Commodities in Cultural Perspective*, 64–91. Cambridge University Press, Cambridge.

Kroeper, K. 1996, Minshat Abu Omar – burials with palettes, in A. Spencer (ed.), *Aspects of Early Egypt*, 70–91. British Museum Press, London.

Largacha, A. 1986, Las paletas Egipcias Predinasticas algunos aspectos y significados, *Boletin de la Asociación Española de Orientalistas* 22, 203–217.

Lehner, M. 2000, Fractal house of Pharaoh: ancient Egypt as a complex adaptive system, a trial formulation, in T. A. Kohler and G. J. Gumerman (eds.), *Dynamics in Human and Primate Societies; Agent-based Modelling of Social and Spatial Processes*, 275–353. Oxford University Press, Oxford.

Lucas, A. and Rowe, A. 1938, The ancient Egyptian *Bekhen*-stone, *Annales du Service des Antiquités de l'Égypte* 38, 127–156.

Mann, G. 1989, On the accuracy of sexing of skeletons in archaeological reports, *Journal of Egyptian Archaeology* 75, 246–249.

Manniche, L. 1999, *Sacred Luxuries*. Opus, London.

Morrow, M. and Morrow, M. (eds.) 2002, *Desert Rats: Rock Art Topographical Survey in Egypt's Eastern Desert, Site Catalogue*. UCL Press, London.

Parker Pearson, M. 1993, The powerful dead: relationships between the living and the dead, *Cambridge Archaeological Journal* 3, 203–229.

Pauketat, T. 2000, Politicisation and community in the Pre-Columbian Mississippi Valley, in A. Marcello and J. Yaeger (eds.), *The Archaeology of Communities, A New World Perspective*, 16–43. Routledge, London.

Payne, J. C. 1993, *Catalogue of the Predynastic Egyptian Collection in the Ashmolean Museum*. Oxford University Press, Oxford.

Petrie, W. M. F. 1902, *Abydos Pt I*. Egyptian Exploration Fund, London.

Petrie, W. M. F. 1914, *Tarkhan II*. British School of Archaeology in Egypt, London.

Petrie, W. M. F. 1921, *Corpus of Prehistoric Pottery and Palettes*. British School of Archaeology in Egypt, London.

Petrie, W. M. F. 1953, *Ceremonial Slate Palettes*. British School of Archaeology in Egypt, London.

Podzorski, P. 1996, *The Northern Cemetery at Ballas in Upper Egypt: A study of the Middle and Late Predynastic Remains*. Coyote Press, Salinas.

Randall-MacIver, D. and Mace, A. C. 1902, *Amrah and Abydos*. Egypt Exploration Fund, London.

Regner, C. 1996, *Schminkpaletten*. Otto Harrassowitz, Wiesbaden.

Renfrew, C. 1994, Towards a cognitive archaeology, in C. Renfrew and E. Zubrow (eds.), *The Ancient Mind*, 3–13. Cambridge University Press, Cambridge.

Rizkana, I. and Seeher, J. 1989, *Maadi III. The Non-Lithic Small Finds and the Structural Remains of the Predynastic Settlements*. Philipp von Zabern, Mainz am Rhein.

Rowland, J. 2004, *Social Transformation in the Delta from the Terminal Predynastic to the Early Dynastic Period*. Unpublished PhD thesis, University College London.

Shanks, M. 1998, The life of an artifact in an interpretive archaeology, *Fennoscandia Archaeologica* 15, 15–30.

Shennan, S. 1997, *Quantifying Archaeology*. Edinburgh University Press, Edinburgh.

Sherkova, T. 1998, The birth of the eye of Horus: towards the symbolism of the eye in Predynastic Egypt, in C. Eyre (ed.), *Proceedings of the Seventh International Congress of Egyptologists, Cambridge, 3–9 September 1995*, 1060–1065. Peeters, Leuven.

Shiah, N. 1942, Some remarks on the *Bekhen* stone, *Annales du Service des Antiquités de l'Égypte* 41, 189–205.

Stevenson, A. 2004, *The Lifehistories of Predynastic and Early Dynastic Egyptian palettes*. Unpublished MPhil thesis, University of Cambridge.

Troy, L. 1993, Painting the Eye of Horus, in C. Berger, G. Clerc, et N. Grimal, (ed.), *Hommages à Jean Leclant* Volume 1, 351–360. Institut français d'archéologie orientale, Le Caire.

Walker, W. and Lucero, L. 2000, The depositional history of ritual and power, in M. Dobres and J. Robb (eds.), *Agency in Archaeology*, 130–147. Routledge, London.

Wason, P. 1994, *The Archaeology of Rank*. Cambridge University Press, Cambridge.

Westendorf, W. 1982, Schminkpaletten, in W. Helck and E. Otto (eds.), *Lexikon der Ägyptologie, II*, cols. 171–191. Harrassowitz, Wiesbaden.

Wilkinson, T. 1999, *Early Dynastic Egypt*. Routledge, London.

Yoffee, N. 2005, *Myths of the Archaic State; Evolution of the Earliest Cities, States and Civilizations*. Cambridge University Press, Cambridge.

Egyptian Royal Women and Diplomatic Activity during the New Kingdom

Georgia Xekalaki

This paper aims to define the role exercised by Egyptian royal ladies in diplomatic activity, and the power this activity might have given them. During the Late Bronze Age in the Near East diplomacy was exercised through an extensive correspondence that the various rulers and their families exchanged (Moran 1992, xviii, xxii–xxxiii; Cohen and Westbrook 2000, 6–12). Among the surviving texts, the letters mentioning royal women have a special position as they form evidence that the symbolic role of a queen in Egypt incorporated important secular elements (Roth 2002, 67; Troy 1986). However, it is still debatable whether all women with direct links to the Pharaoh by blood or marriage had the right to correspond. This initial question leads us to investigate: (a) the qualities which permitted specific royal ladies to maintain diplomatic contact with their counterparts abroad; (b) the potential these ladies had to mark their position, and to secure additional rights through this correspondence; and (c) the consequences this practice might have had with regard to the diplomatic path of Egypt during the New Kingdom.

These questions will be examined with emphasis on a single event: the negotiations for the first marriage of the 19th Dynasty Pharaoh Ramesses II (*c*.1279–*c*.1213 B.C.) to a Hittite princess. The material used derives from a group of texts coming from the royal archive of the Hittite empire, found at Boğazköy in Turkey and dated to the 13th century B.C. (Edel 1994a; Beckman 1999). Earlier material from the late 18th Dynasty Egyptian royal archive found at Tell el-Amarna is also utilized (Moran 1992). Both groups consist of cuneiform letters exchanged between Egyptian royalty and their counterparts in the Near East (Posner 1972).

What prompted me to initiate this discussion was the text of a particular letter from the Boğazköy archive (Beckman 1999, 132), labelled as 105 (L 2) by Edel (1994a, 216–223). It appears to have been written by a queen and is addressed to a king. The letter's tone and references to certain historical events and circumstances relevant to Egypto-Hittite political affairs indicate that it formed part of the written correspondence between the courts of Egypt and Hatti during the reigns of Ramesses II and Hattusili III (Beckman 1999, 132). The sender has been subsequently identified as the Hittite queen Puduhepa, wife of Hattusili, and the recipient of the letter as Ramesses II. In the text it is stated that the marriage of the Egyptian king to a Hittite princess has already been agreed and that negotiations have reached an advanced stage. However, the Egyptian demands in relation to the dowry were higher than expected by the Hittites, leading them to withhold the princess. In support of the Hittite reaction to the Egyptian attitude, Puduhepa argues that the demands of the Egyptian ruler are far more than the ones made by the Babylonian king for his own diplomatic marriage to a Hittite princess; thus she expresses the feelings of humiliation both of her country and of Babylonia (Beckman 1999, 134). The letter also reflects the queen's concerns about her daughter's safety in Egypt, as it was known to her that communication between foreign royal ladies married to the pharaoh and their home country's authorities was limited. Letter 105 (L 2) contains information about messengers sent from Babylonia to Egypt, who were denied access to the quarters of a Babylonian princess married to the Pharaoh (Edel 1994a, 221, 223; Beckman 1999, 131–135). It would perhaps be possible to interpret letter 104 (L1), also from Boğazköy, as the Egyptian response to Puduhepa's worries, since it contains claims by Ramesses II that the Babylonian bride was allowed to receive her country's envoys and dine with them (Edel 1994a, 215). Nevertheless, it appears that the marriage did take place, after Ramesses had assured the Hittite royalty that their daughter was intended 'for rule in Egypt', as stated in drafts of his letters found in Hattusa: *e.g.* 43 (E 10) (Edel 1994a, 109; Beckman 1999, 136).

A point made in letter 105 (L 2) is that Egypto-Hittite negotiations were continuing long after the initial marriage arrangements, in the form of mutual pressure. The pattern of discourse takes the following form:

- The Egyptian side presents its high expectations in relation to the dowry, ignoring possible future negative Hittite reactions.
- The Hittites delay in dispatching the bride to the Egyptians. At the same time, they attempt to ensure that their princess will hold a high status after her marriage in Egypt, and will be able to contact any Hittite envoys visiting the country in the future. This is hinted at by remarks about the status of foreign wives among the Hittite royalty, and the negative position of the Babylonian princess in Egypt. As a result, although the Hittite queen does not try to prevent the marriage, she does attempt to postpone it until secure assurances have been received that after the marriage her daughter will enjoy a good quality of life, and be accessible through envoys.

Taking account of the remarks stated above, the main question raised for the Hittites is connected to their leading role in both the initiative in the marriage proposal, and the setting of rules that would secure for their princess a position of actual power in the Egyptian court. Subsequently, the analysis of the Egyptian policy has to be focused on the exploitation of the Hittite initiative by Ramesses II, who set out enormous demands of a financial nature at a point when the main marriage arrangements had already taken place.

To explain such matters we have to consider information found in the archives of both Amarna and Boğazköy concerning the rights of a royal wife in Egypt, and especially those of a foreign wife. From what survives from the Hittite archive of Boğazköy, one can see that it was possible for an Egyptian queen to make her mark outside Egypt, by corresponding with her fellow royalty. This archive indicates the diplomatic activity of three Egyptian royal ladies, known through seven letters. Puduhepa would be aware of two of the ladies who evidently corresponded, since they were her contemporary Egyptian queens, Nefertari and Tuya, respectively the chief wife and mother to Ramesses II. The letters seem to have been sent immediately after the Egypto-Hittite peace treaty was agreed in the 21st regnal year of Ramesses II. Nefertari, who appears as Naptera in the Boğazköy archive, is seen twice as a sender of letters – 12 (B6) and 13 (B7) – to queen Puduhepa (Edel 1994a, 42–43). Two further letters – 93 (I13) and 94 (I14) – were probably sent from her and her husband to the Hittite royal couple (Edel 1994a, 200–203). Tuya was the sender of two letters – 10 (B4), 11 (B5) – to the King Hattusili, and in a single case she was the recipient of one of his letters – 112 (L 9) (Edel 1994a, 37–39, 232–233). Both ladies' letters were structured according to a formula common in diplomatic correspondence (Edel 1994b, 61–64; Moran 1992, xxiii; Roth 2002, 76–77), ending always with a list of presents.

The content of those letters can be briefly described as follows: (a) addressing the recipient using the expression brother/sister; (b) wishes for the receiver's wellbeing and references to the sender's own situation; (c) wishes for peace between the countries; (d) presentation of a set of presents sent along with the letter.

It is logical to assume that the content of those two ladies' correspondence was the exchange of presents. It is widely accepted that a crucial element of foreign relations was trade. Egypt, rich in physical resources but also in skilled artisans, was always active in this sphere (Bard 2000, 66–67). Since the value of presents exported might be expected to equal the value of the incoming ones (Zaccagnini 1973, 117–124; Liverani 2000, 25), it is possible to consider exchanges such as the ones reflected in the two ladies' letters (and in many other letters in the Boğazköy archive) as a form of trade between rulers. However, a special characteristic of those commodities is the restriction to royal contexts, since it seems that usually both the provenance and destination of this kind of commodities were royal estates (Bleiberg 1996, 100; Cochavi-Rainey and Lilyquist 1999, 195). This is shown by the personal character of some presents, their luxurious nature, and also the requests of foreign rulers for commodities intended for the creation and embellishment of royal edifices: *e.g.* EA 3, 21 (Moran 1992, 7, 50; Zaccagnini 2000, 147). As a result, the use of a general term such as 'trade' to characterise the gift-exchanging practice might be too restrictive, making it difficult to discriminate certain very specific characteristics of this practice that permit us to understand its function at a deeper level. It is therefore better to follow the classification of Bleiberg (1996, 114), and to classify the commodities presented in the letters as something other than mere trading goods.

With regard to the use of foreign gifts by the Egyptian royal estate, Egyptian written sources mention a number of economic institutions, connected with the royal palace and various state temples (*e.g.* the estate of Amun) which benefited from income deriving from foreign countries. This income is indicated in Egyptian sources by various terms, but mostly by the word *inw* (Bleiberg 1996, 3–4, 13–28, 90*ff*; Warburton 1997, 226–231), and it has been linked to a number of factors such as temple donations, maintenance costs of the royal court and payments to royal workmen (Bleiberg 1996, 100–114). Nevertheless, all of these uses are connected with the expenses of the Palace and, consequently this procedure can be seen as a means of funding the royal estate. In the Wilbour papyrus (Warburton 1997, 165) the income of the Palace appears to be divided into multiple estates associated with each other: the King's Estate, the Queen's Estate, and the Royal Harems of Mer-wer (in Kom Medinet el-Gurob) and Memphis (for an example of this see Gardiner 1948, 19). The state of these separate estates as economical institutions has not previously been extensively studied (an exception is Reiser 1972), since research (Bleiberg 1984; Warburton 1997) has so far focused on the direction of goods received from the Palace (as an entity) to the funding of royal projects and separate institutions (*e.g.* state temples). However, it is safe to assume that if the Palace was receiving a number of commodities, these would be subsequently directed as needed between the minor economic units forming it. Among them would be the Queen's estate and the Harems (Reiser 1972; Robins 1993, 39), where specific women were evidently involved in manufacturing activities and had minor administrative roles (Davies 1908, pl. XXVIII; Robins 1993, 40; Warburton 1997, 150). It is thus possible to assume that queens could participate in international trade as possessors of commodities themselves, exchanging goods deriving from their own personal estates.

A matter of serious concern is the possible expression of political thought through the royal wives' letters. The term 'political thought' might be defined here as any indication of active participation of the individual in politics; this might take the form of personal statement relevant to political matters, or the expression of an initiative in relation to diplomacy. As a result statements with a political character in letters written by, or addressed to, royal women can reflect an active participation of such individuals in the support, if not the making, of diplomatic decisions (Bryan 1996, 36; *pace* Roth 2002, 80) and must therefore indicate an exceptional status for them.

The surviving indications of political thought in Egyptian royal women's letters are relatively rare. Both clear examples come from the later part of the 18th Dynasty. The most convincing case is presented in a letter surviving from Hattusa, addressed to King Suppiluliuma I, where an unnamed Egyptian queen expresses her wish to marry a Hittite prince. The letter survives as an independent text, part of the original Egypto-Hittite correspondence of the end of the 18th Dynasty (Edel 1994a, 14–15), but also as part of the annals of Suppiluliuma's reign, as compiled at the end of the 14th century B.C. by his son and successor Mursilli II (Güterbock 1956, 94; Pritchard 1969, 319). The Egyptian queen in question, who must have lived at the end of the Amarna period, has been speculatively identified as Ankhesenamun, since the letter clearly mentions a threat to her royal line due to the lack of a male heir to the throne (different opinions about the identity of the queen are stated by Reeves 2001, 176–177 and Gabolde 1998, 213–226). In the letter, after the standard expressions of wishes, the queen mentions that she is virtually the only surviving member of the royal family, and proposes to the Hittite king that he send one of his sons for her to marry, thus effectively making him king of Egypt. Whatever strategy was pursued by the queen (Bryan 2000b, 81–82), the letter definitely shows potential for an Egyptian royal lady to express political thought abroad.

Judging from the Egyptian archive at Amarna, Tiye, wife of Amenhotep III and mother of Amenhotep IV/Akhenaten, played a significant part in the international politics as 'advisor' to her son after his accession. References to her as a correspondent are found in letters EA 26, 27, 28 and 29 (Moran 1992, 84–92), but none of her own letters survive. However, in EA 26, addressed to her from the Mitannian king Tusratta, she is asked to advise her son Amenhotep IV about all matters relevant to politics, based on her late husband's policy (Moran 1992, 84–85). Amenhotep IV is also encouraged to consult her for foreign policy matters concerning Mitanni (Moran 1992, 94–96). Other Amarna letters show that Egyptian queens could correspond with other queens abroad, while their precise association with their kings was well-known by Great Kings and vassals. Such is the case with Tiye, and also with her granddaughter Meritaten when she was consort to Akhenaten. An unnamed Egyptian queen is the recipient of letters EA 48 and 50 from a vassal's female relative, probably from Ugarit (Moran 1992, 120–121).

The information given by the Amarna archive for the royal ladies' position in the Egyptian court presents a completely different situation to the one of isolation which Puduhepa, driven by the case of the Babylonian princess, was worrying that her daughter would face as an Egyptian queen. So the question of the reliability of the source of information – "the messenger of the King of Babylonia" (Beckman 1999, 135) – remains to be examined. Records from the Amarna archive suggest that there might have been a large element of truth in Puduhepa's remarks, at least as far as life in the late 18th Dynasty court was concerned. EA 1 shows that a princess who had been sent to marry Amenhotep III was not recognised by ambassadors from her own country who visited Egypt some time after her marriage (Moran 1992, 1–3). In the letter, a scene is described where envoys of Babylonian origin find Amenhotep in his palace, surrounded by all his wives. Since they are looking for their princess, and do not recognise her, they ask for her. Subsequently, they are shown one of the Pharaoh's consorts and they are told that she is the princess they are looking for. As the letter shows, they were still perturbed, since the lady was not recognisable. An interesting remark is the statement that "she did not open her mouth" to speak (Moran 1992, 1). Such references to the ladies' state in the Egyptian court, as seen by the Babylonian envoys, allow some speculation as to whether strong rules in relation to public presentation were required for certain royal consorts (Liverani 2000, 26).

Similar questions are raised with reference to written communication undertaken by the royal women. EA 1 contains a statement of Amenhotep III to his Babylonian counterpart: "should she make some acquisition, I will send it to you" (Moran 1992, 2). This phrase shows that: (a) any of the wives could acquire personal wealth; and (b) it was the Pharaoh's choice and responsibility as to whether this wealth would be kept by the royal wife herself or sent to her father (if she was from abroad). The latter indicates possibly that the wife had no right to control what she acquired (Bryan 2000b, 83–84) and most importantly that, after the marriage, her ability to keep personal contact with her father and her country was dependent on the Pharaoh's will.

The above information indicates that there are controversial elements in the descriptions of a queen's life in Egypt. On the one hand certain consorts of the Pharaoh, generally referred to at present as his 'chief wives', are well-known to their foreign counterparts for their advisory role beside their husband. They were also widely famous through further correspondence relevant to gift-exchange, by which they were aiming both to improve the quality of the countries' relations with each other and to increase their wealth. On the other hand, there are indications that lesser wives may have led a relatively isolated life, since their contact with the outside world was controlled, if not non-existent, and any gain depended on the Pharaoh's good will. However, it is questionable whether any formal difference between these two groups of royal women would be connected to diplomatic activity.

Looking back at the royal wives who were evidently active, one can see some common characteristics in that: (a) their presence in Egyptian monuments of their time is extended and; (b) despite slight differences in importance between them they all share the title of *ḥmt-nsw wrt* 'Great Royal Wife'. This is evident for Tiye, Nefertari and Meritaten. As for Tuya, despite the lack of surviving monuments identifying her as Great Royal Wife (Troy 1986, 168, 19.2), she is assumed to have carried this title, given her importance in her son's reign. Even if she did not, there was another title, similarly prominent that she evidently did hold: that was *mwt-nsw* (King's Mother). This title was also held by Tiye, and it was in this capacity that she acted in the Amarna letters. Additionally, it is known that the power of the King's Mother was traditionally extended in both Egypt and the Near East, and that may be connected with symbolic (Robins 1993, 40–41) as well as political (Bryan 2000a, 253) reasons. Based on this evidence, it can be argued that the title of *mwt-nsw* would give similar rights to the title of *ḥmt-nsw wrt*.

To examine a possible connection between the title of Great Royal Wife and the role of royal women in diplomatic correspondence, it is worth looking at the case of princess Meritaten, daughter of Amenhotep IV-Akhenaten and his wife, Nefertiti. This lady was later (*pace* Robins 1981, 75) given the title of 'Great Royal Wife' and full queenly status (supported by relevant iconography), as she was probably replacing her mother by her father's side (Green 1996, 10–11; Reeves 1999, 92–93).

The response of Meritaten towards specific requests made to her by foreign rulers may be crucial for the observation of differences between the role of a chief queen in comparison with that of any other royal lady in diplomatic activity. As shown in EA 10, 11 and 155 (Moran 1992, 19–23, 241–242), Great Kings and vassals appear to know her relationship to the Egyptian king as a princess (EA 10, 11) and later as a chief queen (EA 155). Initially Mayati, as she is addressed in the letters, appears in EA 10 from the Babylonian King Burna-buriyas, who clearly mentions her as the Egyptian king's daughter and sends a present with the order for it to be given to her.

It seems that through this indirect way of sending her a present he aimed to encourage the return of a similar present from her (Moran 1992, 19). However, in EA 11 it is stated that he never received a present from her and he does not seem to send her anything (Moran 1992, 22). He also seems to avoid any praising words for the princess, since he simply addresses her by her name and does not mention her position in the court or her relation to the Pharaoh.

Meritaten's failure to respond can be seen as negative behaviour towards a friendly initiative, as well as neglect of the custom of reciprocity (Liverani 2000, 25, Zaccagnini 1973, 100), which was crucial in the process of diplomatic relations between countries during the Late Bronze Age. Thus, it cannot be explained in a framework where what was targeted was the promotion of friendship between two countries. Consequently, Meritaten's neglect of the Babylonian initiative might lead us to suppose that there was some reason preventing her from replying to the king.

The situation described in EA 11 is in strong contrast to that of EA 155. This letter was sent to Akhenaten by Abi-Milku, king of Tyre and a vassal to Egypt (Moran 1992, 241–242), to ask for the renewal of his alliance with the Egyptian Pharaoh – "the breath of life" (Bleiberg 1996, 96) – and seek help with regard to his kingdom's financial and political problems. Interestingly, the ruler of Tyre addresses his queries not only to the Pharaoh, but also to Meritaten, who is addressed as "my mistress", while Tyre is mentioned as "the city of Mayati". This approach to the lady by the vassal ruler is an indication that she might have had a kind of political or economic authority over Tyre that permitted her to share diplomatic discussions with the king. There are hints of an economical nature to the lady's involvement with Tyre. Abi-Milku's approach to the Pharaoh can be seen as an attempt to improve his country's difficult economical situation by restoring financial bonds with Egypt. There is textual evidence (Wente 1990, 94, 95) that Meritaten held a personal estate that might have included cities as a whole (Kitchen 1962, 20). Under this light, the abundance of praise expressions for Mayati, and the declaration of Tyre as her city leads to the possibility that Meritaten's authority over Tyre might have included exploitation of the city's resources, commercial exchanges and royal gift-exchanging (Kemp 1978, 7–57; Shaw 2000, 329). As a result, although EA 155 does not indicate any delivery of commodities to Abi-Milku by Meritaten, the possibility that the lady was involved in Tyre's economy cannot be ruled out.

Overall, the approach seen in this letter cannot be irrelevant to the fact that Abi-Milku was a vassal seeking help from the Egyptian king. Still, the fact that Meritaten is a high-profile recipient of his request for support gives her central role in the letter. Such prominence might indicate that: (a) she was the chief queen at the time the letter was written; (b) she was considered to have some authority over Egypt's vassals, that permitted her to act politically on the Pharaoh's side; or (c) she might have had a special connection with Tyre in reference to financial matters concerning her personal estate.

In the case of EA 10 and 11, factors (a) and (b) are significantly different. Contrary to the full praise given to Meritaten in EA 155, she is mentioned merely as the daughter of the king in EA 10. In EA 11 the title of 'mistress of the house' is probably used for a lady other than herself (Moran 1992, 22, 23), indicating that at the time the letter was sent Meritaten was not the chief queen. More awkward to explain is the lack of connection between her possession of personal property and her using it to further the diplomatic correspondence. In none of these cases does Meritaten appear to exchange presents. Since Meritaten already possessed an estate, her failure to send presents to the Babylonian king cannot be explained in terms of lack of property. A possible justification for her behaviour would be the absence of the right that permitted her to participate in the gift-exchange procedure.

If an Egyptian princess was generally unable to maintain diplomatic correspondence, it is problematic why the Babylonian king would have tried to establish correspondence with a princess. The ironic tone of EA 11 implies that the king was not only targeting the fact that there was no present sent, but was criticising Meritaten's behaviour towards him. A single letter from Amarna, EA 12 (Moran 1992, 24), indicates that a princess's participation in diplomatic correspondence was generally accepted in the Near East. However, that was not the case for the Egyptians. There is no surviving letter from Amarna or Boğazköy in which an Egyptian princess corresponds with a foreign ruler. A case from Boğazköy may be indicative for this situation. In a collection of letters relevant to the Kadesh treaty, the Egyptian royal family appear to exchange wishes with the Hittite royalty (Edel 1994a, 30–41; Archi 1997, 8); the senders are Ramesses II, queens Nefertari and Tuya (in the letters stated above), prince Setherkhepeshef and other princes (Edel 1994a, 30–33, 34–37; Fisher 2001, 58– 59; Roth 2002, 76–77), but no princesses. It seems that diplomatic correspondence between foreign countries in the form seen in the Amarna and Boğazköy letters was introduced to Egypt long after its generalization in the Near East. As a result, the Egyptians had to follow long-time established rules (Roth 2002, 78–80). However, they chose to participate in the diplomatic affairs in a modified way, so that the newly brought diplomatic customs would not clash with their own broad cultural background and the traditional viewpoint about Egypt's position in the world (Archi 1997, 6–9; Meier 2000, 168). They therefore seem to have bestowed the opportunity to correspond on a small number of women whose symbolic role at the Pharaoh's side was traditionally very strong, such as the Great Royal Wives and the King's Mother (Robins 1993, 40– 41; Troy 1986, 54– 72). Why the Egyptians did not follow the example of the East in the case of the princesses, whose function was also imbued with heavy symbolism (Raymond Johnson 1998, 87; Wente 1969, 85) is not known. Since the female princely titulary, unlike the queenly equivalent, contains hardly any titles relevant to political leadership (Troy 1986, 152–170, 194–197), it is possible that these individuals were kept away from any kind of formal secular activities, and this practice was therefore also followed for the diplomatic correspondence too. Overall, Meritaten can be seen as having the potential to participate in diplomatic correspondence as daughter of the Pharaoh according to the Eastern rules of diplomacy, but only the title of Great Royal Wife and the equivalent status would give her the right to correspond independently as an Egyptian lady.

From what has been said above, the right to diplomatic correspondence in Egypt seems to be reduced to a very small number of women. If a princess was excluded from diplomatic action for cultural/functional reasons, the case was similar with the Pharaoh's lesser wives (*ḥmt-nsw*), including those of foreign origins (Troy 1986, 165, 18. 21, 18. 22, 18. 23). Since the dowry these foreign ladies would bring with them was considered as a marriage gift to the pharaoh (EA 22; Moran 1992, 57), their personal possessions would be minimal (Bryan 2000b, 81). Also, since the custom of diplomatic marriage in the way that it took place in the 14th-13th century B.C. was relatively new to Egypt, the creation for the lesser wives of a symbolic-cultural framework of a similar nature to the one related to the Royal Mother and Great Royal Wife role is highly unlikely. Thus, the foreign brides would be considered as married to the Pharaoh, would stay in the palace but would not have the same rights as a Great Royal Wife. Of those, the right to participate in foreign relations would be of high importance if the royal woman was another king's daughter, since: (a) she would lose contact with her father; (b) she could not communicate with her country's envoys; and (c) she could not make commercial exchanges. It is true that the continuity of friendly contacts with Egypt was a considerable benefit for those foreign countries. However, it has to be added here that sending a bride to the Pharaoh would not always result in further benefits, such as military alliance and safety; the case of Mitanni, which was left to its fate despite the continuous diplomatic marriages of its princesses to Egyptian Pharaohs (Bryan 2000b, 71–84), is indicative.

The situation that prevailed in the Egyptian court concerning foreign wives would not prevent the foreign kings considering that giving a daughter as wife to the Pharaoh was a way to wield a kind of authority in Egypt, following a century-long Near Eastern mentality (Meier 2000, 170–171). Also, they did not hesitate to demand a high status for their daughters in Egypt, as well as their access to minor diplomatic activity. As demonstrated in EA 1 and 105 (L 2), kings such as the rulers of Babylonia would at the very least expect their daughter to be in personal contact with her country's envoys on occasions that they visited Egypt. Furthermore, letters EA 17–25 from the correspondence between Egypt and Mitanni might indicate expectations by the Mitannian king that his daughter Taduhepa, then betrothed to Pharaoh Amenhotep III, was to be 'the mistress of Egypt'; the expression is used in EA 20 (Moran 1992, 47), while Queen Tiye's name is absent from any letter concerning marriage negotiations (Bryan 2000b, 80).

In the mid-13th century B.C. it appears that the Hittites, especially queen Puduhepa, shared with the 14th century Near Eastern kings the expectation of authority over Egypt (Archi 1997, 12), marked by the demand for the Hittite princess to become Great Royal Wife. This expectation is revealed by comparisons of the Hittite princess with the daughters of the other Great Kings, who had previously married Ramesses II, in 105 (L2) and in 104 (L1) (Beckman 1999, 132–133, §2; Meier 2000, 171– 172). Nevertheless, after more than a century of relations with Egypt, the Hittites would have acquired enough knowledge about the situation in Egypt to be fully informed about the benefits Hatti would have in the event that the princess was given the title of Great Royal Wife. Exploiting personal property, and communicating with Hittite authorities of any kind, the Hittite princess would benefit her country commercially and diplomatically. She could communicate the views of Egypt to her envoys and probably influence Egypt positively over Hatti. She could also send much of the precious material that she would gain as presents back to her country. All of these possible benefits were precious for a country that from time to time suffered from internal instability (Van den Hout 2000, 1109–1110, 1113–1115; Van Dijk 2000, 298), as the royal family would have a powerful ally forever. It is notable here that the Hittite attempt to gain some kind of political influence in Egypt might have eventually been so successful that it led to overturning of core points of Egyptian diplomatic customs. Ramesses II actually had a daughter by the Hittite princess, and if the interpretation of Roth (2002, 102) on the basis of certain material from the Boğazköy archive – 68 (E 35) (Edel 1994a, 166–167) – is correct, then, this king might have been asked by the Hittites to send this daughter to Hattusa for a prospective diplomatic marriage. In that case, the daughter of Ramesses and his Hittite wife, would have been treated more as Hittite than as Egyptian royalty, and the Egyptians would have broken a century-long diplomatic taboo (see EA 4 in Moran 1992, 8).

From the Egyptian point of view, the presence of a Hittite as queen in Egypt would indeed reduce Ramesses II's freedom to handle Egypto-Hittite relations in the way that he wanted. From this aspect, a marriage designed to suit the Hittites would not have been so profitable for Egypt. But since Hatti continued to be the most significant country in the Near East (Roth 2002, 102), the Egyptians would not be willing to jeopardise an alliance that took years to build. Hostility with Hatti would mean expenses that Egypt, even at that time, would not be able to afford after years of wars (Spalinger 2005, 229–230). As a result, the Egyptians could not turn down a diplomatic marriage proposal from Hatti.

The response of Ramesses II was to ask for an enormous amount of commodities as dowry from the Hittites. The practice of financial pressure was common in foreign diplomacy, as was the ploy of withholding a princess if the demands of one party were not accepted by the other; it appears in different versions in Amarna (*e.g.* EA 4 in Moran 1992, 8–10; Westbrook 2000, 382) and it has even been considered as one of the basic steps followed in the procedure of establishing a diplomatic marriage (Artzi 1987, 24). On the one hand, the use of financial pressure by Ramesses would give the king time for further negotiation, while at the same time perhaps providing economic benefit. On the other hand, the method of withholding the princess, as in the case of Puduhepa, seems to have been very effective in the past; EA 5 and 11 indicate that the marriage mentioned in EA 4 seems to have taken place (Moran 1992, 10–11, 21–23). However, the acceptance by the Egyptians of the Babylonian demands stated in EA 4 would not result in any unprecedented political/diplomatic change. The same would happen in the Egypto-Hittite case, with the additional benefit that financial profit would be secured (Kitchen 1995, 769).

From this perspective, the outstanding point in the Egypto-Hittite diplomatic bargain is not simply Puduhepa's boldness, but the fact that the main outcome of those negotiations was the appointment of a Hittite princess as Great Royal Wife in Egypt, with all the rights this position would evidently give. As a result, the first Hittite marriage of Ramesses II was not just the culmination of the two countries' good relations. It also has to be seen as the result of mutual pressure and compromise on behalf of two countries forced by historical circumstances to maintain alliance so as to avoid disaster. This pressure indicated the mastery of both sides in diplomatic techniques developed over centuries, as well as a deep knowledge of each other's court-life details and royal customs.

Thus, the conclusions of this discussion are the following:

- Of all the Egyptian royal ladies, the Great Royal Wife (*ḥmt-nsw wrt*) had additional rights over the rest of a Pharaoh's wives (*ḥmt-nsw*) in the possession of personal wealth and ability to exploit it, of corresponding with their foreign counterparts, and of expressing diplomatic opinion. Consequently the title *ḥmt-nsw wrt* might be given by the Pharaoh to any woman he wanted to bestow these rights upon. The royal mother did not need to be given the title, since women holding this title already possessed these rights traditionally in both Egypt and the Near East.

- If a foreigner was a *ḥmt-nsw wrt*, her role would have been crucial for her country's relations with Egypt. That is possibly the reason why this practice was avoided by the Egyptians in the times prior to Ramesses II.

- Due to the mutual need for Egypto-Hittite alliance in the 19th Dynasty, a diplomatic marriage proposal from the one to the other would not have been neglected. Since the Hittites proposed the marriage and set their rules, the Egyptians could not refuse. In this situation, they would probably have just been waiting to gain time, hoping that the Hittites would change part of their demands and at least allow them to acquire some more wealth.

- The marriage negotiations show an advanced knowledge in diplomatic language by both sides, which, for the Egyptian side resulted in unprecedented innovations relevant to customs with regard to the royal family and for the Hittite side strengthened the political gains achieved with the treaty of Kadesh (Archi 1997, 6).

University of Liverpool

References

Archi, A. 1997, Egyptians and Hittites in contact, in *L'Imperio Ramesside: convegno internazionale in onore di Sergio Donadoni*, 1–15. Università degli studi di Roma "La Sapienza", Roma.

Artzi, P. 1987, The influence of political marriages on the international relations of the Amarna Age, in J. Durand (ed.), *La femme dans le Proche Orient antique: compte rendu de la XXXIIIe Rencontre Assyrologique Internationale, Paris, 7–10 juillet 1986*, 23– 26. Editions Recherche sur les Civilisations, Paris.

Bard, K. 2000, The emergence of the Egyptian state, in I. Shaw (ed.), *The Oxford History of Ancient Egypt*, 61–88. Oxford University Press, Oxford.

Beckman, G. M. 1999, *Hittite Diplomatic Texts*. Scholars Press, Atlanta.

Bleiberg, E. 1984, The King's privy purse during the New Kingdom: An example of INW, *Journal of the American Research Center in Egypt* 25, 155–167.

Bleiberg, E. 1996, *The Official Gift in Ancient Egypt*. University of Oklahoma Press, Norman.

Bryan, B. M. 1996, In women good and bad fortune are on earth; status and role of women in Egyptian culture, in A. K. Capel and G. E. Markoe (eds.), *Mistress of the House Mistress of Heaven: Women in ancient Egypt*, 25– 46. Cincinatti Art Museum, Cincinatti.

Bryan, B. 2000a, The 18th Dynasty before the Amarna period, in I. Shaw (ed.), *The Oxford History of Ancient Egypt*, 218–271. Oxford University Press, Oxford.

Bryan, B. 2000b, The Egyptian perspective on Mittani, in R. Cohen and R. Westbrook (eds.), *Amarna Diplomacy; the beginnings of international relations*, 71–84. The Johns Hopkins University Press, Baltimore and London.

Cochavi-Rainey, Z. and Lilyquist, C. 1999, *Royal Gifts in the Late Bronze Age Fourteen to Thirteen Centuries B.C.E.* Ben-Gurion University of the Negev Press, Beer-Sheva.

Cohen, R. and Westbrook, R. (eds.) 2000, The Amarna System, in *Amarna Diplomacy: the Beginning of International Relations*, 1–12. The Johns Hopkins University Press, Baltimore and London.

Davies, N. 1908, *The Rock Tombs of El-Amarna, VI.* Egypt Exploration Fund, London.

Edel, E. 1994a [1986], *Die ägyptisch-hethitische Korrespondenz aus Boghazköi in babylonischer und hethitischer Sprache, I: Umschriften und Übersetzungen*. Westdeutscher Verlag, Opladen.

Edel, E. 1994b [1986], *Die ägyptisch-hethitische Korrespondenz aus Boghazköi in babylonischer und hethitischer Sprache, II: Kommentar*. Westdeutscher Verlag, Opladen.

Fisher, M. M. 2001, *The Sons of Ramesses II, I: Text and Plates*. Harrassowitz, Wiesbaden.

Gabolde, M. 1998, *D'Akhenaton à Toutankhamon*. Université Lumière-Lyon 2, Institut d'archéologie et d'histoire de l'antiquité, Lyon.

Gardiner, A. H. 1948, *The Wilbour Papyrus, 4.* Oxford University Press, London.

Green, L. 1996, The royal women of Amarna: who was who, in D. Arnold (ed.), *The Royal Women of Amarna: Images of Beauty from Ancient Egypt*, 6–15. The Metropolitan Museum of Art, New York.

Güterbock, H. 1956, The Deeds of Suppiluliuma as told by his son, Mursili II, *Journal of Cuneiform Studies* 10, 41–68 and 75–130.

Kemp, B. J. 1978, Imperialism and empire in New Kingdom Egypt, in P. D. A. Garnsey and C. R. Whittaker (eds.), *Imperialism in the Ancient World*, 7–57. Cambridge University Press, Cambridge.

Kitchen, K. A. 1962, *Suppiluliuma and the Amarna pharaohs: a study in relative chronology*. Liverpool University Press, Liverpool.

Kitchen, K. A. 1995, Pharaoh Ramesses II and his time, in J. M. Sasson (ed.), *Civilizations of the Ancient Near East,* II, 763–774. Simon and Schuster Macmillan, New York.

Liverani, M. 2000, The Great Powers' Club, in R. Cohen and R. Westbrook (eds.), *Amarna Diplomacy: the beginnings of international relations*, 15–27. The Johns Hopkins University Press, Baltimore and London.

Meier, S. A. 2000, Diplomacy and international marriages, in R. Cohen and R. Westbrook (eds.), *Amarna Diplomacy: the beginnings of international relations*, 165–173. The Johns Hopkins University Press, Baltimore and London.

Moran, W. L. 1992, *The Amarna Letters*. Johns Hopkins University Press, Baltimore.

Posner, E. 1972, *Archives in the Ancient World*. Harvard University Press, Cambridge Mass.

Pritchard, J. B. 1969 [1950]. *Ancient Near Eastern Texts Relating to the Old Testament,* (3rd edition). Princeton University Press, Princeton.

Raymond Johnson, W. 1998, Iconography and theology, in D. O'Connor and E. Cline (eds.), *Amenhotep III: Perspectives on his Reign*, 87–94. University of Michigan Press, Ann Arbor.

Reeves, C. N. 1999. The royal family, in R. Freed, Y. Markowitz and S. D'Auria (eds.), *Pharaohs of the Sun; Akhenaten, Nefertiti, Tutankhamun*, 80–95. Thames and Hudson, London.

Reeves, N. 2001, *Akhenaten, Egypt's False Prophet*. Thames and Hudson, London.

Reiser, E. 1972, *Der königliche Harim in alten Agypten und seine Verwaltung*. Notring, Wien

Robins, G. 1981, "*ḥmt nsw wrt* Meritaton", *Göttinger Miszellen* 52, 75–79.

Robins, G. 1993, *Women in Ancient Egypt*. British Museum Press, London.

Roth, S. 2002, *Gebieterin aller Lander. Die Rolle der königlichen Frauen in der fiktiven und realen Aussenpolitik des ägyptischen Neuen Reiches*. Vandenhoeck and Ruprecht, Göttingen.

Shaw, I. 2000, Egypt and the outside world, in I. Shaw (ed.), *The Oxford History of Ancient Egypt*, 314–329. Oxford University Press, Oxford

Spalinger, A. 2005, *War in Ancient Egypt*. Blackwell, Oxford.

Troy, L. 1986, *Patterns of Queenship in Ancient Egyptian Myth and History*. Acta Universitatis Upsaliensis, Uppsala.

Van den Hout, T. P. J. 2000, Khattushili III, King of the Hittites, in J. M. Sasson (ed.), *Civilizations of the Ancient Near East, II*, 1107–1120. Simon and Schuster Macmillan, New York.

Van Dijk, J. 2000, The Amarna period and the later New Kingdom, in I. Shaw (ed.), *The Oxford History of Ancient Egypt*, 272–313. Oxford University Press, Oxford.

Warburton, D. A. 1997, *State Economy in Ancient Egypt: Fiscal Vocabulary of the New Kingdom*. Fribourg University Press, Friburg.

Wente, E. 1969, Hathor at the Jubilee, in G. E. Kadish (ed.), *Studies in Honor of John A. Wilson*, 83–91. University of Chicago Press, Chicago.

Wente, E. 1990, *Letters from Ancient Egypt*. Scholars Press, Atlanta.

Westbrook, R. 2000. Babylonian diplomacy in the Amarna Letters, *Journal of the American Oriental Society* 120.3, 377–382.

Zaccagnini, C. 1973. *Lo Scambio dei Doni nel Vicino Oriente Durande i Secoli XV–XIII*. Centro per le Antichità e la Storia dell' Arte del Vicino Oriente, Roma.

Zaccagnini, C. 2000. The interdependence of the Great Powers, in R. Cohen and R. Westbrook (eds.), *Amarna Diplomacy: the beginnings of international relations*, 141–153. The Johns Hopkins University Press, Baltimore and London.